Queer Lyrics

Queer Lyrics

Difficulty and Closure in American Poetry

John Vincent

QUEER LYRICS
© John Vincent, 2002

First published 2002 by PALGRAVE MACMILLAN™
175 Fifth Avenue, New York, N.Y. 10010 and
Houndmills, Basingstoke, Hampshire, England RG21 6XS.
Companies and representatives throughout the world.

PALGRAVE MACMILLAN is the global academic imprint of the Palgrave Macmillan Division of St. Martin's Press, LLC and of Palgrave Macmillan Ltd. Macmillan® is a registered trademark in the United States, United Kingdom and other countries. Palgrave is a registered trademark in the European Union and other countries.

ISBN 0–312–29497–2 hardback

Library of Congress Cataloging-in-Publication Data
Vincent, John.
    Queer lyrics: difficulty and closure in American poetry/
    John Vincent.
        p. cm.
    Includes bibliographical references and index.
    ISBN 0–312–29497–2
        1. American poetry—History and criticism. 2. Homosexuality and literature—United States. 3. Closure (Rhetoric). 4. Sex in literature. I. Title.

PS310.H66 V46 2002
811'.009'353—dc21   2002068443

A catalogue record for this book is available from the British Library.

Design by Newgen Imaging Systems (P) Ltd., Chennai, India.

First edition: November 2002
10 9 8 7 6 5 4 3 2 1

Printed in the United States of America.

For Ben

Contents

Acknowledgments

Michael Moon made this book possible. He and Eve Kosofsky Sedgwick gave me the permission to write it. Each, wellsprings of curiosity, rigor, and brilliance, modeled whole new ways of reading the world. Not to mention poetry. Barbara Herrnstein Smith is the fairy godmother of the project. Her incredible work in poetics inspired me through the slow times, and her conversations sponsored the fastest and most furious. My affair with poetry began under the tutelage of poet and critic Louise Glück. She made poetry matter. I am humbled to include each of these luminaries in my genealogy; I'm full of gratitude for their support and warmth.

Rafael Campo and Richard Morrison are presences throughout. Michael Hardt was grounding and generous. Joan Aleshire was a great help with my work on Hart Crane. Larry Levis, Heather McHugh, and Carol Frost each taught me how to think in and about poetry.

While writing this book, I lost my friend Brian Selsky. We read *Self-Portrait in a Convex Mirror* aloud together. He bought me the foot-long version of *As We Know*. Most ideas held within were conceived on his kitchen table. He would like how perverse that sounds.

Ben Weaver, Jennifer Doyle, José Esteban Muñoz, Gus Stadler, Nigel Alderman, and Katie Kent all provided friendship and conversation that were crucial to this project. David Glimp, Leslie Bow, Russ Castronovo, and Michael Rothberg inspired me and kept me engaged while at the University of Miami. The English Department there also allowed me the freedom and time to work.

Kevin Kopelson read the manuscript and made incredibly helpful suggestions with a panache and erudition I envy. Kristi Long made the project happen.

Marc Brudzinski, Steve Monti, Kristin Bergen, Siobhan Somerville, Allan Isaac, and Christopher Matthews were generous with themselves.

My parents have cheerfully sponsored my entire career. For some reason they have always wanted a writer in the family, and I fear they got one. Their support and love mean the world to me.

Q-bert and Grub each made me inordinately happy while I was and was not writing. And Ben Peacock, well, he's made the last decade worth it.

Permissions

Grateful acknowledgment is made to the following:

Portions of Chapter 3 originally appeared in *Twentieth Century Literature,* Summer 1998 issue (Vol. 44, No. 2), pp. 155–75. Reprinted with permission of *TCL.*

Also, a slightly different version of Chapter 2 appeared as "Pulling Close and Pushing Away: Rhetorical Suspense, Sexuality, and Death in Whitman's 'Calamus' Poems," reprinted from *Arizona Quarterly* 56:1 (2000): 29–48; by permission of the Regents of the University of Arizona.

Reprint in its entirety the poem "The Grapevine," from *Some Trees,* by John Ashbery. Copyright © 1956 by John Ashbery. Reprinted by permission of George Borchardt, Inc., for the author.

Excerpts from "Fragment" and "Soonest Mended" from *The Double Dream of Spring.* Copyright © 1970, 1969, 1968, 1967, 1966 by John Ashbery. Reprinted by permission of George Borchardt, Inc., for the author.

"A Blessing in Disguise" from *Rivers and Mountains.* Copyright © 1962, 1963, 1964, 1966 by John Ashbery. Reprinted by permission of George Borchardt, Inc., for the author.

"Fairies' Song" from *The Vermont Notebook.* Copyright © 1975, 2001 by John Ashbery. Copyright (c) 1975 by Joe Brainard. Copyright © 2001 by the Estate of Joe Brainard. Reprinted by permission of George Borchardt, Inc., for the author.

Excerpts from "Litany" and "As We Know" from *As We Know.* Copyright © 1979 by John Ashbery. Reprinted by permission of George Borchardt, Inc., for the author.

"Or in my throat" from *Shadow Train.* Copyright © 1980, 1981 by John Ashbery. Reprinted by permission of George Borchardt, Inc., for the author.

Preface

My title uses the term "queer" doubly, as adjective and imperative. I myself would find this pun precious if it weren't actually still odd to see the words "queer" and "lyric" conjoined. This is not to say that there are not excellent studies of lyric poets that "queer" the meaning of their works, lives, and reception. The lyric itself, however, as a literary form, has not been examined for its relation to queer meanings.

In part, I believe that the lyric, as genre, has been neglected by queer theorists due to an interest in historical readings of texts and an allergy to approaches that appear transhistorical or formalist. Suspicion about such approaches is justified. Queer communities have had to work, and continue to work, to uncover and recover their history. Form appears ahistorical. The lyric, imagined as a record of a single voice speaking to one person or no one, seems to have been puked up whole from the whale of English Literature onto the beach of the present.

In this book, however, I argue that lyric form, particularly in relation to, and in the relation of, difficulty and closure, has transmitted queer meaning across the span of American Poetry, both from poet to reader and from poet to poet. Lyric devices have been, since Whitman, used as tools in powerful survival and world-making strategies. These queer poetic innovations include but exceed thematics. Queer lyrics do not simply record lives lived and feelings felt. At their best, they offer performances, or demonstrations, of living and feeling.

Despite the lyric's reputation for being an over-refined genre, it is quite *ill-defined* in contemporary critical discourse. Flummoxed by stubborn singularities, critics have been reduced to describing the lyric, as Northrop Frye has recently, as primarily "anything you can get uncut into an anthology" ("Approaching" 31). We can still, with relative confidence, say what an epic is or what a drama in verse is. These genres, the traditional foils of the lyric, have maintained much definitional integrity, while their main characteristics, narrative and enactment, have seeped into the lyric. The lyric genre is difficult to define because its boundaries are precisely the location of some of the most notable experiments in the poetry of the last century and a half. T. S. Eliot tried to define the genres of poetry in a typology of address, but, as we will see in more detail in Chapter 5, he was not satisfied calling Marianne Moore's poems "lyrics" because their correspondence to the material world seemed at least as important as the voice that spoke them. Moore's peculiarities lead him to coin the term "descriptive poetry," a term whose use he dropped directly after its invention. Furthermore, as we will see, both Walt Whitman's use of the series and Jack Spicer's self-proclaimed invention of the "serial" poem vex the notion of the lyric as a single unit. Even the lyric's trademark univocality is challenged by the poets I discuss. John Ashbery is notorious for his mid-sentence shifts of voice, and Spicer claimed that his best poems were beamed in by Martians or written by dead people.

Sidestepping Queer Theory's aversion to form, one finds that the lyric is, by its nature, the queerest of genres. It is the genre that, in Charles Altieri's terms, counters the "impulse to lucidity." "Lyricism," Altieri suggests, "... refers to the many ways post-Enlightenment literature counters [lucidity's] reduction of the mind's cognitive powers into analytic operations by developing frameworks to express the full affective life of the psyche.... The lyric poem ... momentarily transcends the limits of lucid self-consciousness" ("Motives" 656). Lyricism, according to Altieri, is the impulse to challenge sense-making apparatuses; the lyric moment strains categorical definitions of feeling and identity.

Eve Kosofsky Sedgwick argues that such strains on meaning will inevitably cluster around the binarism of homo/heterosexuality. In *Epistemology of the Closet*, she argues that "major nodes of thought and knowledge in twentieth [and now twenty-first]-century Western culture as a whole are structured—indeed fractured—by a chronic, now endemic crisis of homo/heterosexual definition..." (1). If heteronormativity can be understood as the impulse to lucidity writ large, then queer lives and performances impel themselves, by their nature, toward lyricism. "Queer," if we agree with Altieri, is always already lyric. As Sedgwick writes elsewhere: "... one of the things that 'queer' can refer to [is] the open mesh of possibilities, gaps, overlaps, dissonances and resonances, lapses and excesses of meaning when the constituent elements of anyone's gender, of anyone's sexuality aren't made (or *can't be* made) to signify monolithically" (*Tendencies* 8). The centrality of homo/heterosexual definition in Western culture aside, I will be locating my investigations around the meaning production of particularly queer poets. This will, even without the argument that the terms "queer" and "lyric" are fundamentally interdependent, always press the one term against the other.

My treatments of the poetry of Walt Whitman, Hart Crane, Marianne Moore, John Ashbery, and Jack Spicer focus on their lyrics as they challenge heteronormative meaning. These poems are queer in the sense that they doggedly explore the epistemology, ontology, and phenomenology of nonheterosexuality. Defying dominant modes of meaning production as they do, the poems are inevitably difficult. A difficult poem requires its reader's participation to arrange its formal, syntactical, thematic, and/or sonic patterns. Allen Grossman notes that difficult poems "lack an intra-textual interpreter" and "delegate[] to the reader the role of exegetical participant" (226). The reader, as intrapoetic exegetical participant, is more present in the arrangement of words on the page than in a nondifficult poem. Indeed, while every poem requires readerly participation, a difficult poem requires the reader to construct it *as a poem.*

Difficult poetry, by limiting any local univocal authority, often inspires critics to grand statements. "This poem," for instance, "is about how language fails to mean." Or, "This poem is about how language is overfull of meaning." Such pronouncements occlude the poems that inspire them. Conversely, a way to keep a difficult poem constantly in sight is to perform a detailed, almost clinical, close reading. Here, while the poem does remain in sight, its *difficulty* is occluded. Difficulty gives way to method and full-blown sense. Critics have been faced with this awkward choice: Keep the poem or keep the poem difficult. Balancing between these poles is the difficulty of difficulty for exegetes and is not, as far as I can tell, avoidable. My method in this book has been more often than not tipped toward sense making on the level of individual lyrics. By this reading technique I do not mean to suggest that the poetries I discuss are solvable; rather that one can find fingerholds in even the most difficult oeuvre. If I do err on the side of lucidity, it is in the interest of offering a way in to a poem or poet's work. I do not intend for the clarity of my readings to be synecdochically applied to groups of poems, books, or entire oeuvres.

My own experiences with difficult poems, and my own deep desire to continue reading them, has to do with the hypnotics of the oscillation between sense and ur-, super-, meta-, semi-, or non-sense, to mention a few varieties. This oscillation can replace typical narrative tensions or lyric framing devices to create motion and emotion, that is, feelings of departure and arrival, without a story line or sustained ligature of repetition. Each new book by John Ashbery, for instance, recently a nearly annual event, represents to me, his avid reader, less a bundle of discrete insights or moments of poetic virtuoso than it does an experience of being pleasurably lost. In the Ashbery mood, I feel blood refilling my linguistic vascular system to no particular end but the tingling effects of having a vigorous circulation. In *Queer Lyrics,* I offer heuristics to locate effects within difficult poems that I hope will enable the near meaning to be enjoyed with more and not less, to borrow one of Marianne Moore's favorite words, gusto.

At the heart of my heuristics is poetic closure. In her groundbreaking, 1969 study of the subject, *Poetic Closure: A Study of How Poems End,* Barbara Herrnstein Smith identifies closure as the most basic generic requirement and the single dependable pattern in lyrics across the history of the genre. Closure is the feeling of finishedness a reader has at the end of a poem. Herrnstein Smith makes the important distinction between the end of a lyric and its closure. The end of a poem is where the poem stops; closure gives the reader the feeling that it stopped for a reason.

Herrnstein Smith argues that concluding gestures have a special status in poems due to their relation to poetic structure:

> Poetic structure is, in a sense, an inference which we draw from the evidence of a series of events. As we read the poem, it is a hypothesis whose probability is tested as we move from line to line and adjusted in response to what we find there.... [T]he conclusion of a poem has special status in the process, for it is only at that point that the total pattern—the structural principles which we have been testing—is revealed. (13)

The difference between the end of a poem, where the poem stops and white space begins, and the closure of the poem, where the reader feels that the patterns of the poem are completed, allows an approach to the most difficult of the genre.

In a sense, closure is an effect of the fact that a lyric is a unit. A lyric has to end somewhere; the poet makes a choice where. Closure implies a sense of purpose from which one can hypothesize backward about the poem as a whole. The feeling of ending purposefully inserts agency into poems that might not otherwise exhibit anything decipherable as meaning. This does not mean that closure will always provide a way into a difficult poem; however, this book will primarily be interested in difficult lyrics in which the purposefulness of closure provides a starting point for exegetical work. While it does not provide a key to difficult poems, closure does offer a place to begin reading their patterns.

My readings will always attend to the effect of sexual identity on the meanings in the poem. Each of the poets I discuss is in a very active, and different, relation to "the closet." Ashbery, Crane, and Spicer are self-avowedly homosexual, but each in a different way. Further, the impact of their sexuality on their literary reception and reputation could not be more different. For instance, Crane's homosexuality is taken as an important aspect of his life and work, while Ashbery's has largely, until quite recently, been ignored. Spicer was the least closeted of all the poets I discuss, but during his lifetime, his brave avowals of his sexuality served to keep his readership small, and in a sense, produce the least available and most "closeted" writing. Whitman, while not exactly self-avowed, as I will discuss in more detail below, has come to stand for homosexuality in America the way that Wilde has in England. Marianne Moore never made a commitment to any particular sexual identity, and I will not suggest that she was a lesbian. Nor will I suggest that she was heterosexual. Her college crushes were on girls and her closest friends were lesbians, which is just to say that her resistance to sexual identity was neither naïve nor passive. All of these poets have very complicated relations to the avowal or disavowal of sexual identity in their lives, and there is no reason to imagine that the relation of this identity to their literary work would be any less complicated.

Eve Kosofsky Sedgwick shows how "in the vicinity of the closet, even what *counts* as a speech act is problematized on a perfectly routine basis" (*Epistemology* 3). The authors of the difficult poems I treat are all irrefutably "queer," but the "queerness" of their difficulty risks being crushed beneath the dead weight of an argument that they were busy either concealing their sexuality by their difficulty or using their difficulty as a specialized language with which they spoke to a specialized audience. While concealment and disclosure are activities that difficulty sponsors or frustrates, I want to take Sedgwick's statement more seriously than that. She suggests that concealment and disclosure *themselves* are problematized around the closet. Obfuscation and truth telling, in the proximity of issues of sexual definition, are not simple.

Michael Lynch tells an anecdote that succinctly illustrates the troubling effects of the closet on truth telling. When Walt Whitman was asked for confirmation of his homosexuality by an overly pressing John Addington Symonds, Whitman replied that he had six illegitimate children. This seems like a claim of heterosexuality: Whitman sired children. However, as Lynch points out, "Whitman was trying to disprove his homosexuality by claiming paternity in an argument to a homosexual who had a wife and four children" (93). In this example, Whitman both avows and disavows his homosexuality.

The operation of Whitman's comment to Symonds troubles the very idea of truth. In one sense, he is allying himself to Symonds as a homosexual by not forthrightly rejecting Symonds's suggestion, but in another, he is denying his connection to Symonds and homosexuality.

While Whitman's answer is in some sense pleasing to Symonds, it is concurrently, and perhaps overridingly, frustrating. Symonds desires *an answer*. Only so far as Symonds takes the lack of a negative response and the parallel between himself and Whitman to heart is Whitman's answer pleasing: but then it is incommunicable, because it depends on Symonds's own position as interlocutor.

In Lee Edelman's terms, Whitman's comment to Symonds is a perfect embodiment of "homographesis," which is "on one hand, a normalizing practice of cultural discrimination (generating, as a response, the self-nominalization that eventuates in the affirmative politics of a minoritized gay community), and on the other, a strategic resistance to that reification of sexual difference" (*Homographesis* 10). A homograph, as in the examples Edelman provides of the words "lead" or "bear," bears more than one meaning under the same sign. Homographesis, "in its deconstructive sense," troubles what it is finally to mean at all.

> It articulates the difference, that is, from the binary differentiation of sameness and difference, presence and absence: these couples wedded to each other in order to determine identity as sameness or presence to oneself. In this sense homographesis, in a gesture that conserves what it contests, defines as central to "homosexuality" a refusal of the specifications of identity (including sexual identity) that marks out the very space within which to think "homosexuality" itself. (14)

Sustained homographesis in the lyric was described by Keats as "negative capability," meaning a state in which a reader can "dwell in opposites." Negative capability can model, I suggest in the pages that follow, queer ontology. For Whitman, rhetorical suspense of meaning holds off death, maintaining the poet in a state of undeath. Ashbery uses paradox and polysemy to suggest that homosexuality is a spoiled identity, but in being spoiled it is also, always, stubbornly *alive*. Moore, in her late lyrics, also maintains paradox at her closures for purposes of liveliness; however, her efforts are directed toward the expression and sustenance of ecstasy. Crane in some ways provides the mirror image of Moore's ecstatic poetics. His poetics finds success in failure; in order to treat his poetic subjects properly, he must mind his "trespass vision." Crane models his ethics of poetic witnessing on the dynamics of pleasure in anal sex. His resignations more fully assert his agency. Finally, I discuss how Jack Spicer disembodies himself in his poetry in order to be with an impossible beloved. In a sense, Spicer flips over Whitman's embodying maneuver: He dematerializes himself in order to be with his disembodied beloved.

The "queer" in my title is also hortatory. Embedded in each lyric I discuss is an imperative to read differently. The reader, faced with innovations in the lyric form, must perform queer readings, that is, readings that go against the grain of heteronormative reading practices so as to participate in the construction of the patterns of meaning that constitute each lyric. A simple illustration of this occurs in another polyvalent title, that of John Ashbery's poem "Or in My Throat." The title might be read as announcing a poem meditating on artistic production: There is "ore" in Ashbery's throat. Only someone willing to imagine the speaker fellating another man can read the title as an utterance about where a sex partner might ejaculate. Determining the gender of the speaker does require a peek into the poem where the "poet" is referred to as "him." The alternative offered by the "or" suggests the perversions of frottage, a "money shot," a group situation, or passive anal intercourse, and a weighing of the pleasurable outcomes of each. This title alone insists on queering the poet/speaker's body; it conjures a male body that can be penetrated and ejaculated into. In Chapter 3 I will read "Or in My Throat" in depth, but here I only wish to show how even the very basic act of punning in a poem's title can map a queer body. This mapping is a function of the reader's ability or willingness to read male bodies as penetrable and to imagine a subject who might offer his partner an option for climax or who might mull over the relative advantages of having this partner come in his mouth. This queering, as I have mentioned above, is at the most basic level of "reading differently."

But Ashbery's title also emphasizes an aspect of the lyric that is not unrelated to imagining all bodies as penetrable. Is the poem in the poet's throat or in the reader's throat? The voice that speaks the lyric is and is not the reader's; identity slippage and interpenetration is central to any lyric. A confusion of tongues (whose tongue is in whose throat?) occurs between the poet, persona, or speaker(s) and the reader. This is unique to the genre. At moments, one is aligned with, and at others gagged by, the voice of the lyric. Reading a lyric is as embattled, embarrassing, ennobling, and euphoric as belting along to the car radio or singing karaoke. And I hope this book stands as testament to my belief that it is *at least* as fun.

Chapter 1

⌒

Snags and Gags: Cruising the Difficult

Poetic difficulty often marks the furthest reach of poetic meaning. It serves as a trace of drift or pulsion into the unmeaning, unknowable, and unspeakable. Much of the most exciting modern and contemporary poetry hovers at this edge, its lexical and affective power arising from unmappable, but somehow accessible, journeys out of and back into the known. Poetic difficulty lives at the site of poetry's central node: the conflict between what can and cannot be said. Because of this, poetic difficulty is as various as poetry itself. To make any generic claims about difficulty would be flawed in the same way that generic claims about the whole of poetry are flawed. The excitement of invention and discovery would drop out of material whose most characteristic urge is toward invention and discovery.

Some poets dwell in this conflict more than others just as some poets, for instance, experiment with the interplay of narrative and lyric more than others. A poet who is remarkably difficult in one poem may be the standard of clarity and availability in another. "Difficulty" is relatively new as a free-standing critical term. In the history of criticism the adjective "difficult" has mostly acted as minion of the critical term "obscurity." Still, the relation between the two has by no means become clear; "obscurity" currently has an entry in the *Princeton Encyclopedia of Poetry and Poetics* while "difficulty" does not. However, the term "obscure" is falling away from critical discourse, mostly because it attaches to texts with no forthright reference to a reader. "Difficulty," on the other hand, references the reading process: The text is only difficult insofar as it is "difficult" to decipher or read. In another register, "obscurity" suggests that there may be no identifiable patterns in a poem while "difficulty" generously considers even a lack of pattern as its own kind of pattern.

A quick comparison between John Press's 1958 study of obscurity, *The Chequer'd Shade: Reflections of Obscurity in Poetry,* and George Steiner's 1978 study "On Difficulty" helps index the critical drift from "obscurity" to "difficulty" in recent decades. Press and Steiner share every node of study as well as a typological method (from examinations of problematic or unknown vocabulary to examinations of the "nature of poetry") but examine them under two wholly different rubrics. Press finds obscurity to be both a complaint leveled against a poem by a frustrated audience as well as an effect a poem produces based on its traffic in unknown vocabulary, systems of thought, reference, public and private knowledges, themes, and so on. Steiner locates difficulty in the reader's comment: "This is a difficult poem." This reader is less exasperated than curious. Steiner asks and attempts to answer the question "what do we mean when we say: 'this poem, or this passage in this poem is *difficult?*'" (18). While there is no definitive moment where we can locate the shift from one term to the other, recent critical trends toward explicit and implicit considerations of readerly interpretation give "difficulty" an advantage over "obscurity," because "difficulty" keeps the processual nature of reading at the fore.

Steiner offers provisional definitions of four types of difficulty in his essay. He locates difficulty as that which does not happen in a text but in the reader's reception of it. As such, his typology's central goal is to catalogue snags: encounters a reader has with texts that challenge him to refer to outside authorities, fine-tune his sensibilities, wrangle with a dissimulating but yielding author, or reconsider the implicit contract of sense making between author and reader. Steiner asks the particular question of how it can happen that "[t]he individual reader or a group of readers find that they cannot understand this or that passage in a poem, or indeed the poem as a whole" (19). While the questions Steiner asks are provocative and illuminating, the readers he figuratively imagines reading poems are frustratingly unvarious; they are readers with the goal of making sense of the poem as it appears on the page.

When, in extreme cases, at the far end of his progressively more complicated typology, sense cannot be made in a poem, the reader must import it from discourses that hover around poetry more generally: what, for instance, a poem says about speech acts and their limits. While Steiner is appreciative of the stubbornly difficult, unparaphrasable poetry of Mallarmé or Celan, he suggests that "certain Dada and surrealist collages" are simply "nonsense or planned obfuscation" (46).

Steiner celebrates the extreme edge of sense making, but decries and disregards nonsense making. His typology of snags holds when a reader's only desire is the desire for sense, elastically defined but referencing a fantasy of sheer lucidity. However, generalizing and typifying the reader of poetry for whom this only can specify exclusively, for whom all resistances must yield or be explained in their unyielding, seems as naïve as a food critic suggesting that the exclusive love of vanilla ice cream is the organizing ontogenic principle and reference point of desert-lovers' palates.

For Steiner, "difficulty" signifies "snag," "snarl," or "knot" in its shoelace, Boy Scout or Gordian varieties. His typology is not complete in its catalogue of difficulties, not because he misses some or because there is more work to be done, but rather because the project of cataloguing difficulty disregards the fundamentally constitutive vastness and variety of interpretive communities and readerly desires.

Steiner identifies four types of progressively intricate difficulty, the first and most basic he calls "contingent difficulty." Steiner suggests that contingent difficulty is by and large what readers mean when they complain that a poem is difficult; it is difficulty's colloquial register. These are difficulties that arise from a reader's lack of information, difficulties solved by the right dictionary or index. Steiner metaphorizes these difficulties as "stick[ing] like burrs to the fabric of the text" (27). Interestingly, he suggests that while contingent difficulties are places where the reader gets stuck reading, so are they themselves stuck onto the text. These burrs, after a trip to an authoritative reference work, actually turn out to be pearls in the "fabric" or some such detail swallowed by the poem's pattern. This metaphor, in its fuzzily constructed relation of text, fabric, burr, and reader can serve as itself a burr stuck to Steiner's text, a catch in his scholarly treatment of difficulty. Diagrammed in figural space, we find a before-and-after ad. Before, the ignorant reader stumbles; after, with the proper linguistic vitamin supplement, he bounds over the obstacle that seemed insurmountable. This does describe a moment of dictionary-supplemented localized epiphany with which all readers are surely familiar, however, it also participates in a fantasized temporality (before/after; unknowing/knowing; burr/pearl) that freezes a readerly relation to texts. Already, in this simplest form of "difficulty," Steiner posits readerly unknowing as difficulty's cause, and while certainly describing a kind of epistemic temporality, his definition requires a fantasy of a peculiarly scholarly leaning readerly project that locates its readerly pleasure in a text/fabric's knit, weave, or pattern as it refers to patterns or authoritative structures of meaning outside of itself. Alternatively, one can imagine a reader who adores undefined but contextualized archaism, dialect, technical specificity, neologism, slang, or argot without any desire to reach outside of a poem for definition (19–21).

A formulation Eve Kosofsky Sedgwick makes about queer reading practices offers an entrée to imagining this reader, a reader who reads for disjunction rather than in order to obviate it. She writes:

> I think that for many of us [queer readers] in childhood the ability to attach intently to a few cultural objects ... whose meaning seemed mysterious, excessive, or oblique in relation to the codes most readily available to us, became a prime resource for survival. We needed for there to be sites where the meanings didn't line up tidily with each other, and we learned to invest those sites with fascination and love. (*Tendencies* 3)

While Sedgwick does not suggest that queer readers are precisely readers who don't look things up, she does offer a powerful account of why queer readers might not read like George Steiner's fantasized reader. This "perverse" reading style, which is insistent about taking pleasure in the disjunct, the places where dominant codes of meaning, identity, identification, or desire are held off by mysteriousness, excessiveness, or obliquity, might find the burrs on a text the most delectable bits of it *because* of their burr-likeness, because they do not simply flatten into the fabric, because a perverse reader can attach to the unattachedness of these moments.

The understanding that Steiner locates at the center of questions of contingent, as well as his other modes of, difficulty, shorn as it is from an explicit circuitry of desire and readerly motivation, implicitly constructs a reader who wants meanings to line up, to conform to codes. Sedgwick offers a tool to pry the lid off this construct; what if, she asks, a reader's fondest and most intense moments of reading are places which do not settle down into codes and, therefore, allow excessive attachment? Understanding, then, becomes a verb-leaning means to pleasure, a creator of tension, rather than a noun-ish tension reduction.

Considering understanding as a means, amid other means, to pleasure rather than as *the* pleasure of reading is rather like considering nonpenetrative sexual activity as truly sex. No penetration, heteronormative sexual and poetic codes demand, no pleasure. Steiner's poetic scene features texts that resist and readers who seek penetrative comprehension. When Steiner describes the "authentic, immensely rare, poem" in Heidegger's language the sense of penetrator and penetrated tweak his philosophic musing rather comically. This supreme, rare, and authentic poem frustrates understanding based on an understanding of understanding as penetrative. This poem is "one in which 'the Being of language' finds unimpeded lodging, in which the poet is … an 'openness to', a supreme listener to, the genius of speech. The result of such openness is not so much a text, but an 'act,' and eventuation of Being and literal 'coming into Being'" (46). This is a poet who not only gets fucked, but gets *literally* come in, not by the reader (not in this "supreme poem") but by the "genius of speech." I point this out as much to show penetrative metaphors on the highest floor that Steiner's theoretical elevator reaches as to demonstrate how perverse reading, in its unauthorized interventions, yields readings that can flank, or even sometimes reinvigorate and undergird, not just a richer understanding, but a richer sense of the term "understanding" itself.

Coextensive with this idea of a differently motivated reader must be a sense of an author with this perverse reader, or community of perverse readers, in mind. By "in mind" I do not wish to lean too heartily on the concept of authorial intention, rather to suggest that the textual patterns an author might create can be vectored toward nonpenetrative reading practices as organized by a community, a community whose very organizing principle might be "perverse" reading.

While the possibility of a perverse reader or reading community does not necessarily diminish the usefulness or descriptiveness of Steiner's first type of difficulty, it does, at this basic level of his typology, offer a whiff of what, as the "levels" become more and more complex, becomes a stench. Modal difficulty, Steiner's second level, "falls to one side of the operative distinction between surface-understanding or paraphrase on the one hand, and penetrative comprehension on the other" (29). While contingent difficulties arise from the "obvious plurality of word and world," modal difficulties "lie in the eye of the beholder" (33). Here, the reader experiences the state of not inhabiting the subjectivity, or epistemic position, that could make sense of a poem. The reader understands the terms used in a poem but is missing the glue to stick them together.

Steiner's central concern is the recession of older texts, "the tragedies of Voltaire … [or] the epic poetry of Bioardo, Ariosto, and Tasso," from the contemporary reader's grasp (32). Vernon Shetley helps generalize this temporally based scheme to any text that eludes, in Steiner's words, not "reconstructive acquaintance achieved by the virtue of knowledge and archaeology of feeling," but "authentic apprehension, [and] penetrative inscape" (Ibid.). Shetley writes that "[w]hat Steiner sees as the results of temporal change, however, we might recode in terms of interpretive communities; contingent and modal difficulties occur when works travel across the boundaries of interpretive communities, and such passages can take place spatially as well as temporally" (9). Modal difficulty, without Shetley's amendment, would be banned from contemporary texts due to Steiner's lack of ability to imagine, or lack of concern with, differences between readers as they intersect with interpretive communities that occur simultaneously in time. Even with Shetley's addition, modal difficulty is based on the fantasy of a reader plugging in to, penetrating, the geist of a text in which there is only one plug format and only one geist. This fantasy underdetermines the rhythms and patterns of a text that Steiner holds cannot be described and overdetermines the pleasure of inhabiting, embodying, standing beside, listening to, overhearing, disavowing, or fixating on such rhythms and patterns. So, while suggesting that some knowledges cannot simply be had but must be felt, it adds that the feeling difficult texts convey must first and foremost tickle the reader's sense of being in the know. This double movement, a conflation of epistemology and ontology writ large (doing neither any favors), if accepted, cuts the legs out from under any critical approach that seeks to further define difficult texts or theorize why readers read them.

The idea that the writer creates obstacles intentionally fits into Steiner's third kind of difficulty, "tactical," which he defines as what occurs when, " ... [t]he poet [chooses] to be obscure in order to achieve certain specific stylistic effects. He may find himself compelled towards obliquity and cloture by political circumstances: there is a very long history of Aesopian language, of 'encoding' and allegoric indirection in poetry written under pressure of totalitarian censorship (oppression, says Borges, is the mother of metaphor)" (33–4). The difference between difficulty created by the reader's lack of knowledge and that created by the writer's willful obliquity is evidenced in the reading process. Thus, in Steiner's scheme, a reader reads the writer's oscillation between two poles: wanting to be easily understood and not wanting to be easily understood. If it seems the writer wants to be understood, we have contingent or modal difficulty, if not, tactical or ontological difficulty. The reader calculates when it seems that his or her understanding seems impeded or impelled by the writer. "Tactical" difficulty implies a level of intentional obscurity on the author's part as interpreted by the reader, which "we are meant to understand slowly," while "ontological" difficulty "puts into question the essential suppositions that lie behind poetry as we have known it"(45; 41). These, the highest level of Steiner's difficulties,

> cannot be looked up; they cannot be resolved by genuine readjustment or artifice of sensibility; they are not an intentional technique of retardation and creative uncertainty (though these may be their immediate effect).

> *Ontological* difficulties confront us with blank questions about the nature of human speech, about the status of significance, about the necessity and purpose of the construct which we have ... come to perceive as a poem. (41)

Ontological difficulties, one suspects, can only happen in poems "we" somehow already know are great poems, written by poets we *already know* are great poets.

John Ashbery presents a problem for Steiner's types; he deploys purposeful difficulty and obliquity, even to the point of questioning what a speech act is, but on the level of the contingent. My example is based on a novel, but holds the same shape as contingent difficulty as Steiner describes it in his poetic typology, which he suggests is applicable across "literary texts as a whole" (47). While the nature of prose may enable Ashbery's located and lucid description of his deployment of contingent difficulty, since it is based on closure and closure is an oft considered generic moment in thinking about the novel, it does not disqualify it as the sort of snag Steiner describes. In an interview, when asked whether he's ever played a "gag" on his readers, Ashbery replies:

> A gag that has probably gone unnoticed turns up in the last sentence of the novel I wrote with James Schuyler [*A Nest of Ninnies*]. Actually it's my sentence. It reads: "So it was that the cliff dwellers, after bidding their cousins good night, moved off toward the parking area, while the latter bent their steps toward the partially rebuilt shopping plaza in the teeth of the freshening foehn." *Foehn* is a kind of warm wind that blows in Bavaria that produces a fog. I would doubt that many people know that. I liked the idea that people, if they bothered to, would have to open the dictionary to find out what the last word in the novel meant. They'd be closing one book and opening another. (Stitt 36–7)

For Ashbery, here and elsewhere, deployed contingent difficulty is a producer of glee, as exemplified throughout his oeuvre by his seemingly random insertion of the names of archaic musical instruments. My use of this example, while it does not deny that Steiner's typology has some descriptive use-value, suggests most of all that Ashbery is a "difficult" writer by design: Even at the simplest level of difficulty, he calculates and strategizes. Further, it suggests that perverse writerly designs on difficulty are what fall out of Steiner's typology. Ashbery hides nothing behind "foehn" beside the desire that the reader go to the dictionary. Thus, this word's presence is both contingently and tactically difficult, while in fact really, as I will suggest, properly being neither because it yields no sense that smoothes back into the pattern of the text, nor delays the reader en route to "penetrative comprehension." Suggesting that there is a single type of either readerly attachment to texts or of a writer's demands or designs on a reader undergirds (while it is finally that which erodes) the distinction between Steiner's types.

Ashbery's gleefully played gag in *A Nest of Ninnies,* already a novel stylistically aimed to readers of the sort who appreciate the perverse as it has been explored by the fabulations of style in Ronald Firbank's campy novels, highlights both Ashbery's awareness of readers who do look things up and his desire to pervert contingent difficulty by offsetting its proffered closure, ("I, reader, will find the answer and close the case"). The novel's closure opens outward for the hell of it. Just as opening up the dictionary perverts the novel's closure, so does finding the definition of "foehn" offer little traction within the novel. The final sentence, after all, does not take place in Bavaria, where foehns generally occur. It is, in the end and in ending, an empty gesture that references nothing but itself. This foehn does what foehns more generally do, it blows in fog.

And while it would be unfair to hold Steiner's self-admitted "rough and preliminary" classifications to task for their roughness or preliminariness, it seems just to interrogate the assumptions about reading and writing that underwrite his authoritative, if sketchy, approach to the general topic of "difficulty" (47). He has, after all, become an unavoidable figure for critics discussing difficulty, being the first to offer a typology, and provisionariness has not stopped his scheme from becoming central to our discussion of it.[1] Steiner's typology offers more by the way of describing critical approaches in the face of difficulty than in describing difficulties themselves. Each term implies a different readerly project: looking up, getting in tune, climbing obstacles, and referencing what a speech act is in the first place (even if the result is blank). However, as shown in the following example, poems can shift in the face of their audiences' projects, and often (particularly around homosexual meaning) more than one locatable audience is being addressed at a time.

Ashbery's "The Ongoing Story," as read by Thomas Yingling, "locates the act of cruising as one stable field in a life otherwise uninterpretable and unstable" (119). In Yingling's reading, cruising offers both a way into the poem, that is, a way of interpreting the poem, as well as a refuge from unknowing for the speaker within the poem. Nowhere does the poem name cruising; the poem's only action is answering the phone, all the rest takes place behind the sheer curtain of the hypothetical. The poem begins:

> I could say it's the happiest period of my life.
> It hasn't got much competition! Yesterday
> It seemed a flatness, hotness. As though it barely stood out

From the rocks of all the years before. Today it sheds
That old name, without assuming any new one.
I think it's still there. (*Wave* 11)

"It" is an unspecified period of time, which between "yesterday" and "today" shifted its mien. It seemed almost describable yesterday through two figures, a stretch of hot, flat asphalt and a rock atop a pile of rocks. Yesterday's explanatory metaphors did not quite fit together, but today's are even more tentative: "it" has become nameless and has possibly come to an end, an end held off only by the suspicion that "it" still exists. The second stanza retools this pronoun in order to describe the present crisis of missing a formerly more comfortable "it": "It was as though I'd been left with the empty street / A few seconds after the bus pulled out. A dollop of afternoon wind." Since "it," a self-made periodization, helped place the speaker in his own life, "it"'s absence or near illegibility force the speaker into a new fantasy of place. The stanza ends with useless suggestions that others might make to ameliorate the speaker's felt situation: "Plan to entertain, / To get out" (Ibid.).

The last two stanzas meditate on this self's misplacement. "What good," the speaker asks are all the "great ideas," "if you can't remember one / At the moment you're so to speak mounting the guillotine. ..." Why pursue eloquence and great thoughts if these both abandon you in times of crisis? The speaker suspects that knowing always buckles in the rush of a very pressing present. Furthermore, he wonders if in fact the great ideas are "covered in a course / called Background of Great Ideas" and therefore are, by their formulaic nature, *a priori*, useless. These kinds of knowing are elbowed out of place by the more sufficient "knowledge that people live close by ... ." This poem suggests that the immanence of knowledge is less sustaining than actual or fantasmatic jostling with people whom one does not know. It offers a poetics whereby a cruising reader does not look to "get to know" the poet or speaker, but rather seeks an encounter with a poet or speaker who will afterward walk away still anonymous.

The final stanza literalizes the cruising fantasy by offering an address to a cruised "you." The speaker directly addresses:

... you,
In your deliberate distinctness, whom I love and gladly
Agree to walk blindly into the night with,
Your realness is real to me though I would never take any of it
Just to see how it grows. A knowledge that people live close by is,
I think, enough. And even if only first names are ever exchanged
The people who own them seem rock-true and marvelously self-sufficient.

The "I think" reinstates the usefulness of intuition as it was practiced in the first stanza in which assertion actually performed the continuation of a vaporously nominalized temporal period. Here, once again, intuition modestly nudges forward a solution to a seemingly unnamable problem. Cruising, walking into the night with a stranger who might only be available on a first-name basis, offers evidence of life, while it does not offer, properly patronymically speaking, locutionary or epistemic purchase. It gives a feeling of proximity that, the speaker suggests, may be the height of epistemic searches in the first place. It hikes the epistemic into the ontic. Michael Warner avers, "Contrary to myth, what one relishes in loving strangers is not mere anonymity, nor meaningless release. It is the pleasure of belonging to a sexual world, in which one's sexuality finds an answering resonance not just in one other, but in a world of others" (*Trouble* 179). The realness that "is real to me though I would never take any of it" offers an alternative readerly position to Steiner's "penetrative comprehension." This speaker is neither a penetrative nor an acquisitive (the import of "comprehend") reader of others. The "ongoingness" of any story, this poem postulates, takes precedence over epistemic immanence.

As Yingling suggests, cruising is the central node of this poem; eroticized encounters with strangers are both its literal and figurative ground. A reader who cannot imagine such encounters as they exist for real in gay lives, and thereby as a fantasmatic organizing principle for these meditations, cannot follow the arc of the poem as it moves from general ponderings on unnamable doldrums in life to specific cruisy strategizing around and about them. Such a reader will read the poem as moving from generalization to generalization without touching down. There undoubtedly could be some pleasure in such a reading since the shifts between the thoughts are clever, and the thoughts themselves sparkle sonically as they oscillate between colloquial and metaphysical speculation. There could likewise be pleasure in reading the poem as an address to the reader about his own position in the poem. However, without cruising as a thematic node, the poem does not develop past its first stanza. It is a neatly set-up stage, but nothing happens on it. While I would not want to suggest that this poem invites or requires "penetrative comprehension," it does require that its linguistic forms take life from a mimetic relation to life itself. This poem wants to be cruised, wants the "rock-true and marvelously self-sufficient" nature of the reader to be felt reciprocally and simultaneously with its own. A reading that does not cruise the poem may take pleasure in the poem's polyphony but does not bring the poem's own insights about such taken pleasures to bear on its meanings. So, while cruising is not the key that unlocks the poem—this is a poem that theorizes the pleasures of incomplete access—it is fundamental to the poem's lyric operation.

If, as is often the case in criticism of contemporary poetry, critics implicitly assume that the audience is straight and that a homosexual writer is either frankly informing the audience of the vocabularies and practices of their (homophobically constructed fantasmatic) "sexual community," or withholding willfully, then all modal difficulty around gay subtexts or texts is, in Steiner's scheme, tactical. The author is holding out on purpose, the logic goes, knowing that part of his audience is straight. Such a construction of the "honest" (straight) reader is especially easy to access in violently negative reviews of Ashbery's work.[2] In a particular type of antihomophobic project, on the other hand, a critic might concentrate on the "gay reading" of this poem, as Yingling does, where cruising is a given. While the latter approach is far more "honest" about its assumptions and goals than the former (allowing for many audiences but specifying one), neither do much to trace the mechanics of how difficulty happens in this poem, or how the poem demands itself be read, and both depend on a stabilization of the audience, as having or not having a particular knowledge. So while the concept of "modal" difficulty helps locate the difference between what happens between this poem and its various readers, it does nothing to describe or trace the text's own attitude toward, or strategy of, difficulty. Contingent difficulty certainly does not describe the central operations of "The Ongoing Story" for a straight and/or uncomprehending reader but what is to say that the difficulty he experiences is not tactical, since Ashbery could have had skirting homophobes and writing to a gay audience in mind? Further, what is to say that this poem is not ontologically difficult insofar as it does, in its shifty relation to audience, actually thematize and actualize a difficulty of human speech, offering to unknowing readers a blank, unanswerable question about their comprehension, or to a knowing reader: an evanescent moment of presence that cannot properly be known but only felt as proximity, challenging, that is to say, the reader's unknowing, but *also* his knowing. The intention embedded in both "tactical" and "ontological" difficulty presents a special problem for reading texts that involve gay meanings.

As I have discussed above, Eve Kosofsky Sedgwick shows in *Epistemology of the Closet* that the closet always functions around gay meanings, as well as around any moment of definitional crisis in the binary homosexual/ heterosexual. Structures of knowing and unknowing are always thrown into overdrive around locutions and performances of or about homosexuality. The system of knowing and unknowing upon which Steiner bases his typology of difficulty uses knowing as a privileged category for a reader's response. While this seems an important *part* of describing difficulty, it leaves out what are crucial textures, mechanics, and strategies of unknowing that a reader or author can bring to a text. In "The Ongoing Story," for instance, the desired proximity to others includes a willful unknowing on the speaker's part, one imbricated in the knowledge of cruising but not subsumed by it. The pleasures of this particular knowing/unknowing are what the author offers the reader in the structure of his poem both intra- and extra-textually.

While Steiner's terms offer a stepping-off point for discussions of difficulty, a different apparatus will be necessary to approach difficulty in queer texts. When the embedded narratives in Steiner's typology are explicated, his labels look less useful than prohibitive: force fields keeping poems safe from unauthorized readers. This is partly a fault of a typological approach, especially when such an approach is meant to be all-purpose. With any label of "all-purpose," as with household cleaners, there are some purposes, such as cleaning one's contact lenses, that are adamantly not included. A typology offers labels and examples while poetic difficulty marks most of all unexemplifiable and un- or antireferential experiences of reading. Difficulty, at its most magnificent, consists of unexpected breakages and resettings and breakages—or as an Ashbery poem title has it, meaning that is "Lost and Found and Lost Again." This is not to say that difficulty cannot be described at all, but rather that the flux of its status as something describable is fundamental to its constitution and must be central to any definitional project. Such flux can seem hobbling to a literary critic, because it insists that he or she return to the most basic and apparently bodiless and unanswerable questions such as: "Why do readers read difficult texts at all?"

Asking such questions, however, is fundamental not just to the successful criticism of difficult poems but also to the successful maintenance of readerly pleasure in the face of the difficult. As in a cruising situation, boredom, disenchantment, fear, shame, and even disgust are likely components of desire and excitement.

The sheer variety in difficulty's party mix of affect struck me when I was talking to a friend with whom I share many poetic tastes, as well as opinions and despairs about the state of poetry. He could never be that excited about Ashbery, but knew that I was, and tried to cathect Ashbery's work. He couldn't. Over the phone he reported that he was about to give up and told me, sheepishly, that he just didn't *get* Ashbery; I agreed, nor did I really.

Somehow, my commiseration in my friend's "not getting it," as he tells it, made all the difference. The next day he went out, bought *Flow Chart* (arguably Ashbery's most unwieldy volume), gobbled it up eagerly, and has been enthralled ever since.

Chapter 2

Rhetorical Suspense, Sexuality, and Death in Whitman's "Calamus" Poems

Across the 39-poem span of "Calamus," Whitman creates and sustains thematic and rhetorical suspensions. He manifestly dismisses the reader, as we will see in "Whoever You Are Holding Me Now in Hand," reserves his affections for a particular reader, in "These I Singing in Spring" and "To a Western Boy," declares himself unreachable, in "Are You the New Person Drawn toward Me," or dares "not tell in words" the core of his motivation and emotion, in "Earth, My Likeness" (270–1; 272–3; 277; 284; 285). These are only several of the most obvious examples. Simultaneous with these forthright rejections of the reader, Whitman's poems declare that the reader is holding "him," not his book, in hand, and that for the right person he is wholly available. Similarly, he opines that the crucial ingredient that would make any man the proper recipient of his poems and affections "has always been waiting, latent in all men" (285).

More locally, Whitman creates rhetorical suspensions with a structure of repeated negations followed by an initially positive but finally frustrated assertion, what I will call the "not ... not ... not ... but" structure. Five of the sequence's poems are dominated by this structure, offering huge lists, each line headed by "Not" or "Nor." Other poems use a less-extended version of this structure as their closure, offering a single or double "not" and an ultimate "but." In each case, extended or brief, Whitman holds off meaning, which implies an ultimate provision of meaning, and then proffers something of a different category in place of what was expected. This rhetorical bait-and-switch corresponds to the thematic oscillation between absolute availability and absolute unavailability, materiality and ghostliness, and between the proffering and withholding of "the truth" about the poet's sexual identity. In order to trace the development of these devices and themes across the span of the group, I begin by mapping the thematics of the sequence's first three poems, which declare the ambitions and scope of the cycle, move to the middle of the sequence and look more closely at the most vivid examples of the "not … not … not … but" structure, and then examine the closure that the last few poems offer the group. Closural effects happen at the level of the group of poems, that is, there are individual closures to each and every poem in the cycle, but also, the cycle itself has an arc: a development from beginning to end that entails and organizes the thematics and rhetorical moves of the individual poems.

Issues of concealment and revelation of homosexual thematics are central to Whitman's "Calamus" poems. The first poem of the group "In Paths Untrodden" declares at its cymbal-crashing conclusion Whitman's intention: "To tell the secret of my nights and days, / To celebrate the need of comrades" (268). Throughout the sequence, what can and cannot, or will and will not, be revealed rivets the reader. It is difficult to read the cycle without wishing that through some adjustment one could be their true recipient, or conversely, without believing that perhaps, in fact, one is. With this dynamic in mind, some critics have set about locating a particular man to whom these poems were addressed or about whom these poems were written. Such approaches see the teasing moments of "Calamus" as the broken up pieces of a scholarly and historical puzzle rather than as primarily *poetic* effects.

Alan Helms, in his article on a sequence of 12 poems that Whitman titled "Live Oak with Moss," suggests that the "Live Oak" series is the "Calamus" group's less-closeted origin (185–7).[1] Helms suggests not only that each group starts off homo-affirmative and then gutters in the chill wind of homophobia, but also that Whitman, further capitulating to homophobic pressures, obfuscates the courage of the "Live Oak" narrative in its metamorphosis into the "Calamus" series. Helms argues that the sequentiality of the "Live Oak" poems revealed too much and that the sequence had to be broken from its "fairly simple story of infatuation, abandonment, and accommodation"(187). In order to prove that Whitman's poetry is directly biographical, Helm's quotes a note found on the back of the manuscript of the "Live Oak with Moss" poem that reads:

> A Cluster of Poems, Sonnets expressing the thoughts, pictures, aspirations &c
> Fit to be perused during the days of the approach of Death.

> (that I have prepared myself for that purpose.—
> (Remember now—
> Remember then
> (qtd. Helms 186; final punctuation absent in text)

Helms uses this fascinating note to show that the "Live Oak" poems are about events that actually happened to Whitman, which Whitman then sets about to remember. Helms further suggests, following Charles Shivley, that these poems are likely about Fred Vaughan. This note, Helms contends, points to a transparent connection between the group of poems that was to become the "Calamus" poems and Whitman's life. That is, the homoerotics in these poems have real and robust roots in lived experience. One can understand the impulse to make such a move in the face of homophobic insistence on proof of Whitman's sexuality. This proof is strangely but notoriously difficult to produce.

As I mentioned in the Preface, Michael Lynch points out an excellent example of Whitman being both inside and outside the closet when he was asked for confirmation of his homosexuality by John Addington Symonds. Whitman's reply that he had six illegitimate children seems like a claim of heterosexuality, except for the fact that "Whitman was trying to disprove his homosexuality by claiming paternity in an argument to a homosexual who had a wife and four children" (93). In this example, as I will argue is also true in the "Calamus" poems, Whitman inhabits the site between avowal and disavowal. The operation of Whitman's comment troubles the very idea of truth. Whitman is both allying himself to Symonds as a homosexual and, at the same time, denying his connection to Symonds and homosexuality. Thus, while Whitman's answer is the one Symonds wants, it is concurrently frustrating because Symonds desires an answer that can stand independent from his own position as interlocutor. Only so far as Symonds takes into account the parallel between himself and Whitman is Whitman's answer pleasing, but then it is not transportable, because it depends on Symonds's own particular position.

My treatment of Whitman's "Calamus" group will not show that Whitman was concealing or divulging his lived sexuality, nor that the organizing principle of the final form of the these poems is obfuscation—both assertions negate aspects of poetic craft and linguistic performances that seem crucial. Rather, I will show that Whitman's understanding of the operations of his readers' (and his own) desire to know "the truth" about sexuality and death underwrite the group's most impressive poetic effects. Whitman was, I argue, privy to the operation of "truth" in the proximity of oppositional sexuality and used this knowledge to create exciting lexical events.

Kevin Kopelson, in an essay on "Wilde, Barthes and the Orgasmics of Truth," suggests that "... [f]or those who, like Wilde and Barthes, would speak (about themselves, about 'their true sexuality') from positions of symbolic alienation, the only viable alternative, the only essential discourse of truth, the only reliable rhetorical figure, is the paradox, the negation of the stereotype" (28). Whitman fits this description uneasily since, as Michael Lynch explores in his seminal essay on "adhesiveness" and the relation between phrenology and the development of the category of the homosexual, homosexuality was not yet, in Whitman's day, a stereotypology. However, Whitman does write from a position of "symbolic alienation" about manly love, even if "homosexuality" had not yet fully emerged as *the* stereotype. One can argue, in fact, that the structures of negation that Whitman charts in "Calamus" have some relation to the firming up of the stereotypology of homosexuality itself.[2] That is, Whitman's tactics against one configuration of stereotypology (Kopelson suggests all *paradoxa* is damned to become *doxa* or shared opinion) can finally, perhaps inevitably, metamorphose to a stereotypology of its own.

Kopelson shows how Barthes and Wilde desire to convey their sexuality but can only convey what it is not. The "*doxa*" of dominant modes of identity and belief must be transferred to "*paradoxa*," but such a transformation is not an end point. "Truth," as these authors create it must be utterly mobile in order to escape popular opinion, which is ever encroaching. Any simple negative, furthermore, would shore up rather than hold off the dominant (stereo)typology. This is to say that any "truth" of oppositional sexualities will not show up as "truth," but rather, as trouble, as activity that will not settle down.[3] Whitman's negations, above all mobile and unsettling, become signs of neither truth nor lies. In their restless activity, they pass through negation to something that might better be called "true lies." Further, the operations of truth around sexuality and truth around death are so intertwined in this sequence that Whitman's epistemological restlessness about truth coincides with, and shores up, an ontological restlessness. The poems are concerned less with aliveness or death as single states than with an impossible mix of the two: undeath. It is in the state of being undead that the sequence finds troubled rest at its close, and also, I will argue, troubled comfort.

From the very beginning of the sequence, regardless of discussions of the real people this sequence might be about, to, or for, there is no single or easily located recipient. "You" restlessly shifts, expands, and contracts throughout the cycle, just as "I" eludes discovery, capture, and even materiality. The second poem of the sequence, "Scented Herbage of My Breast," ends with a lengthy apostrophe to death who "will someday take control of all ... may-be you are what it is all for, but it does not last so very long, / But you will last very long" (270). The act of writing the sequence is openly declared as an attempt to mime or borrow death's "tone" that is intimately ensnared with love. "Give me your tone therefore O death, that I may accord with it, / Give me yourself, for I see that you belong to me now above all, and are folded inseparably together, you love and death are" (269–70). This poem, coming immediately after the introductory "In Paths Untrodden," follows up the first poem's clarion call to tell "the secret of my nights and days," and further suggests that borrowing death's "tone" will help the poet "give an example to lovers to take permanent shape and will through the States" (269). "Death" is a theme, a persona, an operation, and an exemplar. Just as deictics fuzz in Whitman's treatment, so, relatedly, do states of being. "Death" stands for permanence that has a lesson to teach about steadfastness, the shortness of time, the mobility and mutability of forms of life, the exhilaration of extremity, and the temporal shiftiness of written texts.

"Death's tone" takes the form of speaking about a time long after the poet's death in "Recorders Ages Hence" (the eighth poem in the sequence), in which Whitman imagines a time well past his own. He shows less interest in preparing his legacy than in using the idea of his legacy to gain more access to the present moment; the poem utilizes the structure of defining the present for an imagined future audience in order to describe and delight in an embodied and unambiguous present. This temporal scheme gives rise to a tender immediacy whose final image is a sharp-focused, hand-in-hand stroll with "his friend" that sweeps away all the present anxieties about returned love, unrequited insomniac longing, and other constituent malaises of lived love affairs. The poem builds from images of the poet pining for the lover and moves progressively toward the climactic touching. He has "lonesome walks," "lay[s] sleepless," has "sick dread" for the possibility that the lover is indifferent. But out of musings on the loss of everything, including his own life, and in the form of describing himself to future recorders, Whitman produces a moment of embodied imagination, enacted and metaphorized as a touch.[4] This end point, a very highly imagined present, as well as a release from anxiety about loss, must be seen as the goal of the poet's projecting himself past his own death. Such projection affords him intimacies more piquant and less vexed than those available without the foreground of utter loss. In this poem, Whitman shows how "inseparably folded together, you love and death are," by declaring his legacy as having been "the tenderest lover" (269; 276). He manages to create the kind of trademark participle presence he enacts and thematizes in the leaping "ings" of "We Two Boys Together Clinging." Adding death to the stew of the present moment gives that present more emotional punch and clears away lived obstacles like momentary absence or imagined future loss, showing death to be a clarifying and vivifying principle.

Helms, in pursuit of transparent biographical connections, does not pursue the verso note's transparent declaration that these are poems *particularly* "[f]it to be perused during the days of the approach of Death." Nor does Helms comment on the oddness of the note's mechanics, most specifically the strange charge created by the double syntactical strain of "that I have prepared myself for that purpose," which is amplified by the ultimately unclosed serial parentheses. The "Fit to be perused" line could mean: I have prepared *these songs* myself in anticipation of the approach of death, or I have prepared *myself* for the approach of death. These are similar but do not collapse completely into one another. Preparing the songs for "some day in the future" when death approaches is different from preparing oneself "right now" for death.

The open parenthesis indicates unfinishedness, but also, and more eerily, that the "now" and "then" of the statement are both simultaneously, utterly immediate. That is, the open parentheses gesture to a spillage from the moment of writing to the moment of reading. It is as if the meditative and wistful "remember now, remember then" actually ended off the page at the scene of reading the incantation. The absence of a final parenthesis gestures to the fact that the imperatives are coexistent with their performance in the world. In a small but persistent way, this missing punctuation mark reminds that the boundary between word and world is permeable. This reminder of permeability is not solely aimed at the reader, but is also directed at the writer as reader of his own work. Every reader, no matter how close to or distant from the site of writing, is included in the "now" to which Whitman gestures. However, we are also included in the "then" in the same way that the approach of death is far off in the future and immediately at hand in the "that I have prepared myself for that purpose" line immediately before it. The verb "remember," in its repetition, further insists on the proximity of past, present, and future.

Kenneth Burke, in *The Philosophy of Literary Form,* offers a useful tool to describe this moment when he suggests "three subdivisions for the analysis of an act in poetry": dream, prayer, and chart. Burke describes "dream" as "the unconscious or subconscious factors in a poem," "prayer" as the "communicative functions of a poem," and "chart" as "the realistic sizing-up of situations that is sometimes explicit, sometimes implicit, in poetic strategies" (6–7). The "Calamus" poems, when read as strictly autobiographical, are in the "dream" and "prayer" categories. Whitman is setting his powerful poetics loose in his memory and at the same time addressing, even imploring, a figure from his past. The "chart" aspect of the poems is largely underregarded. A "chart" attempts to translate an operation in the world into an operation of words on a page. Once written, a "chart" serves as evidence of its subject in the world but also as a starting point for strategically approaching this subject.

The "Live Oak" poems, according to the note Helms uncovered, are meant to perform the function of taking down "the way things are," which will help somehow during "the days of the approach of Death." This series and the "Calamus" series that follows it are a chart of insights into the world and being that will jog the poet or reader's memory at a moment when that being and that world are about to change drastically. These insights cluster around the suspension of the reader (who is also the author since his inscription addresses the poems to himself in the future). These poems act out a combination of attractions and repulsions with the reader in mind meant to prepare the reader for death. The group charts the effects of desiring the truth about sexuality, about death, and finally, about life after death, and the way those desires can be metamorphosed into a tool for being and dying. The group is a preparation, like other preparations of "calamus" or sweet flag, in the sense that it is meant to soothe, to comfort.[5]

In the third poem of the sequence, "Whoever You Are Holding Me Now in Hand," following his poems declaring this sequence about the secrets of his love and about his concerns and strategies for dealing with death, Whitman tells the reader several times frankly to go away. Even after the reader is dismissed as an inadequate disciple and a bad companion, the poem that dismisses the reader and the poem sequence itself still carries on. In the third stanza, Whitman lists increasingly prohibitive reasons why the reader might think twice about continuing to read. The climax of the reasons is an outright dismissal.

> The way is suspicious, the result uncertain, perhaps destructive,
> You would have to give up all else, I alone would expect to be your sole
>   and exclusive standard,
> Your novitiate would even then be long and exhausting,
> The whole past theory of your life and all conformity to the
>   lives around you would have to be abandon'd,
> Therefore release me now before troubling yourself any
>   further, let go your hand from my shoulders,
> Put me down and depart on your way. (270)

Whitman, several stanzas later, explains that not only is it useless to become his disciple but that he has eluded the reader even before he began to desire to be a disciple. The poet anticipated the reader's desire and began toying with him before the reader noticed.

> But these leaves conning you con at peril,
> For these leaves and me you will not understand,
> They will elude you at first and still more afterward, I will
>   certainly elude you,
> Even while you think you had unquestionably caught me, behold!
> Already you see I have escaped from you. (271)

This is far from the last poem in the "Calamus" group, and it requires some work on the reader's part to place these dismissals as sincere, or more important, perhaps, to place the poet in a position in which these dismissals are not a sign of an endemic insincerity. In these poems particularly, sincerity is at stake since the poems are declared as standing in for, or even being in the first place, the poet's body.

The reader had to glide over the first dismissal, "put me down!", and the declaration that the reader will never understand the poems, "Already ... I have escaped from you," in order to get to the final stanza of the poem where an even stronger dismissal takes place.

> For it is not for what I have put into it that I have written this book,
> Nor is it by reading it you will acquire it,
> Nor do those know me best who admire me and vauntingly praise me,
> Nor will the candidates for my love (unless at most a very few) prove
>   victorious,
> Nor will my poems do good only, they will do just as much evil,
>   perhaps more,
> For all is useless without that which you may guess at many times and not
>   hit, that which I hinted at;
> Therefore release me and depart on your way. (271)

Allen Grossman uses this poem to show that "Whitman's 'Calamus' is an *esoteric* pastoral, a narrowing of the genre of the pastoral text toward the problematic of its fundamental motive, knowledge of other minds, or more precisely, *instruction* in the knowledge of other minds" (115). Grossman reads Whitman's fundamental lesson or thematic as the "incommensurability of the person," which seems right in its reference to pedagogy and impassable boundaries but limited in its willingness to subsume all other thematics to this single one (121). The instruction that takes place seems divided between this global lesson that subjectivities are immiscible and the local lesson, the practical reading tool, of refusing to be bucked from this particular author's rejections. This poem seems intent not on blocking the reader but on teaching the reader how to jump the fences of prohibitive utterances or boundaries. Whitman stages these rejections not as a sign of some huge unjumpable obstacle, but rather as a training ground for readers who are meant, in future, to remember that they possess the agility and means of bucking the authority of authorial dictum.[6]

The epistemological drive that speeds the reader through the "nors" of the final stanza of "Whoever You Are" is in direct conflict with the manifest content of those lines that are about the difficulty of being Whitman's disciple. While the attempt to follow the poet is announced to be impossibly difficult, the repetition makes the reader's movement from line to line easy. There are no new grammatical patterns: We are shuttled along by the series. This ease is also created by the expectation that this list will distill itself into a positive assertion that stands in contradistinction to each and every one of the negative assertions. However, while the principle of distillation makes the movement through serial negations quick, the final positive assertion is never delivered. *What is* is never delineated. In its place, the poet issues a command; however, this self-same command has already been twice-issued and twice-disregarded.

The opening poems in the sequence introduce the major theme of the group, the intertwining of sexuality and death, take the poetic elements of address and pronominal shifts for a test drive, and give a lesson in hurdling linguistic obstacles. These first poems are also some of the longest in the series; the poems get significantly shorter as the cycle moves on, until, near the end, three or four whole poems fit on each page. The middle and late poems are shorter because they mostly consist of a single sustained rhetorical gesture, while the first poems involve more than one, as we saw most strikingly in "Whoever You Are," in which one gesture is repeated in three variations. It is as if Whitman is suggesting, by his order, that the cycle's structure, once it develops through linkages of theme and technique, takes the reins from lyric structure and becomes the organizing principle of his poetic material. That is, the titles of the late poems serve less as titles of poems than they do as markers for gestures within the cycle, which then becomes more like a long poem with titled sections. The distinction between poems in series and a poem in parts is mostly one of strong and weak contiguity; a single part of a poem in sections declares that it could not stand alone, whereas a poem in a group of poems could be plucked from the group and do just fine. The "Calamus" cycle works as both. Most of the early poems could stand alone, however, many poems further along in the cycle cannot. Two poems, the three-lined "Here the Frailest Leaves of Me" and a rather slight poem, "I Dream'd in a Dream," are the clearest examples of this. "Here the Frailest" is *about the sequence itself* and therefore requires the sequence, and "I Dream'd" is a textureless observation if removed from the thematic support of the poems that precede it. The cycle develops thematic strands of manly love and urban space that this poem twines in a dreamscape (*Leaves* 283–4).

The first striking instance of a single gesture lyric is also the most extended "not … not … not … but" list of "Calamus." "Not Heaving from My Ribb'd Breast Only" features a series of 16 lines of negatives expressing the poet's yearning for his songs to express "adhesiveness" more than in the breath- and blood-driven expressions of his body. The images cluster around the poet's breath and its operations of inhalation and exhalation: speech, grunts, sighs, and murmurs. The poem begins:

> Not heaving from my ribb'd breast only,
> Not in sighs at night in rage dissatisfied with myself,
> Not in those long-drawn, ill-supprest sighs,
> Not in many an oath and promise broken. … (273)

It wends its way through all sorts of "not" expressions, including the very sexy "Not in husky pantings through clinch'd teeth" to the two-line conclusion—"Not in any of them O adhesiveness! O pulse of my life! / Need I that you exist and show yourself any more than in these songs" (274). Whitman's song has absorbed all of these bodied expressions in a series that itself reads like a series of sighs, because like sighs each line includes in its syntax the desire for an absent element and becomes in its utterance a sign of that absence. The reader wants to know what the poet desires and where it might be found if not "only" in any of these proliferating locations. The tortured syntax of the final line indicates that "adhesiveness," the phrenological term for the love of man for man, is what the poet is searching for. The massive-feeling bulk of this poem, then, organizes itself around two fragile syntactic turns.

The "only" in the eponymous first line flips over from a sign of partialness to a sign of complete presence. It turns from a "Not only" into a "Not only here … but also there." But this logical development can only happen after the closure is reached, so that each "Not …" becomes not a negative but a very strong positive. The negatives create suspense and pulsion in the poem but then, at the poem's close, are drained of their negative valence. Just as the rejections of "Whoever you Are" are shown to be encouragements, so are these assertive negatives transformed into positive assertions. Each of these devices creates a homographesis, a place in which immiscibles occur at the same site, and reenact in a different register the way that the "truth" about the sexuality Whitman is intent on singing presents itself only in suspension of the "truth."

Several poems later, in "Not Heat Flames up and Consumes," this same technique is shifted from a "not only ... but also" to a "not these ... but, more than these, those" structure. Three images from the natural world, the way flames consume, the way waves come and go, and the way seed pods float in the wind, are enlisted in their negation to describe the poet's love. None burn more, waft more, or come and go more than the poet "O love, for friendship, for you" (278). While none of these images are quite intense enough, they are the only images in the poem. Again the negatives create rhetorical suspense and at the close of the poem are shown not to be negatives at all but rather signs of intensity. It is because no image could adequately show the poet's love that these images, by their nature, fail. This failure is the truest sign of the just-beyondness of the poet's feeling.

Whitman repeats this device shortly after this rather slight natural image poem with a richer poem filled with an urban landscape instead of waves, wind, and downy seed balls. The same gesture of "not these ... but those" is repeated with a difference. In "City of Orgies" the notted terms do not simply change from negations to assertions, but they also metamorphose in the course of the poem.

> City of orgies, walks and joys,
> City whom that I have lived and sung in your midst will one day make you
>   illustrious,
> Not the pageants of you, not your shifting tableaus, your spectacles, repay
>   me,
> Not the interminable rows of your houses, nor the ships at the wharves,
> Nor the processions in the streets, nor the bright windows with goods in
>   them,
> Nor to converse with learn'd persons, or bear my share in the soiree or
>   feast;
> Not those, but as I pass O Manhattan, your frequent and swift flash of eyes
>   offering me love,
> Offering response to my own—these repay me,
> Lovers, continual lovers, only repay me. (279)

The poet declares that he will make this city famous but that none of its obvious glories actually repay him for his service. The orgies of the title and first line seem to refer to an abundance of color, activity, and conversation. These clearly please but do not fully satisfy the poet. Instead, he is repaid by continual possibility, by the flash of eyes rather than by the constant sensory feast that displays everything outright. The flash of eyes implies all kinds of carnal pleasures fulfilled and unfulfilled, and it is precisely the disconnection of this flash from material reality that gives it its power. One of the joys of cruising, as I explored in the last chapter in Ashbery's "The Ongoing Story," is that the randomness of an encounter allows one to project another such encounter anywhere, revamping public space and charging it everywhere with sexual possibility.[7] The title refers to both sorts of "orgy," but the high valuation of the flash-of-eyes orgy and the way in which the title of this poem is a celebratory shout lean it more toward the orgy of possibility, that is, cruising. The flatly visible abundance of the city is only a way of gesturing toward the greater joys of the serial and expanding visible and fantasmatic abundance of cruising. The suspension created by the "not...not...not...but" rhetoric of this poem coincides with the suspension of the term "orgies" through the course of the poem.

"I Hear It Was Charged Against Me," several poems later, creates a similar suspension with the term "institution," but without the list of negatives. This six-line poem begins: "I hear it was charged against me that I sought to destroy institutions, / But really I am neither for nor against institutions, / (What indeed have I in common with them? or what with the destruction of them?)." The second half of the poem, then, goes on to describe how the poet will establish what is announced in the final line—"The institution of the dear love of comrades" (281). The first assertion of the poem seems to flatly contradict the final assertion. This makes "institution," like "orgy" in "City of Orgies," an active term. One way to try to resolve the tension between the two uses of "institution" is to treat the first "institution" as pure noun and the second as a verb-leaning noun. Another is to treat the first comment about institutions as about the destruction of institutions and the second as about the establishment of institutions. Neither method, however, settles the contradiction; it still lurks in the poem. "Institutions," and "orgies" before it, become active and unsettled terms; the structure of the poems leads to a stubborn suspense of simple meaning that invests the loci of the transformations, the terms themselves, with a power unavailable before their dip in contradiction.

Whitman's suspensions use "Death's tone," or the tricks of the negative, to elucidate and power his mediations on sexuality. As the series reaches its close, the theme of manly love that has been so front and center throughout the series is shifted slightly aside; the negative effects

Whitman has featured in the series begin to cluster more around death, loss, and disappearance. The shift happens in "No Labor-Saving Machine" in which Whitman uses a serial negative but includes some "nots" that are clearly false.

> No labor-saving machine,
> Nor discovery have I made,
> Nor will I be able to leave behind me any wealthy bequest to found a
>   hospital or library,
> Nor reminiscence of any deed of courage for America,
> Nor literary success nor intellect, nor book for the book-shelf,
> But a few carols vibrating through the air I leave,
> For comrades and lovers. (283)

The last rapid-fire evidence that has the usual bang, bang, bang finality of a closed case, "No literary success nor intellect, nor book for the book-shelf," is belied by the fact that this poem did appear, during Whitman's lifetime, in a book for the bookshelf, and was already at least a moderately successful piece of literature. For a poet who at the very end of this sequence writes, "when you read these I that was visible am become invisible," a line fully aware of the physical survival of his poems in print, the final "nots" are especially dissonant (287). The power or even joy of the rejection enacted by saying what Whitman has not done has taken over. The utterance, the vibration, the stimulation of negation outreaches even the obvious truth.

Whitman claims in his "but" to leave something that cannot be left—vibrations. In the "nots," however, he claims specifically not to have left any transcript of those very evanescent vibrations. I think that this poem marks a definitive hollowing out of the "not ... not ... not ... but" structure. The occurrence of the rhetorical device without even some pretense of concomitant closure indicates that the device has been deployed for its own sake, for the pleasure of using it, and that it is itself the source of Whitman's highly valued "vibrations." The poems in the middle of "Calamus" move from single gestures calculated to bring about embodiment of the poet, as we saw most strikingly in "Not Heaving from My Ribb'd Breast Only," progressively toward single gestures that are calculated to bring about the successful disembodiment of the poet, most notably, "No Labor-Saving Machine." The poems that constitute the closure of the group, then, explore complete disembodiment as the truest expression of love between men. The negatives used throughout the cycle to express the love of comrades have by the end become a sign of that love. In the same manner that Whitman uses the device of addressing "recorders ages hence" in order to access an anxiety-free present, so at the end of the cycle does he empty his poems of bodies altogether to reach some absolute expression of queer embodiment.

In the final two poems of the sequence, Whitman reaches the height of his embodiment and disembodiment at once. As I have noted, this is a method of creating a shelter for manly love under the sign of the negative, but it is also a tool for dying. The "remember now, remember then" of the note on the back of the "Live Oak" series is taken at its word as a method of preparing for death: a command to remember the present, remember the past, and, by the situation of the note as a reminder itself, remember the future. The command to "remember" what has not yet happened provides a mobility in time that indicates that even the most apparently impassable boundaries are passable.

If the living and dead are both shadows, the phase change between being one and the other is not all that dramatic. In the penultimate five-line poem of "Calamus," "That Shadow My Likeness," Whitman makes his living self and dead self entirely identical:

> That shadow my likeness that goes to and fro seeking a livelihood,
>   chattering, chaffering,
> How often I find myself standing and looking at it where it flits,
> How often I question and doubt whether that is really me;
> But among my lovers and caroling these songs,
> O I never doubt whether that is really me. (286)

The triumphant "O I never doubt whether that is really me" is offset by the fact that the "really me" is still a ghost flitting about rather than a solid human being. "Chattering" and "chaffering" together stand brilliantly for ghostly and petty activities—they are the sounds of both spirits and shallow pursuits—implying also a correlation between the two: the pettier, the less real. Further, the little crooks that migrate from feet of the t's to the heads of the f's in "chattering, chaffering" perform a variety of ghostly metamorphosis based on petty difference. These effects undergird Whitman's suggestion that in worldly pursuits the poet is a *mere shadow,* but among good love and good song, the poet is secure in knowing that that is *his* shadow, but a *shadow* nonetheless.

The final poem in the sequence, "Full of Life Now," serves as a "but" to the negation of "That Shadow My Likeness" as well, in a sense, to all of the negations and dematerializations that precede it in the cycle. "Full of life now, compact, visible," declares this poem a response, or a kind of sequel, to a complete dematerialization in both the direction of the past and in the direction of the future (287). The first of two stanzas happens in a very specified time and place, a "now" at the moment of writing, "in the eighty-third year of the States ..." while the poet is seeking a reader "yet unborn" (287).

> Full of life now, compact, visible,
> I, forty years old the eighty-third year of the States,
> To one a century hence or any number of centuries hence,
> To you yet unborn these, seeking you. (287)

This stanza has no dominant verb but the ghost verb here is "dedicate." This dedicatory activity happens in the writer's present. Simultaneously, the syntax of the final line places the writer as a ghost "full of life" at the site of a reading of his own poems some time in the future. I am, it declares, full of life *to you, future reader.* The writer is "seeking you" both in the past present and in the future present. He is, that is to say, successfully "full of life," of verbal potential, of the ability to seek, in his own present and far past his own death. Tense has collapsed into the participle present of the activity of seeking that happens, impossibly, in both times.

After this virtuoso performance of his unbound temporality in the first stanza, Whitman shifts his "now" more firmly to mean the reader's moment, long after Whitman himself is dead.

> When you read these I that was visible am become invisible,
> Now it is you, compact, visible, realizing my poems, seeking me,
> Fancying how happy you were if I could be with you and become your
>   comrade;
> Be it as if I were with you. (Be not too certain but I am now with you.)
> (287)

Whitman's imagined reader fantasizes about bringing him materially back from the dead, and Whitman encourages him in his efforts. Whitman never materializes, but instead makes an appearance in an immaterial form that he suggests was always the point and has always already happened.

The poem gets even stranger when one considers that it was published and read during Whitman's lifetime. The second stanza then detaches from the first and speaks to the reader sharing Whitman's "now." The "you" can mean any reader and suggests that even during his life, material Whitman was made immaterial, and then vice versa, by the activity of others reading his poems. Any embodiment of the author by means of the operations of his text (except wherein he himself was reading the poems aloud, which would be queer indeed!) would happen in the poet's absence. It does not actually matter whether the poet is alive or dead, he is still invisible and has sent his poems as an incantation to bring him to the reader. Alive or dead in body, this poet, in his poem, is always undead.

This ghost, all about presencing absence, chafes against the ghost of the poem immediately before which was all about absencing presence. "That Shadow My Likeness" turned Whitman into a shadow, and "Full of Life Now" turns him from body, to ghost, to a ghost embodied in his reader's desire. These "not" and "but" propositions about materiality are led up to by all of the rhetorical suspensions that precede them. This is the ultimate suspension, but suspension in another material and lexical register: The poet is suspended in the solution of the reader's desire.

Whitman's poetic body in his sequence operates exactly like the truth of his sexuality. It can only be known by one person at a time and is as mobile as his book of poems. Kevin Kopelson suggests, when discussing Barthes, that "to pronounce a perfect paradox is never to hear it deteri-orate into a doxa. It is to be strangled while uttering it" (26). Whitman's dematerialization of his own body—he kills himself off while uttering his negations—is both dependent on and constitutive of the mobility of the "truth" of his sexuality. The reader's desire to know Whitman and to know Whitman's sexuality are always already anticipated in Whitman's text. These poems always keep the reader at arm's length, unsure whether the poet is pushing him away or pulling him close—but always *wanting* to know.

Chapter 3

Reports of Looting and Insane Buggery behind Altars: John Ashbery's Queer Poetics

I.

Among critics there is no disagreement about John Ashbery's sexuality. Perhaps that is because Ashbery is actually a registered homosexual. He came out to the draft board and was exempted from military service during the Korean War (Shoptaw 5). On the other hand, Ashbery, while registered with the draft board, often does not "register" as a gay *poet*. For instance, the *Penguin Anthology of Homosexual Verse* (edited by Stephen Coote) does not include him, even though it was published years after Ashbery's *Self-Portrait in a Convex Mirror* won the "Triple Crown" of American poetry prizes: Pulitzer Prize, National Book Award, and National Book Critics Circle Award. Ashbery's absence in this anthology is even more striking when one considers that at the time of its publication by Penguin, Ashbery was one of the "Penguin Poets." Critics do, however, pay enough attention to Ashbery's sexuality to note that the masculine pronoun in Ashbery's poetry can address "a friend," "a lover," or "the poet himself," and when examining him as a love poet, critics make sure to consider the beloved as male.[1] These same critics, though, while they acknowledge that pronouns and reference are transformed in the aura of Ashbery's sexuality, do little but remark the transformation.

Contemporary cultural events like the passage of the Defense of Marriage Act, which made sure that states could deny gay marriages before states were even asked to consider accepting them, underline the huge difference in cultural value between heterosexual and homosexual love bonds. Homosexual and heterosexual desire and bonds, given their different cultural valuation, have entirely different available narratives, legality, forms of expression, as well as different available relations to abstraction, specification, self-definition, community, ritual, temporality, and spatiality. This is not to suggest that there are not overlaps, but rather that any treatment of homosexual desire as simply another form of desire (read, heterosexual) will be fundamentally flawed, if not also in the service of a homophobic fantasy of a world without gay people in it.

This said, there is little argument among critics who have the slightest sympathy for Ashbery's work that "homosexual moments" in a text are interesting and useful ways to tease some of his poems into meaning. Homosexuality enters and then *exits* this critical stage with little fuss, which means it causes little outrage but also attracts little serious, sustained attention. This ease is underwritten, in part at least, by "Ashbery's difficulty." That is, as Helen Vendler has remarked, "... it is popularly believed, with some reason, that the style itself is impenetrable, that it is impossible to say what an Ashbery poem is 'about' " (*Music* 224). Since reading "homosexuality" in Ashbery's poetry allows a point of penetration through grammatical, referential, or epistemic murk, its value as a critical tool seems inestimable. At the same time, the difficulty of Ashbery's poetry allows critics to disregard homosexual thematics when they are not useful to their other projects.

For instance, Helen Vendler, against what she declares is a popular belief that Ashbery's poems are not "about" anything, elucidates some themes in the lyrics in Ashbery's 1980 volume *As We Know.* Vendler suggests that these lyrics are about "growing up, fidelity, about identity, about death, about ... the permanence of art, about construction, about deconstruction, and perpetual creative joy in the face of death" (*Music* 237). Notice how homosexuality is not just missing as its own thematic but is also missing as something that would inflect the other thematics, as in "growing up gay," "fidelity without heterosexual marriage narratives in place," "identity in the face of erasing and phobic cultural forces," "death without a comforting/troubling narrative of reproductive continuation," and so on.[2] These do not seem mere qualifications but are actually constitutive of the themes that Vendler locates. Fidelity, to point out the most striking instance, needs to be positioned in terms of the kind of relations it describes. A gay man has no uncomplicated relation to "adultery" or "fidelity" since these words depict activities and conditions based on a legal marriage bond; in order to use such heterocentric terms about gay people or bonds one needs at least to mention that they are being torqued from their general cultural usage. Furthermore, this is not a volume without explicit homosexual content. Many of the poems entail homosexuality as an inflection of their central thematics, and two poems in this collection are eponymously and frankly *about* male–male relations; they declare themselves up front and go on to meditate on the male–male bonds suggested in their titles.[3] "My Erotic Double" has the poet flirting with an image of his own lazy self, and "The Plural of 'Jack-in-the-Box,'" the final poem of the collection, muses on how homosexual bonds might affect the spatial, mythic, and linguistic boundaries that contain them.

But even in the best cases, where homosexual content is not being actively erased from readings of Ashbery's poems, "homosexual meaning" is treated as a *tool* of reading, or sense making, with the implication that homosexual meanings are best deployed at the service of other, larger, more shared systems of meaning. Such figurations of generality as heterosexual must always be interrogated, because not only do they elbow homosexuality out of the frame, they also deny (by ignoring) any complicated way of inhabiting a *heterosexual* subjecthood.

If there is any one thing that queer theorists can be said to have given the academy, it is the sense of how crucial the homo/heterosexual divide is to Western culture's most central binarisms. This, in turn, fosters the sense that identity is too complicated to snugly fit broad binarisms.[4] Homosexual thematics, styles, and desires are worth examining, in other words, on their own terms. In their specificity, they trouble generality; they highlight and vex the operation of metonymy itself (the correspondence of part to whole, and whole to part).[5] Further, queer people living in this culture, who cut across or through its definitions, require explicit strategies to negotiate linguistic productions of the specific and general.[6] For instance, on a tax form a coupled lesbian may have to mark the box for "single" (for lack of any other box) when she considers herself anything but "single," highlighting the way in which this term inadequately describes her and violently blocks her from the tax and other privileges accorded someone "married." The felt exclusion and misrepresentativeness of this situation make the linguistic markers "single" or "married" active sites of anger, comfort, capitulation, and resistance. The sheer variety of affect, and effect, which can attend this seemingly simple accounting of a subject's relation to her culture, on this the starkest of levels, testifies to the fact that for a gay or lesbian person defining himself or herself within the larger culture requires reading tools that are often, not only not vectored toward, but *against* more general ways of reading.

In this case, a box that might or might not be difficult for a heterosexual form filler can't but give a gay, lesbian, or transgender taxpayer pause. A site of apparently evident definitional simplicity becomes a site of difficulty, deliberation, and decision. This is at least as true in reading poetry where self-definitional strategizing is not one to one, box to attribute. Poets, who traffic in linguistic charge, most of all must be cognizant not only of definitional activity but also of its *effect*. For gay and antihomophobic poets and readers of poetry, homosexuality is not merely a tool by which to reach a more general effect or understanding (a way to clear a blocked path) but a node of linguistic charge itself that can vivify or deflate general effects, as in the world it can vivify or deflate general categories.

In this chapter, I will show how, across the span of Ashbery's oeuvre, a semiotics and thematics of homosexuality jimmies open address and reference, as well as logical, figural, and poetic closure. Frustrated closure, on the level of argument, figure, and lyric, happens often in Ashbery and is frequently remarked by critics as contributing to the tension and play in his work between randomness and deliberate artfulness. However, there is evidence within his poetry of a theoretical standpoint that reconsiders this conflict and posits unclosedness as a strategy that can be deployed against toxic or confining notions of identity, a strategy that does not buck cultural categories but stalls their crystallization and further theorizes about the value and power of that stalling. It is no coincidence that the most explicit and focused experiments of this sort correspond to Ashbery's most explicit and focused treatments of homosexuality. Other critics, most powerfully, John Shoptaw, have traced the semiotics of homosexuality to Ashbery's "misrepresentativeness." That is, Shoptaw suggests that homosexuality enters Ashbery's poesis by a trope of ill-concealed concealment and ill-divulged divulgence. Implicit in this theorization, though it does not directly address the idea of the queer reader in Ashbery's work, is the idea that a queer reader goes to these texts, at least in part, for their power to represent and poetically enact structures of the closet that art makes legible. While this does seem true of Ashbery's work, it downplays the structural theorizing that Ashbery performs. The "misrepresentative" poet figure offers many local interventions based on one grand idea about language and identity. I want to suggest that Ashbery's theorizing is more self-aware and plastic than that. The techniques that he uses to explore identity and its relation to language on a local level, through his experiments, inevitably constitute his grander theoretical frame rather than only being expressions of it. Thus, while I am not suggesting creating a chronology of poetic effects, I want to reverse the above theoretical causality, which means focusing on a poetic technique for its effect on a theory of poetics.

The closural effects I will examine are only several types of poetic difficulty in Ashbery's quiver, but are bound together by the goal of providing very particular effects for queer readers.[7] These poetic moments hold off closed meaning, providing architectural liminality, which mimetically gestures to a site, real and linguistic, in which queer people can live, and these effects offer themselves pedagogically as examples of carving liminality, or inhabitable space, from the larger culture.

I take the title of this chapter from a recent short lyric by Ashbery in which he explores the durability of dominant culture in the face of attacks. In the scene of "The Military Base," even though "the house took a direct hit / ... it didn't matter; the next moment / it was intact, though transparent" (*Can You Hear, Bird?* 117).[8] There were not even any injuries from the sudden attack. Everything returns to the idea the culture had of it, whether that idea still matches reality or not, and when everything is over, "There were no reports of looting / or insane buggery behind altars" (117). This poem suggests with its final, oddly specific negation (no "insane buggery behind altars") that odd specificity is one way to sneak such reports under the apathetic inertia of a world that will not collapse. Poetry may not be able to bring the house down, but it can salvage reports of the queer attacks that happen on quotidian and other unreportable levels, attacks that may simply take the form of queer lives quietly lived. Following typical Ashberian reasoning, the report of the absence of reports of looting and insane buggery is itself both a report of looting and insane buggery and *is* looting and insane buggery. Following Ashbery's musings about seemingly meaningless linguistic messengers in "Litany," "It is they who carry news of it / To other places. Therefore / Are they not the event itself?" (*AWK* 8).

II. "The Fairies' Song"

The first discussion of homosexual meaning across the span of Ashbery's work occurs in John Shoptaw's *On the Outside Looking Out* (also only the second full-length study on Ashbery). Shoptaw discusses a way to keep homosexuality central to discussions of Ashbery's style, as I mentioned before, without reading homosexual thematics into each of the poems. His heuristic centers around Ashbery's "misrepresentative poetics":

> ... although, or rather because, Ashbery leaves himself and his homosexuality out of his poetry, his poems misrepresent in a particular way which I will call "homotextual." Rather than simply hiding or revealing some homosexual content, these poems "behave" differently, no matter what

their subject. With their distortions, evasions, omissions, obscurities, and discontinuities, Ashbery's poems always have a homotextual dimension. (Shoptaw 4)

Ashbery's poetics are, within this frame, an expression of his theoretically motivated absence from his poems. Because, in other words, Ashbery decides not to name homosexuality, it hypostasizes throughout Ashbery's poems via his style, whose most striking operations are concealment and misdirection. Evasions and omissions gesture back to the missing origin of *the* central evasion and omission, homosexual content. However, these gestures have become, in their own right, invested with the urgencies and erotics of the original evasion.[9] While Shoptaw's theorization is the best offered so far for homosexuality as semiotic access to Ashbery's poetry, it seems itself to misrepresent homosexual content in John Ashbery's poetry. After all, there *are* poems in Ashbery's oeuvre that are obviously thematically centered around homosexuality. Ashbery does not, untraceably at least, leave himself nor his homosexuality out of his poems.

A poem called "The Fairies' Song" from *The Vermont Notebook* (1975) not only takes homosexuality as its explicit theme, but also addresses Ashbery's own position in his poems as a "fairy singing," putting forward a poetics explicitly inflected by his sexuality. This poem outlines and enacts a poetic strategy for dealing with the trials of homosexual identity. It suggests why homosexuals might have a particular relation to songs, that is, poems or verbal expressions in general, and also offers a strategy for keeping this particularity particular. In other words, the poem both is a fairy's song and has as its subject the further production of fairy songs and the encouragement of fairy songs.

"The Fairies' Song" begins with "Clouding up again. Certain days there is a feeling that whatever we arrange / Will sooner or later get all fucked up" (93). That "certain ... feeling" arouses "explosions of a 19th-century, garden-variety form of intellectual rage." But Ashbery suggests that, when confronted with this "certain ... feeling," a fairy is "too far in the glade, the way this is all about harassing." "This" is the condition of being homosexual. A homophobic culture "fucks up" plenty in its harassing, but, Ashbery asserts, being harassed is not the sole defining mark of being gay, though it might sometimes seem it. To get caught up only in the unpleasantness of life in a homophobic culture is to miss not only what pleasures there are in ecstatic moments but also what "charity" there is in "the hard moments" (*DDS* 19). This formulation is offered in "Soonest Mended" from the earlier *The Double Dream of Spring* (1970), and shares the thematic of making the best of a "spoiled" identity with "The Fairies' Song," but is far less explicit in locating its subjects as homosexuals.

"Soonest Mended" takes its title from the cliché "least said, soonest mended," and its performatively absent first phrase could possibly even dictate both a poetics and a politics almost completely in opposition to those in "The Fairies' Song." This title could be advocating discretion or even silence as strategies for negotiating the difficulties of homosexual politics and life in American culture. The later poem, in contrast, while not a battle cry exactly, does call for self-celebrating song. But as is often the case with solitary phrases (even ghost phrases like this one) in Ashbery, "least said" may be embedded in another context of irony, comment, or persona, and refuses to be pointed in any single direction. The title could be the best expression of the culture that "barely tolerates" (*DDS* 17) the speaker and his lover, an expression that then serves as the spur for the utterance that is the poem. The uncertainty that clings to the title must be considered as having its own "charity" as well as humor. "Least said, soonest mended," the cliché, commands terseness and action, neither of which occurs in "Soonest Mended." There is nothing particular to be done and much verbal production about it. In face of the advice to constrict speech and act, Ashbery's poem dilates dreamily, but his dreamy tone takes on a kind of argumentative weight in the proximity of this credo.

"Soonest Mended" begins similarly to "The Fairies' Song"—"Barely tolerated, living on the margin / In our technological society, we were always having to be rescued / On the brink of destruction, like heroines in *Orlando Furioso* . . . ." "Soonest Mended" campily characterizes the speaker and his lover as heroines in a high poetic drama. (The boundary of the "we" shifts to include a larger group of people at several points in the poem, but the default and most common mode of the second-person pronoun here is singular, and this single other person seems a lover: They have "made a home" together.) However, as we shall see, "The Fairies' Song," the later, more explicitly gay poem, ends not with the assertion that carrying on living is enough, "For this is action, this not being sure," which the earlier poem ends on, but rather with the assertion that the action of living in a "spoiled" identity is intense and exciting, and, in fact, a source of lyric vivacity. Both poems do, however, start by proclaiming a crisis and close with an argument about closure and action, suggesting that true action is often inaction, or undecided-ness, and true closure often allows opposites to coexist in tension rather than either repeating and therefore instantiating (and fulfilling) a pattern or following the chemical model of a positive and negative charge canceling each other out to reduce tension.

The second stanza of "The Fairies' Song" shows the result of fairies being harassed and taking harassing as what being gay is all about:

> Sometimes one of us will get included in the trash
> And end up petulant and bored at the multiple opportunities
>   for mischief,
> Screaming like a seagull at vacuity,
> Hating it for being what it is.

Ashbery hopes to provide some alternatives to this result, thus the parat-actically generous "there are ... there are ... there are" structure of the middle stanzas of the poem. It is not that "we" can prevent "our" num-bers from ending up in the trash, but rather that "we" can forge responses different from "screaming like a seagull at vacuity, / Hating it for being what it is." The "there are"s catalogue sites of waste. Pastoral "Manure piles under the slop and surge of a March sun," "pale plumes of dullness," and "insipid flowering meads" begin to bend toward more abstract and less pastoral wastes: "Wastes of acting out daytime courtesies at night, / Deadfalls of resolution, arks of self-preservation / Arenas of unused indulgence" (93–5). In the midst of this list comes a stanza describing a moment of subdued but expressed desire:

> Thunderheads of after-dinner cigar smoke in some varnished salon
> Offer ample cover for braiding two coat-tails together
> Around the clumsy arm of an s-shaped settee.
> In a screech the occasion has disappeared, the clamor resumed like a
>   climate.

The "braiding" of coat-tails can only occur under a smelly, dark cloud, around the "clumsy" arm of an awkward piece of furniture. This moment of expression occurs in silence and evaporates in a queeny "screech" and "clamor." The list of images, pastoral and abstract, insists on the presence of waste and discomfort in any momentary beauty or landscape the fairies can achieve. At the close of the list, Ashbery asks when this wild ride of waste and exaltation stops: "Where do we get off / The careening spear of rye?" (95). His answer to this question is the proposition that "we" don't, but that "we" need to theorize the mixture of good and bad from the position of someone who has to drink sour milk telling himself: "But it all gets mixed up in your stomach anyway" (95). Ashbery suggests a change of point of view, or what I have been suggesting is a declared theoretical standpoint: It's not how the milk tastes, it's that it fulfills a nutritional need. Thus, experiences might never be unmitigatedly good for fairies, but it is possible to rethink the mixture of good with bad not as good or even satisfactory but as at least livable and postulate livability as the possibility for exaltation.

The final image of the poem is one of unrestrained limpidity, where after declaring that "we," fairies, "dance on hills above the wind / And leave our footsteps there behind. / We raise their tomatoes. / The clear water in the chipped basin reflects it all: / A spoiled life, alive, and streaming with light" (95). The final lyric movement suggests that what is called "spoiled" or even "furtive" is "alive, and streaming with light" when seen from the fairy's-eye view above the crisp image of a sink. A lyric moment, gazing at oneself reflected in clear water, jumps into lucidity, producing a self-preserving comment: While seemingly hidden and wrecked, homosexual identities are on the contrary filled with lyricism and light partly because of their banished condition from other forms of visibility and order. Ashbery's poem offers testimony that fairies' lives are lived and sung.

This poem is a straightforward lyric, but with a strategizing plot, an arc moving from the clouded to the limpid, passing through a Whitmanesque list, coming to rest in an ecstatic moment. The interesting thing about the poem, considering its rather typical form, is that it neither finds redemption in the spoiled nor spoilage in redemption, but is instead is a supreme example of Keats's "negative capability," "where a man is capable of being in uncertainties, Mysteries, doubts, without any irritable reaching after fact & reason" (qtd. in Preminger 824–5). It is not an ecstasy *because* of, or *despite*, waste and spoil, it is just there, right along with its opposite, testament to their possible/impossible coexistence. Ashbery does not make sense of how this coexistence can happen; instead he states that it does while he demonstrates that it does poetically: The press and anxiety of the excess detail of spoilage impels the poem to saturation, whereupon adding a single temporally locatable scene, a single present rather than a continually spiraling possible future, creates a precipitate of clarity.

This example alone shows that homosexual meaning does not *always* misrepresent itself in Ashbery's poetry. Here it is not only explicit in, but also explicitly fundamental to, a lyric. It also offers a glimpse as to how Ashbery writes homosexual lives as *difficult* on a quotidian, lived level, a difficulty that invites an analogy to his own poetic *difficulty.* Interestingly, the only time the word "homosexual" appears in Ashbery's poetic oeuvre, it elucidates just this connection between the "pain" of life (which Ashbery so often thematizes in a general way), homosexual lives, and difficult writing. The first poem in Ashbery's seven-part "Haibun" series addresses the import of his entire body of poetry to future generations of gay readers. He writes:

> I'm hoping that homosexuals not yet born get to inquire about it, inspect
> the whole random collection as though it were a sphere. Isn't the point of
> pain the possibility it brings of being able to get along without pain, for
> awhile, of manipulating our marionette-like limbs in the straitjacket of air,
> and so to have written something? (*W* 39)

This part prose, part haiku poem suggests that difficulty is a way of
preserving the constructability of his poems for homosexuals not yet
born, preventing the poems from being "claimed by the first person who
happens on them" (39). Ashbery declares that he wishes to preserve his
poems' power to name, and therefore hold and reduce, pain for this
particular "not yet born" audience. While this does not suggest that his
poetry is *only* addressed to homosexuals, it does suggest that he has particular designs for serving an audience of homosexuals; he wants to aid
and abet a particular use of his poetry in the midst of other uses, trying
to ensure that other critical and readerly appropriations do not interfere
with his transmission of the "possibility of getting along without pain,
for awhile" to future gay readers. More general meanings, as discussed
above, are not being dismissed out-of-hand but are considered possible
obstacles in the way of this poetic project.

Shoptaw's scheme, then, with these readings in mind, proves useful,
not insofar as it accounts for a hypostatization based on the absence of
homosexuality but rather that it accounts for a hypostatization simultaneous with its presence. This general sense that homosexuality infuses all
of the poetry seems helpful insofar as it carves irrigation canals by which
gay readers and readings can reach the poems, but, when forwarded in
the absence of homosexual thematics, it flattens the peculiarities and
specificities of influence that homosexual meaning has in poems across
Ashbery's career. I want to argue that Ashbery does precisely *not* leave
homosexuality out of his poems, while they *still* "behave differently."

Homosexual thematics arise from both readings of single poems and
from readings of Ashbery as a theorist across poems. The difficulty associated with these thematics is not just self-protective in the sense that
protects the author from persecution, but is more often self-protective in
the sense that the homosexual meanings are precisely that which *is being
protected.* Ashbery's misrepresentative poetics are partly symptomatic of
what types of articulations around gay desire are available in culture and
language, but they are also willful refusals to settle into narrative, lyric, or
imagistic wholeness without registering by disjunction and breakage the
realness, specialness, and particularity of gay meanings and lives.

III. Shifty Pronouns: "The Grapevine"

Some readily available sites of this different behavior are Ashbery's famous shifty pronouns. Critics often quote the interview with Ashbery where he discusses pronominal shiftiness directly. "The personal pronouns in my work very often seem to be like the variables in an equation. 'You' can be myself or it can be another person, someone whom I'm addressing, and so can 'he' and 'she' for that matter and 'we'" (qtd. in Perloff *Indeterminacy* 258). Ashbery suggests that the "point" to this shiftiness is that "we are all somehow aspects of a consciousness giving rise to the poem and the fact of addressing someone, myself or someone else, is what's the important thing at the particular moment rather than the particular person involved." He then makes the much-grasped-at comment, "I guess I don't have a very strong sense of my own identity and I find it very easy to move from one person in the sense of a pronoun to another and this again helps produce a kind of polyphony... which I again feel is a means towards a greater naturalism" (Ibid.).

Ashbery suggests three things that seem to contradict one another, and critics usually just highlight and dwell on the not-very-strong-sense-of-my-own-identity strand without disimbricating it from the others. Dissecting this very statement, we note a shift, if not a shiftiness. There are three seemingly contradictory statements: (1) Pronouns shift in Ashbery poems because inside his poems they are less important than the form of address; that is, the speaking voice breaks down the barriers between pronouns as it sees necessary to balancing its "equations." (2) Voice, and thus the equations it formulates, exists in conversation, boundary-crossing traffic, with its subjects such that subject–object relations in his poems inform the speaking voice. In other words, the "equations" formulate and are formulated by their variables in a give-and-take that defines the very speaker who utters them. And (3) Ashbery has a weak sense of his own identity. The first proposition places the speaker in a dominant and the second in a subordinate relation to its subjects; the last proposition, then, seems to contradict the first two propositions by its claimed naïveté about identity. However, I think, differently inflected, this last statement is more of a manifesto than a confession. From the above two propositions it is clear that identity and subject–object relations are very much at the forefront of Ashbery's poetic practice and consciousness; his statement suggests that he does not have a very strong sense of "identity" as a flatly formulated condition. Identity is precisely what Ashbery is strongly active in critiquing, strategizing about, and reformulating at both molecular and molar levels in his writing. His comment, inflected with this sense of his investment in interrogating identity, suggests that his work with identity aims toward a mimesis of not his own private "weak" sense of himself as a bounded individual but of identity as it is more complicatedly formulated than in the colloquial "sense of oneself."

The equations in which Ashbery's pronouns are variables do not often have simple resolutions heralded by poetic equal signs. He suggests a way to consider his poems' analogy to mathematics in "Litany," where he writes: *"I want to write / Poems that are as inexact as mathematics. I have been / Sitting making mudpies, in the sparkling sunlight, / And the difficulty of giving them away / Doesn't matter so long as I want you / To enjoy them. Enjoy these!* (*AWK* 91). "Mathematics" and "mudpies," as Ashbery configures them in these lines, are structures of meaning upon which he models, and in whose light he considers his poems. Mathematics are internally coherent but difficult to translate from the abstract (therefore "inexact"), and mudpies are internally incoherent but coherently categorically constituted by their translation into gifts. The smeared juxtaposition of these two suggests that this speaker/poet sees the internal coherence of math and the external, purely relational coherence of mudpies as equivalent: Both are systems and gifts, and their desired giftness outreaches their internal coherence as systems. Thus the logically organized and the pleasurably unorganized share the problem of translation into the world, and the translation requires a willing receiver. But that the chosen recipient is willing to receive them is less important than the maker's desire that he or she enjoy them. This is the organizing principle of math, mudpies, and poetry for Ashbery. In other words, equals signs in Ashbery's poetics, equivalences and closed analogical structures, are at the service of wanting "you / To enjoy them," at the service of the reader's pleasure as the author imagines it. This offers a more coherent sense of what pronouns are meant to do in Ashbery's poetry than does the usual inflection inflicted on the oft-quoted interview.

As simple as it may sound, it has not yet been stated in Ashbery criticism: The shifts in pronouns are first and foremost meant to provide readerly pleasure. They may cause delight with their irreverence, surprise, and sentimental identification in their breakages, which offer unauthorized attachment or pleasing breaks from category by their disarrangement of gender and number. The confessional "I" can slip into the royal or chummy "we," what was a crowd can condense to a "she," and the solitary lyric tone of a single utterance can splinter into a rowdy group discussion. "Most reckless things," as Ashbery said in a lecture to the Yale Art School, "are beautiful in some way, and recklessness is what makes experimental art beautiful, just as religions are beautiful because of the strong possibility that they are founded on nothing" (*RS* 391).

While I think moments of recklessness are underregarded aspects and pleasures in Ashbery's poetry, they do not lend themselves to more than satisfied or disgruntled local responses unless lashed together in a project of deployed recklessness. Thus, I would like to focus, for the sake of my discussion of pronouns, on mathematics over mudpies and consider how moments of reckless pronominal usage can crystallize around bigger projects of recklessness. "The Grapevine," a poem from Ashbery's first published book, *Some Trees* (1956), offers a good example of Ashbery's mathematical pronouns. Its sense of poetic equation centers on homosexuality as an epistemic issue, wherein lies its recklessness. It is poised on the edge of coming out at a historical moment when gays and communists were being hounded out of their professions, if not their lives. John Shoptaw tells how months before Ashbery finished *Some Trees*, F. O. Matthiessen, one of Ashbery's professors at Harvard who was also gay, jumped from a twelfth-story hotel window just before he was scheduled to appear before the House Un-American Activities Committee (Shoptaw 35). Besides being reckless in a simply poetic sense, aligning and misaligning pronouns around gay meanings at this time performed a kind of political recklessness that organizes and depends on these more textual recklessnesses. While it might be argued that Ashbery's shifts are often pointless and arbitrary, in the case of "The Grapevine" they are certainly neither; a real point is being made with the poetic material at hand, and it addresses an urgent political reality.

The poem is not parsible in the simplest sense, because it torques its pronouns out of typical relationality and referentiality. One needs to treat the pronouns in it, the "you," the "we," and the "them" as algebraic variables, like X, Y, or Z. As the poem proceeds, the values, the people these markers stand for, change. Grammar, relations between the terms themselves, and optic, epistemic, spatial, and temporal shifts modify their referents, or in mathematical terms, their value. So, parsing cannot result in a satisfactory reading, though it is necessary in the service of figuring out just what are the terms of the equation. The very epistemological situation the poem puts forward is itself a kind of function, where every X that undergoes its indicated operation comes out a Y, though X and Y are never flatly given referents.

THE GRAPEVINE

Of who we and all they are
You all now know. But you know
After they began to find us out we grew
Before they died thinking us the causes

> Of their acts. Now we'll not know
> The truth of some still at the piano, though
> They often date from us, causing
> These changes we think we are. We don't care
>
> Though, so tall up there
> In young air. But things get darker as we move
> To ask them: Whom must we get to know
> To die, so you live and we know? (*ST* 19)

Shoptaw's reading of this poem is informative but limited:

> In this word-of-mouth network of "fruits," not only have the names
> been withheld but the pronouns have been changed at every opportunity.
> Who committed, who detected, these fatal acts, "we" or "they" or "you"?
> To "you" (including the readers), the investigating "they" uncomfortably
> resembles the uncovered "we." ... The revenge of those found out consists
> of planting seeds of doubt and suspicion among those knowing. They
> themselves may be subject to investigation. (21)

Shoptaw's connection of Ashbery's poetry to the McCarthy years and
the deep structure of suspicion and homophobia in America around the
time that *Some Trees* was written is a necessary addition to Ashbery
criticism, but this poem seems more than a simple rewriting of "it takes
one to know one." The poem also suggests an attraction to a network of
homophobic knowing whose motor is also paradoxically that of a
homosexual community.

The poem is an allegorical address to a plural "you" who remain the
intrapoetic audience throughout the poem but drop from sight as soon
as they are invoked in the second line. The "we" and "they" set up in the
first line are developed as antagonistic groups, "they" ferreting out "us."
As Shoptaw suggests, this first "us" consists of homosexuals, and the first
"they" consists of people enforcing homophobic laws and cultural norms.
"They," the pursuers, die at the end of the first stanza and take to
the grave the "truth of" some people "still at the piano," truth that often
dates from the "us" themselves. This "truth" consists of whether those
"still at the piano" are gay or not. Homosexuals, along with homophobes,
are interested in identifying other homosexuals, as the final lines of stanza
two suggest, in order to constitute a gay community. The "young air" of
the final stanza seems the celebratory and heady part of either entering
the community of other gay people or of collectively imagining "ourselves" *as* a gay community. "Things" then "get darker" when the self-
identified members of this particular, or allegorically, *the,* gay community

"move / To ask" those still at the piano the poem's only question. The question poses the possibility of an inquisitive community "dying," no longer *wanting* to know, but rather *knowing*. One way to make sense of the resurrection of "we" in the last line is to read the speaker's use of "we" as itself algebraic. The first "we" is the we of the present, inquisitive, and the second, the "we" of the desired future, secure enough in its knowing that it no longer wants to know more. The former "we" desires its own demise, since its desire to know gets in the way of "you" living. The poem imagines pronouns aligned in a utopic and differently epistemologically driven gay community. Rather than knowing the "truth" of one individual's sexuality, the final stanza suggests that there is *someone* to get to know. *Knowing* in this stanza turns to *acquaintance*. With this shift "we" who know *about people* can "die" and be transformed to "we" who know *people*, who participate in a community.

This poem really seems less concerned with destabilizing the homophobic "they," as Shoptaw suggests, than it is in reimagining a homosexual "we." "The Grapevine" starts in this poem as a system of homophobic knowledge and ends as the fantasized living tissue that holds clusters of fruits together. Such a network is excessive, it outreaches epistemology and is logically unrealizable. However, the poem's own creation of such a network, the "we" that is resurrected, offers both articulated reasons to urge toward such a network and a semantic performance of one.

IV. Address Shifts: "Or in My Throat"

One vantage up from the shifting pronouns in Ashbery's work are the effects that happen around address shifts. Tense, syntax, punctuation, lineation, pronominal relation, tone, and immediate context give cues both to who is speaking and to whom or what. This whom and what, though, can shift contrarily and with great frequency. But there is a further problem: Many of Ashbery's poems oscillate unannounced between a meditative interior/thought voice and a very definite exterior/spoken voice of the poet, speaker, or character. A speech act can be performed in an intrapoetic scene or can *constitute* an intrapoetic scene. The linkage of locutions is often, however, if taken as one of those elements a reader must parse before constructing a larger comprehension, as difficult to parse as the entire poem itself. Many of Ashbery's later poems, from *And the Stars Were Shining, Can You Hear, Bird?, Wakefulness,* and *Your Name Here,* define, and depend on, an arc between their very first developed address situation and their last for their sense of lyric movement and closure.[10]

"Or in My Throat," a poem from Ashbery's collection *Shadow Train*, utilizes homosexual thematics as the axis along which address shifts occur. Different from his later poems in which address shifts often offer the only identifiable arc, "Or in My Throat" uses address shifts at the service of thematics. The scenes in which the shifts happen are not made available by internal distinctions of voice and must be constructed with the help of gestures the poem makes toward scenes that can only be completed based on knowledges of cruising: its spatiality, its mechanics, and its emotional texture.

The poem consists of four quatrains, as do all of the poems in this book, and it begins by offering two possible interpretations of an unstated object or situation. "To the poet as a basement quilt, but perhaps / To some reader a latticework of regrets, through which / You can see the funny street ..."(25). The first line seems not to relate immediately to the title in a metaphoric or a metonymic sense. It places both points of view in the basement though, looking out a window at "the ends of cars and the dust ... ." "You" operates as a colloquial figure for "one" ("through which / You can see the funny street"), as well as splicing the two interpretive positions into one single interpreter's vantage (you are in the basement and are noticing how this single object can be interpreted two ways by two missing figures, the poet, who once again is presented as a speaker, and the reader). This object that one can see through causes coziness for "the poet" and a feeling of melancholy for "the reader." [11]This spatialization of viewer divided by a lattice from the outside is then figured for a "him," for whom "The two ends were the same except that he was in one / Looking at the other," describing the feeling of being divided from the world of which one is a part by regret, or considering this as a deep innuendo, describing some particular despair in relation to a sexual partner. The two ends can refer to the two ends of the human body's alimentary canal: the mouth and the anus. Penetrating one with a supine partner offers a view of the other. This innuendo receives strong support as interpretation from the title where the throat can figure as an alternative receptacle for a partner's ejaculate.

Either metaphorical spatiality causes the reader, or the "him" who might have shifted from "the reader," "the poet," or the "you," serious chagrin: "and all his grief stemmed from that: / There was no way of appreciating anything else, how polite / People were for instance ... ." In a place for serious cruising and public sex, the goal is figuratively to be either in one end looking at the other or to have someone else in this position. Noticing politeness requires that the noticer not be reading that politeness for its participation or nonparticipation in the prelude, midst, or denouement of a sexual encounter.

This interpretation takes hold in the third stanza where the site of pleasure turns into a nightmare landscape of the sort one could encounter at abandoned warehouses or similar places of exhausted production that often house, and concurrently block from sight, anonymous sex. This scene resurfaces in "Litany," where "Some in underwear stood around / Puddles in the darkened / Cement and sodium lights / Beyond the earthworks / Beyond the chain-link fence…" (*AWK* 10). In "Or in My Throat," the "they" that seems to have grown by simple pluralization from the "him" dominating the second stanza, still frequent such sites, and the speaker and his cohort of gay men, "the boys," sometimes hear back from this "them." The speaker and his letter-passing friends occupy a space divided from "them" by the suggestion that they hear from them via mail. They do not bump into them at common haunts, but instead receive letters.

> … and, the dream, reversed, became
>
> A swift nightmare of starlight on frozen puddles in some
> Dread waste. Yet you always hear
> How they are coming along. Someone always has a letter
> From one of them, asking to be remembered to the boys, and all.

As of yet the poem has not relied on address shifts, it is largely addressed to a "you," that could be the poet, a friend, or a group of friends. The speaker began by creating a half-formed image that made way for a sketchy portrait of "him," the singular form of the "they," which in the third stanza slides in to replace "him." The first three stanzas are a setup for the unveiling of the first person in the fourth. This stanza concretizes the innuendo about public sex that haunts the first three stanzas.

> That's why I quit and took up writing poetry instead.
> It's clean, it's relaxing, it doesn't squirt juice all over
> Something you were certain of a minute ago and now your own face
> Is a stranger and no one can tell you it's true. Hey, stupid!

The first line suggests that what separates the first person from the "they" from whom "someone always has a letter" is the act of quitting public sex for the more pristine activity of writing poetry. The second elaborates, but as it moves into the third line, deconstructs itself. The juice that squirts all over the third line is the excessive "flow" Ashbery will later exclusively highlight in *Flow Chart*. This line continues to qualify what already seemed perfectly and pithily in place. The reader understands that the juice that is no longer squirting all over is ejaculate but the poet insists on squirting his own overqualification all over.

"A minute ago" in the fantasized scene that these lines create, the speaker's face was unmarked by the messiness of fellatio, but instead of coming in his throat, the speaker's partner makes a mess of his face, turns him into a stranger to himself. The oddly dangling, "and no one can tell you it's true," indicates, on a literal level, the possibility that no one at a scene of public sex might know you in the first place in order to witness your face's transformation to "a stranger;" but it also means that no one can tell you that poetry (carrying poetry as referent for "it" from the second line of this stanza), which "doesn't squirt juice all over," is true. Poetry does not become literalized by its ejaculate, as here, oral sex does. Its lack of proof and trueness or falseness is a virtue to the speaker. However, the "it" of "no one can tell you it's true" is a moment of poetic juice squirting itself. "It" 's referential multivalence is messy.

The final address shift, the exclamatory, accusatory, or jibing "Hey, stupid!" refers both to the scene of the imagined figure with come all over his face and the poet whose faith in the neatness of poetry as an alternative to messy sex is bucked by his own performance of poetic referential splitting. The speaker of the final exclamation splits based on the split of "it" that directly precedes it. The consistency of voice throughout the poem, which suggests a single speaker, does not settle this final locution into his speakerly position. He could be ventriloquizing playfully accusatory voices that are aimed at him. It could be a taunt that those still having public sex might fling at the prissy poet, suggesting that his alternative to their mess is no more contained or free of carelessly sprayed ejaculate. Or it could be the poet turning his practice of poetry for sex into a kind of evangelical project and teasing the sticky-faced figure in his fantasy about his bespoiled condition. Whichever of these three, or whatever combination of the three takes in a reading, the poem literally ends with an *ejaculation*. And its either-wayness returns to the first mysterious figure of the lattice, which seen from the poet's vantage can be a "basement quilt" and from the reader's a "latticework of regrets." The speaker's decision to choose poetry over anonymous sex is either cozy ("it's clean, it's relaxing") or regretful, depending on one's location. Neither vantage, "quilt" or "latticework of regrets," is disqualified, and both continue to comment on the other. Like "The Fairies' Song," this poem closes by simultaneously affirming two contradictory propositions, but in this case the contradiction is even more striking because *one phrase* expresses both contradictory stances.

V. Ecstasy Rises from Spoil: "A Blessing in Disguise"

"A Blessing in Disguise," from *Rivers and Mountains* (1966), prefigures the lyric plots of both "Soonest Mended" and "The Fairies' Song." Here again, ecstasy rises from spoil in the midst of wonder that the speaker is himself "alive," and linguistic multivalency, or what I will call fuzziness, leads to felt clarity. In this version, there is a more inchoate sense of homosexual content; though with the other two poems in mind, the homosexual content stands out quite discretely. This poem, instead of utilizing a strategy of frustrating closure by paradox to provide a lyric moment for the reader (as in "The Fairies' Song"), explicitly offers pronominal shiftiness as a strategy to bring about the purposeful and exultant frustrations of closure. The reader is given no thread to follow through the referential difficulties of this poem, but is instead offered, at the poem's close, a reason why the pronouns do not have sharply defined boundaries.

The poem begins as a response to an unspecified question or comment from an unspecified interlocutor:

> Yes, they are alive and can have those colors,
> But I, in my soul, am alive too.
> I feel I must sing and dance, to tell
> Of this in a way, that knowing you may be drawn to me.
>
> And I sing amid despair and isolation
> Of the chance to know you, to sing of me
> Which are you. You see,
> You hold me up to the light in a way
>
> I should never have expected, or suspected, perhaps
> Because you always tell me I am you,
> And right. ... (26)

The first part of this poem can be read as an archly funny allegory of reading, and also as a prefiguration of the themes and figures treated more lucidly in "The Fairies' Song." "You," the reader, are following the characters and situations on the page, whose hidden, founding motive is that attention be paid to the "me" who is writing them. Ashbery echoes a similar but more campily delivered sentiment in an interview with Piotr Sommer. "I said to an interviewer recently that I was getting a little jealous of the reputation of my poetry, because it gets more attention than *I* do. When *will* people pay attention to *me* for a while!" ("Interview in Warsaw" 300).

John Shoptaw reads "A Blessing in Disguise" this way, but in the light of "The Fairies' Song" the self-assurance given in "But I, in my soul, am alive too," the "singing amid despair and isolation," and the assertion that "you always tell me I am you" take on yet another level of particularly homosexual allegorical meaning. "You hold me up to the light in a way // I never should have expected" suggests not merely an actual single or plural "you" but rather the entire operation of the pronoun "you." It marks a poetic self-distancing, a way Ashbery often uses "you," as well as a group naming, and therefore constituting, performance. "You" includes Ashbery but also acts on Ashbery from outside, "Because you always tell me I am you, / and right" is a way for the you to win an argument of some kind by absorbing the opposition. However the "rightness" is also a textual correctness (as in "this poem is right on"), and an ontological "rightness" (a sense of fit to an identity via community).

The poem begins as an assertion of aliveness against the evidence that all around him is more alive and colorful, suggesting that the poet must "sing and dance" to make the "you" desire him; but the poet is also part of the "you." This pronominal tangle makes most sense when read as the function of a desiring community. The "you" *is* readers, but I wish go further than John Shoptaw's suggestion (echoed by many other critics) that this or that poem by Ashbery is written to "the lover, the reader, and even the poem itself" and suggest that the lover, the reader, and the poem are bound together in a describable desiring community, a desiring community that has the special quality of vexed articulation around desire (82). The poem supports many levels of allegory, but has not yet been read as an allegory of the vexed articulation that both spoils gay identities and also heightens and exalts articulations of gay desire and community. Read as such an allegory, the poem has the virtue of elucidating the relation between a desiring speaker and a desiring addressee actually bound together as readers, as lovers, and as producers and consumers of the poem. They are not best related by a serial "and" or "or" and do actually have traceable lines of influence on one another. Reading "you" as the operative of a community that is both a member and a tool of inclusion or excision, and reading that community as gay, gives the edges of the "you" in this poem a more definable shape. It also gives real context for the poem's final articulation of exaltation. This exaltation recalls both the "young air" of "The Grapevine" and the aliveness and brilliance at the end of "The Fairies' Song."

The middle of the poem continues the address with which the poem commenced but shifts from exposition of how "you" affects the agency of the speaker to how the speaker's fantasy reshapes "you." Statements situating the speaker's relation to "you" mix and merge with scenic detail. They neatly alternate, as at the end of the third and beginning of the fourth stanza where the focus goes: scene / you // you / scene.

"The great spruces loom. / I am yours to die with, to desire. // I cannot ever think of me, I desire you / For a room...." It is as if the poem cannot decide which is more constitutive of the I/you relation: direct locutions about it or fantasized landscapes in whose shade, on whose chairs, and over whose paths this ill-defined couple (or group) might languish, sit, or stroll. The speaker wants the "you" to be a place, "a room" that is strangely situated in a garden. It is a room but has no ceiling and in it "the chairs ever / Have their backs turned to the light / Inflicted on the stone and paths, the real trees // That seem to shine at me through a lattice toward you."[12] As in "Or in My Throat" the subject/object relation gets spatially arranged by a lattice, but here, more oddly, as if the speaker were standing facing a row of trees through which light is streaming as if through a lattice and the "you" were standing behind him but also facing the same direction and the same trees. The lattice is only one example of difficult spatiality in these middle stanzas; the scene that is set and the relation of the speaker to his subject, "you," is largely unparsible; it refuses to settle to an imaginable scene because it jumps from detail to clashing detail (the room is suddenly in the middle of a garden detached from a house and with no walls) and finally, because the speaker has a "secret you will never know," propelling him through this patchy landscape.

Pronouns and landscapes, this poem argues by its difficult performance, have room for excess meaning. This excess meaning is at once evidence of the inadequacy of speech acts, the speaker is singing "amid despair and isolation," afraid that he himself is the single most colorless item in a landscape unattachable to the thriving evidence of life around him, while it is also his greatest hope and source of a project of remembering that can lead to exaltation. Keeping alive the hope of a "you" who is both plural and embodied in its unembodiedness is evidence of the speaker's own aliveness. Hope or desire with a stubbornly undefined object highlights the will that keeps them in place, and this will looks like a desirably self-determining version of the self.

The speaker muses about how to maintain the "secret you will never know" that will take him on its "wings" into the day. This "secret" cannot be the secret of the speaker's sexuality, this is manifest in the speaker's desire for the "you." It refigures the secret of sexuality into a secret that keeps the speaker separate from the "you." Perhaps it is the secret of "desir[ing] you / For a room" that was already divulged two stanzas ago. But in the midst this poem's pronominal elasticity this phrase, "you will never know," is less a statement of fact than it is performative. This is a "you" who "will never know;" were this "you" to know, it would have to become another "you." The speaker's desire is paring down the contents of "you" throughout the beginning of the poem until he makes desire (desire for knowledge, desire for the speaker who holds the knowledge) constitutive of the "you." The secret is how the "you" functions for the speaker, since the "you" *can* positionally never know it.

The title finally grips in the last stanza where Ashbery explicitates the two central concerns of the poem: "you" and exaltation.

> I prefer "you" in the plural, I want "you,"
> You must come to me, all golden and pale
> Like the dew and the air.
> And then I start getting this feeling of exaltation.

" 'You' in the plural," with its fuzzy outline and difficult to specify contents, is the key to "this feeling of exaltation." It is, in its very impalpability, a "blessing in disguise." Special feelings and feelings of specialness are dependent, this suggests, on a certain fuzzed-out space of fantasy. They are special precisely because diffuse like "air" or "dew," they cannot be completely figured, only named.

The "you" who is a room without occupants dramatizes this: Naming offers the possibility of habitation, but does not require habitation. So, for instance, "you," the pronoun, is exactly a room with no one in it. It can fit one or many, and the idea that a crowd could assemble under the rubric of the directly addressed beloved in a lyric thrills the poet whose erotics are wound up in the mundanity of impossibility and the impossibility of mundanity. Impossibility is essential to this most quotidian and workhorse of pronouns, but similarly, mundanity's mobility and mutability, embodied in this pronoun, are anything but mundane (in the sense of an emotional flatline). Ashbery postulates that location and unlocatability happen (paradoxically, *are located*) in the operation of the same pronoun. Harnessing the power of this node of linguistic production allows the poet, and, by careful attendance to the poet's example, the reader, to experience an aliveness that real life often does not provide. Ashbery's poetry can be approached as both a vehicle for the experience of that fuzziness, which enables exaltation, and also as an articulate celebration of such locatable fuzziness.

VI. The Half-Focused Image

Alan Williamson has named a particular stylistic innovation in Ashbery's poetry that produces just such effects. He calls it "the half-focused image" and describes it as "a kind of borderline structure between the mind and the world, possessing distinct sensuous qualities without ever quite becoming a visualizable object or scene" (122). The room/ gardenscape in "A Blessing in Disguise" is just such a structure: All the sensuous qualities are present but are lacking a principle of spatiality to relate them. Williamson unfortunately leaves "the half-focused image" itself half-focused because he writes, "[t]he effect is hard to describe, but fairly easy to illustrate" (Ibid.). The illustrations Williamson offers, "Our Youth," from *The Tennis Court Oath,* and "Fragment," from *Double Dream of Spring,* both present themselves, in Williamson's reading, as closed images via their sonics, while the "terms of their arguments remain unknown qualities" (Ashbery qtd. in Williamson 124).

While Williamson's sonic readings are interesting, sonic closure does not always attend this "borderline" structure's ghostly visitations. In fact, in "A Blessing in Disguise" the half-formed image of you as room entails a triplet rhyme whose initial and final rhyme is doubled ("through … you," "true," "unto you"). The stanza's final line, "Whom I can never stop remembering," offers a very uneasy sonic closure. The speaker says he wants the "you" for a room where light through trees:

> … seem[s] to shine at me through a lattice toward you.
> If the wild light of this January day is true
> I pledge me to be truthful unto you
> Whom I cannot ever stop remembering. (*RM* 26)

It is such a heightened poetic effect that it resists unnoticed suture into meaning and lands bumpily with the help of the clumsy slant double negative of "cannot" and "stop." The triplet rhyme marks excessive attention to sound that in conjunction with the heightened diction of "I pledge me to be truthful unto you" cannot be folded back in to subtle sonic workings of the poem. It stands up and demands its music be considered artifice. While this is indeed a sonic effect, it does not lead to the kind of sonic closure in light of argumentative unspecifiedness that Williamson identifies as a possible organizing principle of the "half-focused image." These are belligerent sonics that stand out *precisely as* the operatives of argument and do not offer this half-scene closure of any but an ironic type.

Williamson himself suggests "that it is impossible to gauge how much of the effectiveness of Ashbery's half-finished stories and pictures depends on his celebrated musicianship, and its power to induce an irrational sense of completion or suspension" (124). After all, sonic readings of most of Ashbery's poems will produce intensely rich closures or suspensions that may or may not be immediately related to the "terms of" *all of* "their arguments." Sonics may make and conclude an argument while other arguments occur simultaneously; so, while Williamson's sonic readings are welcome and useful, they do not seem to keep questions of explicit argument from influencing or helping to describe the "half-focused image." In other words, Alan Williamson tentatively suggests that because focus in these images themselves is only half-present, sonic focus must enter to locate the reader and allow this technique to work. He leaves other forces that may urge the success of Ashbery's "half-finished stories and pictures" unexplored. One such force, I will suggest, is an explicit thematic about closure itself, and an explicit project aimed at a queer reader who reads, in part at least, for frustrated closures.

It seems possible and productive to argue that the halfness of these focusings is not merely offering new closural effects that happen because of or at them, but that they offer readers spaces whose resistances to closure and meaning are sites of lyric and self-imagining possibility. By this I mean that by resisting completion, these images argue, by their example, for resistance to completion as well as offering sites for such resistance. They can also serve as sites for utopic fantasies of identities and meanings that do not conform to a bowdlerizing fantasy of hegemonic junction. These half things provoke by partialness and therefore offer partialness as a strategy for provocation, for generating the interest that reads as life at its intensest.

The very example Williamson offers from "Fragment" suggests that the explicit thematic argument is well served by blocked closure. He quotes the opening of this long poem that is eponymously concerned with fragmentariness itself and begins interestingly enough with a *closed block:*

> The last block is closed in April. You
> See the intrusions clouding over her face
> As in the memory given you of older
> Permissiveness which dies in the
> Falling back toward recondite ends. ... (*DDS* 78)

What Williamson doesn't quote is the end of this stanza where Ashbery argues that "The sympathy of yellow flowers" (held by a comma and an appositive-feeling line break from "recondite ends") absorbs the meaning of the first scene forcing it out of "permissiveness" and into "recondition" in which it cannot be absorbed nor imagined. After the flowers, the dizain continues: "Never mentioned in the signs of oblong day / The saw-toothed flames and point of other / Space not given, and not yet withdrawn / And never yet imagined: a moment's commandment" (*DDS* 78). The flames and "other space" are not given a point or direction in a structure of sentimentality and emotion that can be summed up in "the sympathy of yellow flowers" where a tight signifier strangleholds a signified whose most cogent attribute is overflow. This thematic of the superiority or relief (permissiveness) of a "space," "not given, and yet not withdrawn / And never yet imagined," coincides neatly with the thematics of homosexually inflected exaltation in the face of spoil we have been examining. Life lives there, Ashbery's explicit thematics argue, and the struggle to live in a vexed identity has to do with deploying structures that keep this space available for habitation.

In "Soonest Mended," Ashbery suggests that the feeling of being held by rules and identities that are not "our" own, speaking sentences that are "Not ours to own ... but to be with, and sometimes, / To be without, alone and desperate" can be combated by "a kind of fence-sitting / Raised to the level of an esthetic ideal" (*DDS* 18). He suggests that holding off meaning, fantasizing, makes one's life (words and acts) particular: "makes it ours."

Half-focusing highlights the reader's act of focusing as well as frustrating a possible readerly desire for complete focus or closed meaning. While it frustrates this particular desire it enables another: that the reader participate in making the poem her own without reifying either the readerly process or the poem. This allows Ashbery's poems to enact what Keats's (also explicitly fragmentary) "living hand" does; it is performatively held toward the reader demanding decision. The technique of half-formed stories and images declares "—see here it is— / I hold it towards you," and offers either the "earnest grasping" of readerly imagining or the icy cold deathliness of violent summary closure (Keats 389). Ashbery's poems are invested in their own livingness as well as in desires to be possessed by readers; they are calls to participation that vivify reader, poem, and poet; this process, as we have seen, is intimately bound to Ashbery's poesis, and moreover to a homosexual poetic project aimed to imagine difficult lives and somehow in the process help make them livable. Ashbery's poetry seeks to reinvigorate a "middle distance" and escape readings that "force" art into "meanings that don't concern us / And so leave us behind" (*W* 71). This attempt is rife with possibilities of failure, but worth it anyway, the poetry argues, because failure has in it the memory of excitement. As Ashbery charmingly formulates in "A Wave:"

> ... the issue
> Of making sense becomes such a far-off one. Isn't this "sense"—

This little of my life that I can see—that answers me
Like a dog, and wags its tail, though excitement and fidelity are
About all that ever gets expressed? What did I ever do
To want to wander over into something else, an explanation
Of how I behaved, for instance, when knowing can have this
Sublime rind of excitement, like the shore of a lake in the desert
Blazing with the sunset? So that if it pleases all my constructions
To collapse, I shall at least have had that satisfaction, and known
That it need not be permanent in order to stay alive,
Beaming, confounding with the spell of its good manners. (*W* 70)

VII. Vaguenesses: "As We Know"

Like "The Grapevine," the title poem of *As We Know* theorizes knowing,
or "sense," as shot through with sexuality. Charles Altieri has offered a
supple reading of this poem in "Contemporary Poetry as Philosophy" in
which he reads its "vagueness" as "a crucial feature establishing the poet's
complex grasp of subjective agency" (217). Altieri remarks that where
Ashbery's "predecessors sought strong images as locales for positing
identities" Ashbery experiments with "the subjective force projected in
deictics and other shifters, hoping that how one establishes one's relation
to utterances and situations provides a sufficient grounding for the range
of identities and identifications that constitutes subjective life" (216). As
I have examined earlier, deictics in Ashbery often open up many locations in a poem, especially at its close, in order to allow even contrary
attachments. "A Blessing in Disguise," for instance, utilizes the deictic
elasticity of "you" to enable a state of exaltation based on "you"'s failure
to specify any particular individual.

My approach, different from Altieri's, is concerned with how these
moments are propelled by homosexual thematics, which require new
strategies for figuring identity. Fuzziness, or multivalency, is for Ashbery
the centerpiece for such a strategy, enabling writer and reader to inhabit
a homosexual subjectivity poetically. Altieri's acute analysis of Ashbery's
theorization and poetics of subjecthood in "As We Know" falls short by
failing to locate the homosexual thematics central to the poem's effects
that enable a whole new level of address, irony, and urgency. Altieri
acknowledges the limits of his reading when he writes, "Having chosen
this example ['As We Know'], I wish I could be more certain than I am
of the specific drama underlying this poem" (216). I would like, while
developing Altieri's critique, to hypothesize about that underlying
drama, which I think is accessible on the level of innuendo. The
poem begins with an "it" that wends its unspecified way through the

first two stanzas:

> All that we see is penetrated by it—
> The distant treetops with their steeple (so
> Innocent), the stair, the windows' fixed flashing—
> Pierced full of holes by the evil that is not evil,
> The romance that is not mysterious, the life that is not life,
> A present that is elsewhere.
>
> And further in the small capitulations
> Of the dance, you rub elbows with it,
> Finger it. That day you did it
> Was the day you had to stop, because the doing
> Involved the whole fabric, there was no other way to appear.
> You slid down on your knees
> For those precious jewels of spring water
> Planted on the moss. ... (143)

Let me start by hypothesizing backwards. The final scene, "you" sliding "down on your knees" for "precious jewels," is a rather transparent scene of fellatio. This activity then retroactively shoots into the "it" that peoples the lines above it. "The day you did it / Was the day you had to stop, because the doing / Involved the whole fabric" suggests that having gay sex troubles the "whole" ontologic "fabric" of the speaker or addressee. It both leads one to reimagine one's place in the world and offers leverage, via a secret that expresses itself everywhere, to reimagine the world itself differently. The steeple becomes "so / Innocent" only in the context of a phallic loss of innocence; its innocence is a product of the landscape being penetrated by "it," the fantasy of gay sex, that could offer the steeple a context in which it would become uninnocent.

The list locating the "it"—"the evil that is not evil, / The romance that is not mysterious, the life that is not life, / A present that is else-where"—gestures with decreasing specificity to homosexuality. "The evil that is not evil" specifies homosexuality in religious discourse; "the romance that is not mysterious" respecifies it in relation to heteronormative courtship suggesting that homosexual romance, shorn of courtly circumlocutions and custom-laden circuitry about sex, cuts to the chase; "the life which is not life" zooms further out to suggest that homosexual lives do not show up on the birth-marriage-death map of heterosexuality; and the "present that is elsewhere" suggests in the largest sense that, because of their banishment from dominant heteronormative discourse, queer lives always happen "elsewhere," they are always temporally spatialized outside of the "present." The poem's first stanza concentrates on homosexuality's movement outward to bigger and bigger othernesses that depend on homosexuality's position as *the* other in a heteronormative discourse of morality, erotics, ontology, spatiality, and temporality, until it "Involve[s] the whole fabric … ."

The kneeling moment in the poem, in its ripple effect on the fabric of reality, makes this "you" teeter "on the edge of this / Calm street … // As though they are coming to get you" (143). Since the whole world has been rearranged in the subjective experience of gay sex, it seems that some regulatory agent should have noticed the anomaly and arrived to eliminate or correct it. But none does: "… there was no one in the noon glare…" (143). Since this ecstatic reorganization met with no external crackdown, and the giddiness and exhilaration of inhabiting an alternative "present" is apparently livable, the speaker moves into the fourth stanza with a new knowledge and approach:

> The light that was shadowed then
> Was seen to be our lives,
> Everything about us that love might wish to examine,
> Then put away for a certain length of time, until
> The whole is to be reviewed, and we turned
> Toward each other, to each other.
> The way we had come was all we could see
> And it crept up on us, embarrassed
> That there is so much to tell now, really now.

The "light that was shadowed" at this moment of reorganization that followed gay sex, the light that hits objects and defines shadows, outlining in its absence, is seen as "our lives." This figuration makes intimacy between two figures in the poem possible: "… and we turned / Toward each other, to each other."

The final lines of the poem suggest both the joys and the limits of narrativizing completely on the basis of moments of outlawed ecstasy: "The way we had come was all we could see / And it crept up on us, embarrassed / That there is so much to tell now, really now." This sets up two lovers looking back on their past, seeing only the way that they had arrived there, and for the first time finding a historical register in which to figure themselves. The "really now" in this reading is a spine-tingling assertion of presentness against the world's insistence that they, as homosexuals, exist in a "present that is elsewhere." There is, however, a critique of this very situation embedded in the lines. The lines also suggest that the vision presently available to these lovers is inhibited by the fact that "the way they had come," their sexuality, is "all they could see." This critique inflects the "embarrassed / That there is so much to tell now" with a bitchy final address shift that is dismissive of how much there is to tell. "Really now" suggests not just a very particular temporality but also a playful, dismissive gesture, the kind of thing one might say to an intimate at the end of a hyperbolic narrative. "As We Know" critiques its own ecstatic knowing while celebrating it. This double move comments precisely on how "we know." "Our" knowledge is embarrassedly shot through with sexuality, a situation that Ashbery earlier explored in "The Grapevine," in which thematic knowing is much more exact: " how do we know who is gay?" But as in "The Grapevine," we need this embarrassment of overlocation as the foundation to further knowledge.

Ashbery's queer poetic project, as we have seen in various poems, uses difficulty mimetically. *Difficult* describes a way lived life feels (full of pain, littered with climbable and unclimbable obstacles), which corresponds to a kind of poetry (full of disjunctions and ellipses, littered with climbable and unclimbable obstacles). This is not a simple correspondence, because any poetic manifestation of difficulty does not just mimic lived difficulty; rather, in its artfulness it offers a vocabularization of the lived and thereby a much-desired momentary respite that can be referenced in a project of remembering or as a way to avoid or rescript future difficulties. Difficulty as a literary effect and difficulty as lived conflict are connected by a theory of literary mimesis to which Ashbery often has recourse in interviews, the "greater naturalism" quoted above, and which recent critics have emphasized. Poetic difficulty is, here writ, a performance of, figure for, and site of lived difficulty. The literary text offers a removed place where naming, untangling, tangling, figuring, and refiguring can take place. As noted in the above quotation from Ashbery's poem "Haibun," by making pain available stylistically within his poems, Ashbery hopes to also make perspectives and strategies for dealing with it available. This rather general project, or theory and practice of difficulty as mimetically deployable, is most convincingly and exactly described or enacted around homosexual thematics in Ashbery's poetry. A critical project that forgoes making homosexual themes obvious for their own sake also forgoes establishing a ground for his very abstract, overflowing, and sophisticated theories and practices of difficulty, which are, by their nature, themselves difficult.

Chapter 4

A Mirror at the End of a Long Corridor: Moore, Crane, Closure

I.

The biographies of Hart Crane and Marianne Moore collide at one much trafficked intersection. Almost every comprehensive critical treatment of either author tells the story of how Moore, when at the helm of *The Dial,* revised and published a version of Crane's "The Wine Menagerie" (under the new title "Again") in its May 1926 issue. Moore cut the poem to less than half of its original length; Thomas Yingling suggests, with an oeuvre the size of Crane's, this is "equivalent to deleting or rewriting one-fourth of a novel by Faulkner ... before publishing it" (*Hart Crane* 108).

Despite the story's ubiquity, each account of this publishing event is "ringed with contradictions and revisions" (*Moore,* Molesworth 219). Crane never directly complained to Moore about her changes; in fact, he sent her a letter of thanks (which I quote below) for accepting his poem, agreeing to the changes in the body and title of the poem. Moore, conversely, takes up the issue only much later when interviewers or friends ask her explicitly about it. Then she tells a simple story, something that once the record is straight seems to require little more comment on her part.

The muddle surrounding the publication of "Again" includes Matthew Josephson, to whom Crane sobbed uncontrollably about the humiliation of having a poem gutted and retitled. Josephson, as he tells the story in his autobiographical work, *Life Among the Surrealists,* wrote a letter to Moore offering to buy back the poem for its original price of 20 dollars. Moore was incensed; and Crane, upon being called into the offices of *The Dial,* denied any part in Josephson's offer.

Josephson's account is the most complete one we have but it has an odd staginess about it, as does all of *Life Among the Surrealists.* This book seems Josephson's attempt to take his hitherto withheld place in literary history, often by retelling his friendships and then his disenchantments with the literary and artistic stars of his generation. For instance, Josephson recounts Crane's emotional response to Moore's rewrite: " 'I would never have consented to this outrageous mutilation,' Hart cried, with tears starting in his eyes, 'if I hadn't so desperately needed the money—only twenty dollars.' When he was overcome by emotion and wept, my wife and I asked him to lie down and rest in a little guest room we had. (As this happened several times, we came to call that room 'Hart Crane's Crying Room')" (296). The words Crane speaks sound as if they were translated out of and back into English; further, the mixture of familiarity, friendliness, and contempt Josephson indicates that he and his wife feel for Crane's alcoholic and womanly behavior give Josephson an almost too perfect proximity to Crane the genius and simultaneous distance from Crane the queer boozer. So, while Josephson's account is the source for almost all that follow, it seems too self-justificatory to accept as the anchor around which the rest of the players and events in this biographical formation crystallize.

The invisible, but possibly most powerful, force in Josephson's account is Moore's annoyance. She took him for a meddler. His narrative, then, seeks to provide his motivation for the favor he did Crane of offering to buy back "The Wine Menagerie." Moore's biographers, conversely, explain how she thought *she* was doing Crane a favor, monetarily, editorially, and poetically. Crane's suggest that his acceptance and then retraction of his permission, and the proliferation of favors everybody did him, were caused by his alcoholic temper and general economic and psychological desperation. Everybody was doing him favors, just the wrong ones.

Part of the appeal of this story is exactly its muddle. It is a mighty little anecdote about a clash of titans of eccentricity that performs all sorts of biographical violence effortlessly. Considering the tale's ubiquity, it is strange that no critic has yet undertaken an extensive examination of what hard and true evidence we do have: the poems themselves. Furthermore, in my own examination, I will suggest that the simplicity and access of outrage in this story around a rewriting of a poem by an editor stops short of understanding the incident as a contact, perhaps a crash, of Crane's and Moore's poetics. These two poets are often treated as radically different in their relation to ecstatic utterances, and by extension, in their relation to poetic utterances in general. Crane is considered sometimes embarrassing in his excesses and Moore stunning in her restraint. Different as they seem, they share certain poetic techniques and tropes with which they express their ideas of the height of poetic power and ecstasy. Central to these is the trope of reflection and the closural techniques that these poets invent to explore it.

The trope of reflection raises issues of what part of one's image constitutes one's self. Lacan dramatizes this in his theory of the "Mirror Stage," in which a child sees his own reflection and realizes that it doesn't have a burbling stomach or clumsy limbs and moves with apparent ease that the child himself cannot muster. Then, to simplify, the child begins to realize the power and usefulness of signs as they stand for him in the world. I offer this here, without any of its theoretical complexity or context, in order to suggest how central reflection can be to a theory of signification. Reflection sets a scene in which the self confronts the not-quite-other but not-quite-self. I do not wish to make any gestures to the early development of Crane's or Moore's significatory practices here; rather, I want to follow Lacan in locating writing (in the broadest sense) at the scene of reflection. Both Crane and Moore utilize this scene to experiment in their writing. Their scenes of reflection make explicit claims about the constitution of the self and enact certain kinds of productions of self.

There are of course various vantages a poet can take on the scene of reflection. She can present the scene as an allegorical structure, offer herself as the reflection of an other, suggest that her self is reflected in the world, or suggest that reflection is the only access any of us has to the world. The poet can imagine her gifts realized when she sees the world reflected in herself or vice versa. The trope of reflection expresses itself as a variety of metaphor: It puts one self in proximity with another not-quite-self and suggests a linkage between them.

Since the association of Crane's and Moore's poetics is all but missing from critical accounts (only showing up in suggestions that Moore was influenced late in her career by Crane, but never deeply and *never* vice versa),[1] a biographical moment like the rewriting of "The Wine Menagerie," even if it is, or especially if it is, a conflagration, deserves attention as a poetic event rather than only as a biographical one. The incident has quite a bit to say instead of just being an inarticulate yawp above the roofs of Moore's finicky bossiness or Crane's drunken sloppiness.

In this chapter I suggest that this story is really outrageous because of its relation to each poet's poetics and theorizations of desire. By "really outrageous" I do not mean to suggest that all critics before me missed the point, or were outraged by the "wrong" things, but rather that they identified an energetic clash but undertheorized it. That said, sometimes it is in fact the case that this anecdote and its attendant outrage are used to bolster easy prejudices that simply interfere with considering this incident and these poets in a complete or rich way. These poems explore basic aspects of the relation of the self to a beloved other. As such they provide access to issues of desire and identification in Crane's and Moore's poetics.

In both versions of "The Wine Menagerie," Crane's and Moore's, the reflection of the self in an othering medium is central. This is in part because Moore's "Again" is only a rewritten version of Crane's poem; she mostly condenses what is already there. I contend however that Moore's version does not thematically or theoretically bring out what is already in "The Wine Menagerie"; her rearrangement and representation fundamentally change the poem's theory of desire. Moore turns Crane's theorization against itself; her version flips his around, as in a mirror image.

Despite its presence in anecdote, "Again," the title of Moore's revision of "The Wine Menagerie," is reprinted in only one of the scholarly accounts that deal with it, Thomas Parkinson's volume of Crane and Yvor Winter's literary correspondence. There, naked, Parkinson means it to stand as evidence of Moore's editorial butchery.[2] In the footnotes, however, Parkinson retracts a little of his crankiness:

> Crane's anger was not entirely justified. Marianne Moore wrote him a very courteous letter requesting permission to make certain changes, and Crane's reply accepted the changes: "I agree with you that the enclosed version of THE WINE MENAGERIE contains the essential elements of the original poem, and inasmuch as I admire the sensibility and skill of your re-arrangement of the poem I should be glad to have it so printed in The Dial. [sic] The title, 'Again,' of course will supplant the original one." The letter is signed "Gratefully yours, Hart Crane." (fn. 162)

Parkinson then suggests that, with this letter in mind, Moore had every right to be annoyed by the fuss Crane made (or rather, the fuss Crane's friends made for him). Moore didn't like fusses. Later in her career, she explicitly admonished: "Poets, don't make a fuss ..." (*Complete Poems* 148).

Scholars have treated the rewriting of "The Wine Menagerie" as a bit of gossip, an anecdote that frustrates the taking of sides but provokes outrage all around. It is difficult, if one has such a mind, to decide which party is more right. Moore seems to have broken an unstated rule about authorship, as well as having broken the explicit editorial policy of

The Dial whereby a poem was to be accepted or rejected as it was submitted. Another incident of Moore's editorial overstepping is delicately detailed in David Kalstone's *Becoming a Poet,* in which he retells a quiet clash between Bishop and Moore when Moore and her mother rewrote Bishop's poem "Roosters" and sent their new version, retitled, "The Cock," back to her with a stern letter signed "Dorothy Dix" (81–8). This slap on the wrist made Bishop recede from Moore's formerly generous and suddenly interfering poetic advice. Bishop bristled and avoided Moore's deep-tissue criticism from there on out.[3]

It seems more than coincidental that the very poet being accused of overstepping bounds and putting words in other poets' mouths is the same one whose corpus is full of the words of others. Her poems are often explicitly or implicitly built out of quotations, marked or unmarked, to the extent that she commented about her poem "Marriage," that it was "a little anthology of statements that took my fancy—phrasings I liked" (*Complete Prose* 551). In the extensive "Notes" to "Marriage" in her *Complete Poems,* she describes the poem similarly: "Statements that took my fancy which I tried to arrange plausibly" (271). The 35 pages of notes at the end of her *Complete Poems* are themselves testament to both how much attention Moore paid to attribution, but also, insofar as they do not solve even near half of the attribution mysteries of her work, testament to how much attribution she withheld, left without comment, or buried. Scholars often admiringly note how Moore indexed her own diaries that are primarily full of quotations. Exactly what is most lauded, innovative, and daring about Moore in her own poems, throwing her voice into other people's utterances, suddenly seems violent and imposing—a scandal— when she speaks a poet's poem, altered and without quotation marks, back to him or her.

Both cases, as a friend to Bishop and as an editor to Crane, seem anecdotally powerful insofar as they suggest that Moore's stylistic collaging was in some way a psychopathology, a kind of quiet megalomania, or Miss Manners (or "Dorothy Dix," a then-famous columnist who gave advice to the lovelorn) gone berserk. Moore was a poet whose precision was one of her strongest gifts and one of her central poetic concerns. To share this gift and concern with other poets seems to require allowing it to act on the poetic material at hand.[4] That she "corrected" and resituated the material in poems by other poets indicates less strongly a desire to interfere than it does a desire to see a poem or poet succeed. This is not to say that Moore's corrections were not performed in an interfering way, but rather that it is possible to argue that her investment in the poetic material at hand, Bishop's or Crane's, was primary to her investment in "correctness" or "cleanliness." This distinction is important because of its insistence that Moore was first and foremost, in these interactions with other poets, a *poet*. That is, her precision cannot be separated from her poetics, and her poetics may include a certain "obsessive" relation to precision or neatness, but this is always mediated by her relation to an idea of what a poetic utterance is. The scoop that biographers seem to think they have on Moore when they cart out example after example of priggishness in her poetic career must be read, if it is not to be a mere pop-psychological reduction of this complex writer's life, through her own poetics.[5]

Marianne Moore was a preeminent woman of letters at the time she had these clashes with younger poets; she was someone whose poetic opinion and products Bishop and Crane both admired. Parkinson, in a book that is very careful about bringing to light and contextualizing the links between Yvor Winters and Crane, goes so far in unwriting Moore as a significant influence on Crane that he suggests that Crane thought her, along with Harriet Monroe, merely a literary "citadel[] to be stormed" (6).

Parkinson's example is a stark one: In the very volume where he presents Crane's vision of Moore as a rung on the ladder to his literary success, Crane himself, in a letter to Yvor Winters, ranks Moore with Poe, Whitman, Melville, Cummings "(at times)," and Frost as artists who give him "a renewed appreciation of what America really is, or could be" (11). Right after this appreciation of Moore's importance, Crane tells Winters about Moore's editorial actions:

> Miss Moore's paces are stubborn, and once, in my case, destructive. "Repose of Rivers" escaped her clutches successfully, as most everything else of mine published henceforth. But that frightful "Again" (what she must have said with lifted eyebrows and a ? mark when she opened the envelope) was the wreck of a longer and entirely different poem "The Wine Menagerie" which I hope you will see in its original nudity when my book, "White Buildings," comes out from Boni & Liveright sometime around December. I was *obliged* to submit to her changes, not only because I was penniless at the time but because I owed money to others at the time equally penniless. When I saw that senseless thing in print I almost wept. (12)

Crane fastidiously separates Moore as editor, whose actions conspired with his poverty to a sad result, and Moore as poet, whose poetry represents what Crane thought was right and powerful about American poetry. But also Crane insists that 20 dollars was all that motivated the above quoted "Gratefully yours," letter of acceptance.

The emphasis on Crane's "*obliged*" seems less explanatory than compensatory, further, his multiplication of pennilessness, while perhaps a fact, sounds defensive. There is, of course, no question that money was a constant problem for Crane; however, Matthew Josephson offered to buy the poem back with his own 20 dollars, and Crane disavowed any complicity in that offer. This would have made Crane 20 dollars richer, and the chop job, "Again," would never have seen print. Further, if Josephson's account of Crane's reaction to the alterations in his poem is correct, we know that he didn't "almost" weep when he saw the poem in print, he wept before it was ever printed at all.

Of course, merely appearing in *The Dial* was an honor and another step toward literary success, and Marianne Moore was not a connection to foul up. Moreover, Crane was not at all insensitive to connections: Upon first moving to New York he had taken an apartment above *The Little Review* in order to better press his poems on its editors. From all accounts, furthermore, Crane had reason to believe that Moore liked him. Elizabeth Bishop tells how "when [Moore] had been talking about her days on *The Dial,* I asked how she had liked Hart Crane when he had come into the office. Her response was ... unexpected. 'Oh, I *liked* Hart! I always liked him very much—he was so *erudite*' " (*Complete Prose* 143). John Unterecker reports that Moore, "genuinely unaware that her well-meant efforts to improve ['The Wine Menagerie'] had not been appreciated—couldn't understand what all the fuss was about," which he supports with a quote from an interview she did with Donald Hall years after the incident.

> Hart Crane complains of me? Well, I complain of *him.* He liked *The Dial* and we liked him—friends, and with certain tastes in common. He was in dire need of money. It seemed careless not to so much as ask if he might like to make some changes ("like" in quotations). His gratitude was ardent and later his repudiation of it commensurate .... He was so *anxious* to have us take that thing, and so *delighted.* "Well, if you would modify it a little," I said, "we would like it better." (Tomlinson 38–9)

In fact, the very same year, 1925, Crane sent Moore's name as a reference with the successful request for financial help he sent Otto Kahn (Weber, *Letters* 224).

One can, even with all this material at hand, draw a picture of simple motivations on both sides. Moore, after all has become famous as the editor who rejected the "Anna Livia Plurabelle" chapter of *Finnegan's Wake* and who, without all the fuss of these other two incidents, cut pages from an essay by Ezra Pound. Moore, the story goes, was schoolmarmish and eccentric, harboring a priggish sense of the correct, and, concomitantly, an overblown sense of her own aesthetic judgments. Crane was impoverished, impulsive, and alcoholic and would have done just about anything for money. Yet, there is a firmness in both of their responses to the incident that makes it seem more than simply an editorial mishap.

II.

Moore's "Again" is a mirror's surface upon which she represents "The Wine Menagerie." The title of Moore's version forthrightly declares itself as such. Moore, much earlier in her career, offers a way to imagine the relation of authors to each other with the familiar trope of reflection in a small poem, "Blake," published in Alfred Kreymborg's *Others,* in 1915 (but which did not make it into the *Collected Poems,* the later *Complete Poems,* or for that matter into any subsequent volume). In "Blake," Moore positions contemporary writers and Blake opposite and facing each other. The poem is short and utilizes a chiastic structure: Blake looking at "us" and "us" looking at Blake.

> BLAKE
>
> I wonder if you feel as you look at us,
> As if you were seeing yourself in a mirror at the end
> Of a long corridor—walking frail-ly.
> I am sure that we feel as we look at you,
> As if we were ambiguous and all but improbable
> Reflections of the sun—shining pale-ly.

The sonic and thematic content of this poem is simple enough. It has a sturdy rhythmic and figural frame. Figurally, a mirror mediates any chiastic traffic between the parties "us" and "Blake." But in an even more concrete way, the sight lines of the poem form a chiasmus. A strong horizontal axis (a figure standing at the opposite end of a corridor from a mirror) in the first sentence shifts to a vertical axis in the second (the sun reflecting in something, most likely a body of water, below it).

The poem performs a high figural compare and contrast between a poet long dead and contemporary artists and to a certain extent it wears its conclusions on its sleeve. We, the speaker announces, cannot measure up to the brilliance of Blake, however hard we try. This simplicity is vexed, though, by the effect at the end of each sentence, where, despite the failure to emulate Blake, the contemporary artist shares the final verb with adverb combinations with him. "Walking frail-ly" and "shining pale-ly" can refer to both "us" and "you" in the poem. We "walk frail-ly" since we are mere distant reflections of Blake—but the poem's grammar suggests the even more grim possibility that Blake himself is "walking frail-ly" and we are even frail-er reproductions of an already frail frame. "Shining pale-ly" is even more complicated because it could refer to how Blake (as the sun) is shining, which is not in any way weak. It describes the color of the sun at the height of its power, as in the phrase "pale fire." "Shining pale-ly" could also describe the sun being reflected palely, not maintaining much of its former illuminatory prestige. Embedded in this final phrase is the idiom "pale reflection," as in "he became a pale reflection of his former self." In some sense, the very device of two subjects sharing referential territory itself splits in its movement from the first to the second sentence. "Walking frail-ly" splits in its relation to the spatiality of a corridor, while "shining pale-ly" both splits in relation to a sky–earth axis and in terms of its adverbial import.

"Blake" shows Moore applying the trope of reflection to temporal influence, imaginative and linguistic coherence, and desire. The visual and the spatial exist in a clear-cut relation of signifier and signified, which is complicated by the shared activity of the participles and modifiers. Thus, Blake is the real, never treated as a reflection of "us," but becomes "reflected" in our activity just as much as we are reflections of him. The "-ly"'s that end each sentence of the poem emphasize yet another chiastic relation: that of adjectives to adverbs. We are "pale" and "frail" but in our relation to Blake we can move from ontic failures to his hopeful successors. That is, we are pale and frail but, with the help of Blake as place holder, develop verb activity and something to aspire to: We can walk stronger and reflect truer.

This poem's closure is unusual for a Moore poem. Usually, her lyrics have either a stronger sense of an end in the shape of an epigrammatic statement or a weaker sense insofar as they stop at the end of an associative strand. This poem is all shape with neither willful closure standing outside of its discursiveness nor willful discursiveness standing outside of its closure. This could explain why it did not make it into Moore's *Collected Poems* (and subsequently her *Complete Poems*), but as many critics remind us, most notably Bonnie Costello, there are many poems that did not make it into *Collected Poems* for no completely clear reasons.[6]

Despite its closural oddity, "Blake" offers Moore's clearest figuration of the perils of seeking one's self in an other. On either side of the looking glass, as it were, reflection falls short. Ideality leaves the perfectly whole other to be disappointed, but this disappointment is part of the odd personification of a dead author and thus seems to hold less immediate import than the fact that the pale, incomplete self must strive and inevitably fail. Humility then is the message for the self: Seek your reflection in others but know you must fail. Fundamentally, however, the "us" in the poem is always a reflection and thus in some way its shortcomings are either caused by distance or by some flaw in the original "Blake." There is, this poem suggests, no transport in the ideality of an other seen as a reflection of the self. Reflection, rather than a way to lose oneself in another, offers no ecstatic experience but rather a perpetually sobering reminder of one's limits.

This message is crystal clear, the very strange thing about it is that this message of imaginative limitations occurs in a poem named after and in praise of William Blake! In some ways this is a meta-poetic chiastic structure of the poem: Moore's theorization of ecstasy is the flipped-over reflection of Blake's. In the notes to one of her most famous poems, "Poetry," (which in the 1967 final revision of *Complete Poems* maintains only the first three of its original twenty-nine lines), she quotes William Butler Yeats about Blake: " 'The limitation of his view was from the very intensity of his vision; he was a too literal realist of imagination, as others are of nature; and because he believed that the figures seen by the mind's eye, when exalted by inspiration, were 'eternal existences,' symbols of divine essences, he hated every grace of style that might obscure their lineaments' " (268). From this excerpt Moore took the phrase "literalists of the imagination" that appeared in her longer version of the poem, also presented in the notes of the final version of the *Complete Poems*. Only when the "poets among us" can be "literalists of the imagination," she asserts in "Poetry," will we have poetry. But this praise of Blake is not simple, because Yeats calls Blake "a too literal realist of the imagination," and the title of the poem that follows this one in the *Collected Poems* (as well as the *Complete Poems*) is "Pedantic Literalist." Moore apparently agrees with Yeats about this characteristic of Blake's vision which is more a characteristic of his poetry than a fault, a constitutive limitation rather than a shortfall. Where Blake offered the imagination, read deep identification with another, as a way of getting outside of the self, Moore suggests the opposite, while also appreciating and deifying Blake himself. Thus, strangely, Moore seeks her reflection in Blake and comes away realizing that she does contain Blake but as a reflection—reversed. Her own poetic project enacts her thematic of failed reflection and suggests that the failure provides an effective site to deploy her agency, a location for the application of "gusto" and "humility." Realizing limits and shortfalls of identification motivates us, for Moore, to reach toward the other.

Warner Berthoff, in a discussion that attempts to right misconceptions that Crane's ecstasy seeking short-circuited his formal and structural concerns, suggests that Crane and Moore share a common "mix of motives": "transcendentalizing ambitions firmly anchored to a free-handed executive practicality" (62). Berthoff shows how Crane's formulation—"There is only one way of saying what comes to one in ecstasy"—puts as much emphasis on the "way of saying" as it does on ecstasy. Berthoff continues: "This is hardly a call for the ecstatic at any cost, without performative mediation. The general position, we might note, is not different from the one announced by Marianne Moore ... in one of her own succinct formulations of what is needed for a consequential poetry: 'Ecstasy affords / the occasion and expediency determines the form.'" While Berthoff's point about Crane and Moore sharing a two-part model of ecstasy's relation to poetry is not only apt but seminally important in criticism of Crane, it fails to remark the possibility that the element these formulations share, "ecstasy," may be fundamentally different in the thematics and enactments of these two poets.

Ecstatic utterances *just look different* in Crane than they do in Moore. Their shared ecstasies over Brooklyn Bridge serve as an excellent example of the difference of what seems a similar tone. Moore suggests that seeing the bridge in one's mind's eye and then *actually* seeing it is constitutive to the ecstasy the bridge creates in its viewer.

> Untried expedient, untried; then tried;
> way out; way in; romantic passageway
> first seen by the eye of the mind,
> then by the eye. O steel! O stone! (*Complete Poems* 205[7])

The exclamations here are both ecstatic utterances of appreciation and of surpassed expectations. These cries are the ecstasy this speaker feels in the face of the bridge, but also the ecstasy caused by the bridge's actuality and its relation to a temporally prior fantasy of the bridge. The doubleness of the exclamations mutes rather than amplifies. Further, the doubleness of the implied scene (imaginary bridge/material bridge), while it allows the celebration of the "bridge" between real and imaginary, mutes Moore's ecstatic cries. Conversely, an appreciation of the bridge by Crane turns up the volume on the ecstatic utterance not least by using a single exclamation point and having a single point to exclaim: ecstasy as threshold not bridge.

> *O harp and altar, of the fury fused,*
> *(How could mere toil align they choiring strings!)*
> *Terrific threshold of the prophet's pledge,*
> *Prayer of pariah, and the lover's cry,—* (*Complete Poems* 44)

Crane performs ecstasy. His poem suggests not the motivation of or build up to this particular ecstatic experience but the constitution of the experience itself. The significant difference between Crane and Moore's tonal poetic ecstasy arises from the fact that Crane is zoomed in on ecstasy in order to enact it for his reader, and Moore produces a wide-angle shot that shows where ecstasy is so that her readers can go and experience it themselves. These are differences in poetic voice, a concept so large as to reward observations and punish generalization, and I do not mean to generalize here about ecstasy throughout the work of both of these poets but simply to show how utterances that seem to fit under the same rubric are modified by their motivation and placement.

III.

The myth on which the psychoanalytic and pop-psychological term "narcissism" is based has a beautiful youth cursed to fall so in love with his reflection that he drowns in the water that reflects him. Anita Sokolsky, in her seminal essay on John Ashbery's "Self-Portrait in a Convex Mirror," explores the accusations of "narcissism" that hover around Ashbery's difficult style. Ashbery's poem is a long meditation on Francesco Parmigianino's Mannerist painting—the "first mirror portrait"—of the same name and is the title piece of Ashbery's most celebrated and well-known book of poems. Ashbery's poetry is "self-involved" to those who dislike it and "self-reflexive" to those who don't. Either way, Sokolsky explains, the assessments of Ashbery's poetry are based on an assumption that narcissism is an "inexcusable vice," and that "self-exploration is justifiable only when it moves inward in order to move, with majestic clarification, out" (233).[8] Sokolsky shows how the lucidity of "Self-Portrait" (it is universally proclaimed as Ashbery's most lucid long poem) is in fact a comment on lucidity's own "illusion of depth" by "taking for granted that narcissism is the implicit subject-matter of art, generating incessant speculation about its own enterprise and the nature of the poetic subject" (234).

In this section I will explore Crane's "The Wine Menagerie," which entails its own self-portraits in convex mirrors (the speaker being reflected on the bellies of decanters and between the tusks of eyelashes) and addresses the very tension between lucidity and narcissism in relation to desiring the other. "The Wine Menagerie" is centrally concerned with issues of the inside and outside of the self and with the extent to which one can breech the boundary between the two. Crane's Narcissus, rather than leaning over a real, wine-red pool, gazes at himself as he is reflected in/on a metaphorical pool of red wine. Alcohol "redeems" the sight in this poem by relaxing it into gazing at itself, removing the inhibition to self-perusal and appreciation. In part, Crane is following up on Rimbaud's project of the disarrangement of the senses, but in another sense, Crane has a notion or theory of where he wants to get with his "disarrangement," making it more of a "re-arrangement." His poem is about reimagining himself in a certain kind of othering medium, not just beside himself, but in a specific mirror. Ashbery's "Self-Portrait in a Convex Mirror" is not only similar to Crane's poem in its central image, it shares a closure in which figures within the poem go on whispering past the end, just beyond the reader's hearing. Both poems end with the indecipherable whispering of imagined figures; "whispers out of time" issue mysteriously from the self-portrait of Parmigianino and from the floating severed heads of Holofernes and John the Baptist.

"The Wine Menagerie" is such a difficult poem and so subtle in its movements from figure to figure that it is worth reproducing whole here.

THE WINE MENAGERIE

Invariably when wine redeems the sight,
Narrowing the mustard scansions of the eyes,
A leopard ranging always in the brow
Asserts a vision in the slumbering gaze.

Then glozening decanters that reflect the street
Wear me in crescents on their bellies. Slow
Applause flows into liquid cynosures:
—I am conscripted to their shadows' glow.

Against the imitation onyx wainscoting
(Painted emulsion of snow, eggs, yarn, coal, manure)
Regard the forceps of the smile that takes her.
Percussive sweat is spreading to his hair. Mallets,
Her eyes, unmake an instant of the world ...

What is it in this heap the serpent pries—
Whose skin, facsimile of time, unskeins
Octagon, sapphire transepts round the eyes;
—From whom some whispered carillon assures
Speed to the arrow into feathered skies?

Sharp to the windowpane guile drags a face,
And as the alcove of her jealousy recedes
An urchin who has left the snow

Nudges a cannister across the bar
While August meadows somewhere clasp his brow.

Each chamber, transept, coins some squint,
Remorseless line, minting their separate wills—
Poor streaked bodies wreathing up and out,
Unwitting the stigma that each turn repeals:
Between black tusks the roses shine!

New thresholds, new anatomies! Wine talons
Build freedom up about me and distill
This competence—to travel in a tear
Sparkling alone, within another's will.

Until my blood dreams a receptive smile
Wherein new purities are snared; where chimes
Before some flame of gaunt repose a shell
Tolled once, perhaps, by every tongue in hell.
—Anguished, the wit that cries out of me:

"Alas,—these frozen billows of your skill!
Invent new dominoes of love and bile ...
Ruddy, the tooth implicit of the world
Has followed you. Though in the end you know
And count some dim inheritance of sand,
How much yet meets the treason of the snow.

"Rise from the dates and crumbs. And walk away,
Stepping over Holofernes' shins—
Beyond the wall, whose severed head floats by
With Baptist John's. Their whispering begins.

"—And fold your exile on your back again;
Petrushka's valentine pivots on its pin." (*Complete Poems* 23–4)

Part of the reason to reproduce the poem whole is to show how it moves.
It begins with a general statement about the effect of alcohol, then
changes the speaker's vision into that of a leopard, and proceeds, following the first situating stanza, to explore the vision that the leopard
"asserts." The second stanza sets the bar scene with its row of decanters
and their very specific reflective activity, an activity that returns four
stanzas later where the rounded reflections on the decanters turn into
the rounded reflections on a human eyeball. The third stanza offers two
characters involved in some kind of erotic conversation.[9] The fourth
stanza returns to the eponymous menagerie and meditates on the
motives of both the speaker and the characters in the poem via the

figure of a serpent. The fifth adds an "urchin" to the human menagerie whose "brow" is "clasped" by neither the "forceps of [a] smile" nor by the vision of a leopard but by "August meadows." Stanza six corrals the four figures into a group. Their images are collected "remorselessly" on the bar's decanters, but simultaneously the images of the decanters are gathered as "roses" between the "tusks" of each character's eyelashes.

In the seventh stanza, after creating a near fun-house effect of reflections, the speaker exclaims that the highest transcendence is to see oneself reflected in the evidence of another's affect, in someone's tear. The fuzzy image of the eye in stanza six clamps to focus in the seventh stanza's incredibly exact and magnified image of the speaker seeing a reflection of himself in another's tear. One would need to be very close to see the tiny centered reflection, and very zoned in on the tear. This figure visually enacts the kind of affective focus it suggests. It also enforces a surreal clarity on the atmosphere in the bar. Intently focused and superhumanly clear-sighted, the speaker zooms in on is his own image. The "competence" is both to acknowledge one's own image in any affective attachment to an other, but also to maintain the intense clarity and attention that would allow one first to find and then follow a welling, spilling, sprinting, and, then, stalling tear.

At this apex of clarity however a crisis brews. The "Until" of "Until my blood dreams a receptive smile" indicates that things were being seen clearly, when something interrupted. The poem suddenly moves from images of precision to images of dispersal. It shifts from the superconcrete image of the reflective tear to the doubly abstracted figure: a personification of a bodily fluid itself imagining "a receptive smile." "Blood" rephysicalizes alcohol's effect and is also the site of the loss of clarity. This stanza pushes affect over the brink of exacting and exact anguish into the insouciant and sloppy maudlin. From this point on, the poem recedes from its pitch of complete affective involvement into commentary on how the recession happened and why. The moment of seeing his reflection in another's eye, or imagining seeing his reflection in another's eye, is the climax of the wine's effect on the speaker. The wine succeeds in allowing him entrance to entrancement, in which he is contained within "another's will." His context becomes another's affect in the same way that his image is surrounded entirely by its liquid medium. The denouement to this climax, however, is disorientation and hallucination—being trapped in another swill.

The end of the poem, wrapping up the energy released by the climax of seeing oneself in the tear of another, relates the poem's thematic and formal aspects in an enclosed closure. That is, the wit that speaks the last three stanzas concludes the poem for and *in place of* the speaker.

The speaker abdicates his role as internal exegete, and the poem closes with an anguished response to the speaker's musings from a voice that is internal to but eerily separate from him. This closure suggests that seeing oneself in another's tear must fail because it is a function of art, and art is gnawed by the "tooth implicit of the world" that does not allow a complete separation from materiality in desire. Similarly, the "wit" suggests, there is a point past which drink's vaunted clarity smashes into scraps of hallucinations. The bottom of the bottle is cruel. Materiality has its revenge, this voice says, but you still have these hallucinated figures of John the Baptist and Holofernes to whisper evidence of your passage into a realm of actualized desire. These severed heads are like your own as it floats in the tear of another, except they float in your own fantasies; thus you can maintain them as you could not maintain your own image in another's tear. These severed heads are, further, homologous to the voice of the "wit" that severs from the speaker and floats off at the end of the poem, never to be recontextualized in its master's voice. The whispers are durable reminders of the speaker's attachment to others. The heads are also homologies of relation of the speaker to his beloved. All is not lost in desiring. And all is not lost in alcohol's trajectory toward, and then sharply away from, clarity. In the speaker's defeat, he has found a kind of relief.

Gregory Woods has makes the interesting observation that the severed heads refer to the severed head of Orpheus. In his myth, he was, "...torn to pieces by women for having recommended men to love boys, his severed head floats off, singing its way down the river and out to sea, towards its final resting place on the shores of Lesbos....The poet's body dies, but the substance of his spirit transcends physique. The head will continue to sing, and be granted the gift of prophesy" (148). The heads at the close of "The Wine Menagerie" seem only to palely reflect the transcendence of the Orpheus myth. Crane is not simply suggesting that when love fails you lose your head (like Holofernes or John the Baptist) even if it keeps singing (like Orpheus). Rather, Crane has crammed all these figureless heads together at the end of his poem as a pile up of failure that is powerfully hallucinatory and therefore, in its own entirely new way, transcendent.

IV. *What she must have said with lifted eyebrows and a ? mark...*

In order to consider what Moore did to this poem and to establish the aesthetic grounds on which her revision was based, it is necessary to compare the texts. Matthew Josephson has famously noted that Moore wrote all the "wine" out of "the menagerie" (296).[10] This quip, however, fails to notice that Moore removed the "menagerie" as well.[11] The sole remaining animal is the serpent who begins the revised version. The "leopard ranging always in the brow," the human specimens, (the urchin who comes into the bar to fill his canister and the two flirting figures: forceps-mouth and mallet-eyes), and the hallucinated heads of John the Baptist and Holofernes (as well as Holofernes' prone body) have all been shaken out of Moore's version leaving only the snake and the speaker's "wit."

Moore changed the thematic closure of Crane's poem but maintained the closural technique; her version still closes with a long quotation. Further, Moore did not simply rewrite the thematics of Crane's closure, she rewrote Crane's thematics *of* closure. She altered what Crane's original poem claimed about its own closure and closure in general. The final stanzas of "The Wine Menagerie" suggest that failed transcendence might transcend failure. Losing oneself in an other with the help of alcohol may not work for long, but the hallucinations that follow are themselves evidence of past immersions. "Again" offers no such denouement, and in its foreclosure of a time after disappointment, suggests that the gusto to start over must spring from some extrascenic source. Moore's version reads:

AGAIN

What in this heap in which the serpent pries,
Reflects the sapphire transepts round the eyes—
The angled octagon upon a skin,
Facsimile of time unskeined,
From which some whispered carillon assures
Speed to the arrow into feathered skies?

New thresholds, new anatomies,
New freedoms now distil
This competence, to travel in a tear,
Sparkling alone within another's will.
My blood dreams a receptive smile
Wherein new purities are snared. There chimes
Before some flame a restless shell
Tolled once perhaps by every tongue in hell.
Anguished the wit cries out of me, "The world
Has followed you. Though in the end you know
And count some dim inheritance of sand,
How much yet meets the treason of the snow."
(qtd. in Parkinson 9–10)

Moore has dropped the original beginning, middle, *and* end of the poem. The first three stanzas, stanzas five and six, and stanzas ten and eleven are gone without a trace. These correspond most obviously to the scenic development of the bar and the characters within it, to the further development of that scene with the addition of the new figure of the urchin, and to the speaker's exit from the bar scene and hallucinatory reentry into the outdoors.

Moore's version is, like the original, constructed around the trope of reflection. The title itself introduces a temporal reflection. The title, "Again," is clipped from the penultimate line of the original, the rest of which does not survive in Moore's version. "—And fold your exile on your back again; / Petrushka's valentine pivots on its pin."[12] In Crane's version, the mobility of "again" is not very strongly emphasized; it creates a backdrop of the weariness of art's vagabondage. It suggests that as "you" took "your exile" off your back, so should you return it to your back. Moore's title suggests: You have done this before and will again and again and again. Moore's "again" is not grounded by any particular activity, even one as figurative as "folding up your exile on your back," and thus ranges freely as a first principle or affective axiom.

Moore's use of "again" as the title seems less a piece of the fabric of "The Wine Menagerie" than it does of Crane's poem "Legend" that was published in *The Fugitive* (accepted by Allen Tate) in September 1925, a year before Crane sent "The Wine Menagerie" to Moore. This poem opens *White Buildings* and serves as a "legend" to the lyrics therein, but also explores the relation of "legendariness" to repetition and the quotidian. "Legend" is a complicated poem, but reflection is its central trope and image. The poem opens by setting a scene in which "as silent as a mirror is believed / Realities plunge in silence by . . . ." Crane declares reflection and repetition the tropes in which his figures will collide and coalesce. The third and fourth stanzas are most explicit in their theorization of acting in a reality where reflection is the linchpin of desire.[13]

> It is to be learned—
> This cleaving and this burning [of, most literally, a moth to a flame],
> But only by the one who
> Spends himself out again.
>
> Twice and twice
> (Again the smoking souvenir,
> Bleeding eidolon!) and yet again.
> Until the bright logic is won
> Unwhispered as a mirror
> Is believed. (*Complete Poems* 3)

Even though "Again," as Moore has arranged it, seems more like "Legend" in its thematic concerns than it does like "The Wine Menagerie," it gives those thematics an entirely different valence. In "Legend," the "relentless caper" of repetition, that is, the way that the accumulation and repeated quality of pain reflects and shores up the rhythmic cries of poetry, only increases the heroism of acting or singing, or as Crane puts it best, "spending [one]self out again." Defeat leaves a residue—a "bright logic is won." "Again" closes without any reaffirmation of the worth of stepping one's "youth into the noon." "Again" softens further the already softened transcendent turn at the end of either "The Wine Menagerie" or "Legend," suggesting that it is not heroic action that would make one undertake action in a difficult reality but rather that all living is followed by disappointment. The mystery then of Moore's rendition is encapsulated in the title. Why, in the face of grim repetition, with only the prospect of treason, which is the nature of things, would one repeat actions that will inevitably lead to disappointment again?

The first stanza offers an interrogative homology between a serpent's symbolic and physical morphology and what that serpent pries. This has biblical overtones that Crane's snake pointedly lacks. The "heap" that the serpent pries is not linked, as it is in the original, to a predatory sexual situation and means here "the world" seen as disorderly and valueless. The second stanza of "Again" focuses on the fantasized reflection of the speaker in another's tear, and the third and final stanza features a meditation on how the speaker's desires might be reflected in another. The poem concludes suggesting that the speaker's desire for "traveling in a tear" is lofty but corrupted by his own attachment to reality. Finally, in Moore's version, the wit suggests that ecstatic loss of the self in another's will is a pipe (or flask) dream. "Again," Moore's title, then, refers to the recurrence of this disappointment: that it has happened in the past and will in the future.

"Again" makes an argument that losing oneself in another person's desires ("Sparkling alone within another's will") always fails because what is seen in the other is always a reflection of oneself. The question about when a lover and his beloved reflect one another ("What in this heap in which the serpent pries, / Reflects the sapphire transepts round the eyes...") is answered in the forced comparison of sand and snow. Reflections shift, liquefy, and sponsor imponderable insights, unownable inheritances, and finally, unfulfillable desires.

The poem itself, in this reading of it, becomes a kind of amulet of mustered strength—the strength to speak in the face of the perceived inability to deeply communicate. Moore's shifts all the verbs to present tense, to a "now" of meditation, an "anytime," rather the meditation in the midst of narrative before, during, and after of Crane's version. "Again" presents a situation that occurred, occurs, and will occur again on the time line. This unbounded allegorical mobility insists that the beloved other *always* treasons.

Crane's poem, alternately, represents one instance shaped like other such instances when "Invariably ... wine redeems the sight. ..." The scenic specificity that develops in the course of Crane's poem resists any simple relation to repetition. The speaker is witness to and reporter of both his meditations and the scene around him. His desires are both parallel to and intersect with the poem's characters' desires and behaviors. Perceiving the failure in their interactions, the speaker acknowledges certain difficulties of his own that correspond to theirs, but finally, he leaves their concerns, the couple and the urchin, to step out on his own into the snow of his own reality (or "prevailing pseudo-reality" as Robert Musil might call it). In Crane's rendition, the snow indicates that winter is both an important felt reality and an important figure in the poem.

Crane's is an exploration of both his poetics *and* a particular scene. The bar is a place where reflections abound; it expresses but does not in itself constitute Crane's poetics.[14] In Moore's version "snow" corresponds only to the highly figuralized "sand"; it plays no scenic role. "Snow" indicates a possible characteristic of an "inheritance of sand"; it inevitably "treasons" by melting or shifting away. Rather than one winter afternoon spent in a bar and the meditations that arise from it, this revision represents any afternoon, perhaps all afternoons. It refuses the concept of an outside to the poem as well as to the poet. The frustration in Moore's version is timeless as the poem is placeless (the snow in the final line, furthermore, no longer specifies an outside because in this version there is no inside).

"Again" is slightly less syntactically and rhetorically disorienting than "The Wine Menagerie": It starts with a question and ends with an anguished answer without letting its figures get tangled in a material scene. Moore has sharpened some grammatical pointers and removed some commas, dashes, and other syntactical speed bumps. However, as I have been reading the two versions, the most striking difference is their diametrically opposed visions of ecstatic experience. Moore did not simply tighten the poem in relation to its contents—removing wine and menagerie—she turned it on its head. This seems to me the real scandal of Moore's revision: not only did she rewrite Crane's poem and smooth out his famously knotty locutions, she rewrote Crane's own utterances *about* those locutions. She undertook not only to revise Crane's poems but *to revise his poetics*.

V. Twice and twice... and yet again: "The Monkeys"

Moore wrote all the characters out of Crane's poem, changed its poetics of ecstasy, and retitled it, but she retained one of the poem's most unusual aspects, its closure within a lengthy quotation. This odd poetic structure was one that Moore herself experimented with in a poem now called "The Monkeys." Kenneth Burke has included this poem in a group he calls Moore's "poems on method" (*Grammar* 502). This poem was published first in Alfred Kreymborg's little magazine, *Others,* where it was published under the title "My Apish Cousins." Subsequently, it was published under its present title in Moore's 1921, Egoist Press published, *Poems* and is included in each successive collection of Moore's poems. The poem consists of four six-line stanzas and is split roughly in half between the speaker's description of a group of animals she saw 20 years ago and the speech of a tiger on that occasion.

THE MONKEYS

winked too much and were afraid of snakes. The zebras, supreme in
their abnormality; the elephants with their fog-colored skin
  and strictly practical appendages
    were there, the small cats; and the parakeet—
      trivial and humdrum on examination, destroying
bark and portions of the food it could not eat.

I recall their magnificence, now not more magnificent
than it is dim. It is difficult to recall the ornament,
  speech, and precise manner of what one might
    call the minor acquaintances twenty
      years back; but I shall not forget him—that Gilgamesh among
the hairy carnivora—that cat with the

wedge-shaped, slate-gray markings on its forelegs and the resolute tail,
astringently remarking, "They have imposed on us with their pale
  half-fledged protestations, trembling about
    in inarticulate frenzy, saying
      it is not for us to understand art; finding it
    all so difficult, examining the thing

as if it were inconceivably arcanic, as symmetrically frigid as if it had been carved out of chrysoprase
  or marble—strict with tension, malignant
    in its power over us and deeper
      than the sea when it proffers flattery in exchange for hemp,
    rye, flax, horses, platinum, timber, and fur." (*Complete Poems* 40)

For a poem whose central figure is a critic of the "symmet- / rically frigid," this poem obeys a strict rhyme and syllabic scheme. Moore's stanzas have been described by Hugh Kenner as "lying on the page ... in little intricate grids of visual symmetry ..."(Bloom, *Moore* 17). The first and second as well as fourth and sixth line of each stanza are strong rhymes (except for "symmet-" and "chrysoprase," which are coupled by assonance), and each stanza's lines contain 15, 16, 10, 10, 15, and 11 syllables (except for the penultimate line of the penultimate stanza, which contains 13 instead of 15 syllables). The shape of the poem is determined by the flush of rhymed lines and the progressive indentation of each new line pattern.

One reason Moore might have been so invested in "lining up" the theory of ecstasy in "The Wine Menagerie" with her own is that it experiments with a closural technique that she herself had set about to master earlier in "The Monkeys." The technique consists of declaring a poem's ambitions and bringing the poem to closure all in the midst of a final extended quotation. Moore experimented elsewhere with closures in epigrammatic quotations, as for instance in "In the Days of Prismatic Color," in which she ends with "truth" figuratively talking, saying " 'I shall be there when the wave has gone by' " (*Complete Poems* 42).[15] This is a small example of anthropomorphization through the gift of speech and provides this poem's closure depth. Such use of quotation adds not only an additional figure to the poem, but offers the figure interiority.[16] This poem differs from "The Monkeys," insofar as the quotation at the end, though a central element of the poem's closure, does not provide both the ascension and the climax of a poetic plot.

Crane also uses quotations to close poems, but his feel less evidentiary and more scenic. In "Pastorale" or "The Hive," for instance, final quotations mark a particular query or comment by the speaker snug within the temporal or spatial scene of the poem. These utterances are directed at the speaker himself and close the poems by providing a sense of clarity. The reader witnesses the speaker literally come to terms with his situation. Crane experiments elsewhere, in "By Nilus Once I Knew" and, though the marks are invisible in this poem, "The Mango Tree," with ending a poem with a character or object's speech.[17] This use is more like Moore's but remains distinct because of its participation with an intrapoetic scene. In any use Crane makes of final quotations he situates the utterance in a scene, whereas Moore's closural quotations generally emphasize the extrascenic control of the poet who is quoting.

The technique of ending a poem with a quotation takes on an entirely different valence in the company of a patchwork of quotation. There it is swallowed up by the poem's convention of borrowing. In Moore's

"New York," "Sea Unicorns and Land Unicorns," "Marriage," "The Octopus," and "Novices," for instance, the final lines are quotations but they are brief and contained by a system of meaning larger than themselves. In other words, these quotations are used as evidence or qualification to shore up a central voice or, more basically, to realize an already declared ambition of the poem.

All of these uses are different from the use of quotation as closure that Moore employs in "The Monkeys." The quotation that closes this poem is one line short of half the whole poem, and its innards both suggest and resolve the poem's central tensions. Further, this poem's closure is different from other Moore poems insofar as the figure who speaks is a physical though improbable speaker, a tiger, and is, at the same time, an abstraction based on a physical figure. The "truth," in "The Days of Prismatic Color," by contrast, is clearly a *figure* when it speaks. Moore's tiger conjures the Aesopian and La Fontainian tradition of moral-speaking animals, and a reader cannot be certain whether to take the tiger as a poetic figure (speaking obviously in place of the poet or being spoken through by the poet) or as an actual character in the poem.[18]

The poem invites us, by its early list of the characteristics of other actual animals, the monkeys who chatter, a parakeet who pecks at its food, etcetera, to take the tiger as an actual animal at the zoo. The reports of the other animals' characteristics and activities invite the reader to take the tiger's speech as more detailed treatment of a zoo's inhabitants. Precedent and pattern lead the reader to expect that all animals will be reported about in a matter-of-fact, detail-by-detail manner that brooks no exaggeration, indeed that aims primarily for precision. For instance, the descriptions of the zebras as "supreme in their abnormality" or the elephant's limbs as "strictly practical appendages" entail an abstract vernacular pitch that foregrounds the speaker's effort to find just the right match of words to animals. These stretches, characteristic of Moore, reassert the poet's presence but with the feeling that this extra presence was required at the service of the material at hand, that which is to be described. All verbal devices are at work, these techniques indicate, to bring the physical animal in question into the living room of the reading experience.

Moore's poem purposely sets up the expectation that it will be reporting a real interaction with a tiger in part to frustrate this expectation with the absurdity of a tiger speaking. She smashes expectations the reader develops for the speaker "through the skylight of our received opinions," as John Ashbery might have it. She suggests, through her lack of comment on this shift in the poem, that the speech of a tiger is another descriptive mode in the same vein as those that precede it or that the authorial hand was just as visible in the depictions of the elephant and the zebra as it is now in the crafty device of a speaking animal. Her lack of comment on the juxtaposition of these two devices, strung on the same speaker's utterance, is itself a comment. The proximity of an "objective" type of poetic description to an "anthropomorphizing" description, considering the lack of an intervening intrapoetic exegesis, implies an equivalency or shared category. Thus, this poem can be said to make an argument for the deconstruction of "objective" description from two directions. Either it shows that anthropomorphic description is just as exact and "objective" as "objective description" or it shows that "objective" description is in fact just as poetically constructed as its less staid cousin "anthorpomorphism." Of course, the poem is not solely about poetic devices, it is about a menagerie of animals. The clash and/or merge of poetic devices dramatizes the thematically central split between thinking that the tiger's words were "actually" spoken and that the tiger's words were translated from his figure.

If this is a fable, the poem describes a speaker who 20 or more years ago went to the zoo and talked to a tiger. If, however, the speaker is the translator of the tiger's demeanor into words, we read the poet's involvement with the tiger as an aspect of the poet's own attachment to the world. In the latter case, the tiger is the spur that enables the poet to visualize and verbalize a position that she then reports as the tiger's speech. Both situations are fictive, but one is more patently fictive (or embedded) than the other, and the oscillation of meaning between these types of fictions is the source of much of the poem's power. "The Monkeys" walks the line between being a poem that contains animals actually speaking and being a poem that foregrounds the fictive nature of the lyric utterance by having it in part be spoken by an impossible speaker.

Moore uses the tiger in "The Monkeys" as an anchor for a meditation and, at the same time, uneasily, but possibly, as a report of what an actual tiger once said. The speech—ventriloquized or delivered by the tiger—challenges accounts of fierce beauty that treat the tiger as an object and spurs meditation on larger aspects of design. For instance, the poem's most available intertext, Blake's "The Tyger," treats this animal as "symmetrically frigid," as Moore's tiger suggests bad critics treat art. "What immortal hand or eye / Could frame thy fearful symmetry?" Blake queries the tiger. Moore does not seem interested in admonishing or really revising Blake's position of wonderment and awe but questions its transference onto man-made objects. It is when critics treat art with the same awe that Blake treats his tiger that steps must be taken. In Moore's poem the tiger is, as an object of beauty, complicated by its relation to a unique voice: both a creator of and a subject for art.

This representation of the tiger is also very different from uses of felines to represent an aesthetic absorption, as in, for instance, Rilke's "The Panther," in which images enter the panther's eye and are irretrievably swallowed by its heart, or his "Black Cat," in which the cat's eye affixes the viewer in the amber of its iris. Part of its difference is the frame in which Moore presents her Gilgamesh cat. Moore's poem makes the tiger the agent of its own threat and beauty; its voice is constituent and/or expressive of its beauty. The tiger seeks to correct or amend poetic renditions of itself. The tiger's very presence remarks on the embodiedness and livingness of its "art." As in "The Arctic Ox (Or Goat)," Moore suggests that it is better to appreciate an animal for its own qualities, than to mythify and mystify those qualities. Here the tiger's very highly aestheticized presence is posited as a full frontal attack on its own aestheticization.

The final figure of "The Monkeys" pits reflection, seeing oneself (or one's mastery) on the surface of the sea, against lucidity, noticing the depth of the water into which one gazes. The tiger suggests that the "malignancy" of the sea is its ability to appear reflective (and calm) in order to pull ships, people, and goods ("hemp, / rye, flax, horses, platinum, timber, and fur") into its waiting, unfathomable depths.[19] The tiger suggests that this effect is what "they," apparently bad critics or over-dramatic connoisseurs, with their "half-fledged protestations" liken to the situation of art, which "we" therefore are not supposed to be able to understand or fathom. The tiger takes issue with the ideas that art is "difficult," "arcanic," "symmetrically frigid," or "powerful" in the way the sea is powerful in its oscillation between appearing to be a surface and revealing itself as a depth. The final item on the list, "fur," also has special importance to a talking tiger, especially when such a tiger undertakes to meditate upon surfaces. His hide has been taken for him in the same way art is taken to be powerful like nature. Naturally, he objects to any such murderous paraphrases.

The trope of reflection is both the material of the poem and the object of the poem's critique. The "sea proffer[ing] flattery" is an image of the sea at its most calm and reflective, and Moore's tiger suggests that reflection in representational art does not necessarily act as the surface of the unplumbable. When the sea is calm the flattery it proffers is expert maneuvering. Art, on the other hand, might offer expert maneuvering at no risk. The sea, when calm, this also suggests, allows people to manage their presence upon it, but this is mere flattery, the prelude to violence begged by the carelessness of the flattered. Further, the tiger suggests that the sea offers flattery as payment for that which it takes.[20]

This poem closes with the same odd effect that "The Wine Menagerie" does. "The Monkeys" descends into quotation and never resurfaces.

One might take Moore's own meditation on the tiger in "Elephants" as her poetic stance: "Who rides the tiger can never dismount..." (*Complete Poems* 130). The closures of both poems imply that the speaker has stepped back from the utterance of the poem but is still the active organizer. The "wit" of Crane's poem or the "the cat" in Moore's are given the last word, and that they are given the last word suggests something about their agreement or concordance with the explicit speaker's opinions or beliefs. Either we take these last figures as ventriloquist dummies, as convenient constructs to speak un-first-personable truths, or we take them as voices that disagree with the explicit speaker's opinions or challenge her. Because they are offered at the close of the poem, at a site of heightened agency, the voices lean toward the poet (in both of these poems the speaker is a poet-figure). The tiger or wit offers voices that convince the speaker of something that she then represents to show how she came to her own beliefs. Thus there is a sense that these speakers reflect *the poet,* even it seems, more than a first-person, poet-figure might. These speeches have been chosen by the poet and represented for their content and their power as poetic devices. That they close the poems suggests: These words stand in for my own to such an extent that the fact that some other agent is speaking them is the climax of my poem.

While the closural devices are identical, Moore's seems more truly a reflective surface of words the poet might speak put into the mouth of her character who without the poet could not speak at all, and Crane's suggests a depth from which a voice emerges, a depth constructed by the fact that the wit has advice for the whole person and addresses the speaker himself as "you."

We must keep in mind that Moore's poem precedes Crane's by several years. It was published (under the title "My Apish Cousins") in her *Poems,* in 1921, while "The Wine Menagerie" was composed between 1925 and 1926. Crane surely read Moore's poem, either in its book form or in its earlier journal form in *Others*; though Crane never appeared in this magazine, he was mistakenly convinced that he would be published in it for several months (Unterecker 72). He had had a correspondence with William Carlos Williams that encouraged him to think, wrongly, that his poetry would soon appear there. Thus, it is reasonable to assume that Crane was watching this publication carefully, likely reading it regularly, and admiring its contents enough to want to take his own place in *Others*.

I think the shared use of the device of using a nonspeakerly voice as closure establishes at least the strong invitation to read "The Monkeys" and "The Wine Menagerie" together if not the material to conclude that

Moore's poem is both an influence on and intertext of Crane's "The Wine Menagerie." Most clearly however, Moore's rewriting of "The Wine Menagerie," and the style in which she rewrote it, strongly supports a claim that Moore took "The Wine Menagerie" to be a refiguring of her "The Monkeys" whether Crane meant it to be one or not. However, I hope that this reading begins to create important and necessary surface area for thinking about Moore's influence on Crane, an undertaking that I am certain will grow to include any number of poets who from some critical blindness have not been read as in debt to or even in the proximity of Moore's powerful poetic presence.

VI.

While the poetic techniques and attempts made by "The Monkeys" and "The Wine Menagerie" indicate that Crane was influenced by Moore, a later poem by Moore, "Armor's Undermining Modesty," shows significant thematic overlap with "The Wine Menagerie." My contention here, as in the earlier section, is not that Moore was influenced by Crane only at this one site (as in the earlier section I did not suggest that Crane was influenced by Moore at a single site); rather, I want to show that more significantly and more generally, these poets shared central poetic concerns and that their concerns were in dialogue. As I have read Crane's "The Wine Menagerie" in this chapter, its "climax," the central desire of the speaker and image of the poem, is the imagined competence "to travel in a tear / sparkling alone within another's will" (*Complete Poems* 24). Moore's 1950 poem "Armor's Undermining Modesty" has exactly the same desire and image at its core but uses it to different ends.

In its first half, this poem meanders. It begins with an image of a moth landing on the speaker's wrist and her mistaking it for "a pest." This leads to an exhortation to "Arise, for it is day" and shifts to musing on faulty etymology and finally on the worthwhile qualities of poetry. The second half of the poem is split only by its subject. The speaker begins, at the end of the fourth stanza, to consider "Knights we've known" and keeps with this subject until the end of the eighth and final stanza. The knights, the reader recognizes, are a readily available allegory for poets, and as digressive as this poem seems to be, it never strays far from poetics as its topic.

The second half of the poem does not meander in the same way that the first does. Its associative shifts from idea to image and back are all grounded in a meditation on knights. A fantasy of chatting with "familiar / now unfamiliar knights who sought the grail," who did not wear ornate armor, and therefore "did not let self bar / their usefulness to others who were / different" (*Complete Poems* 151–2). Moore's mid-poem musings on poetry smear into the poem's final image-cluster of singing the praises of, desiring an audience with, and finally (consolidating praises and audience in one compact image) of the speaker seeing herself reflected in the breastplate of a knight.

The first two stanzas offer the appreciation of an object and faulty conclusions from its observation. The rest of the poem seeks to theorize how a poet might properly treat natural and contingent beauty in a poem without feeling her thunder stolen.

> I should, I confess,
> like to have a talk with one of them about excess,
> and armor's undermining modesty
> instead of innocent depravity.
> A mirror-of-steel uninsistence should countenance continence,
>
>> objectified and not by chance,
>> there in its frame of circumstance
>> of innocence and altitude
>> in an unhackneyed solitude.
> There is the tarnish; and there, the imperishable wish.
> (*Complete Poems* 152)

Moore's convex mirror is not a sentimental Cranian tear nor an artful Parmigianino/Ashberian " 'mirror, such as is used by barbers' "; it is the breastplate of a Grail-seeking knight. Her particular mirror refigures Crane's. His tear suggested that, ideally, one would lose oneself, empathically and poetically, in another person's strong feeling. Moore's image in the "uninsistence" of a breastplate is both "tarnish" and "imperishable wish." That is, her reflection in its "unhackneyed solitude" is the figure for an ideal vision of oneself in another. This "wish" is "imperishable" because it is constant, but that constantness has a second edge: It is constant because the wish is both always desired and never fulfilled. The "tarnish," on the other hand, indicates the gazer's reflection, actually appearing as a smudge on the armor, but also the "tarnish" indicates that the "unhackneyed solitude," which is constitutive of the "imperishable wish," is also the very undoing of that wish.

This recalls a small piece of Moore's long poem "Marriage" in which Eve demands "*I* should like to be alone." The visitor, who one suspects is the intrigued speaker, comes back with: " 'I should like to be alone; / why not be alone together?'" (*Complete Poems* 62–3). The speaker mirrors Eve's words, but shifts the frame. "Aloneness" becomes peace, quiet, and meditativeness rather than actual isolation. Being alone together is an "unhackneyed solitude," a togetherness which enables a sense of discrete self while in relation to a desired other.

The final image of "Armor's Undermining Modesty" serves as its climax; it is the first image in the poem which finds steady footing. All the former images, including the memorable "bock beer buck," participate in an associative logic which does not transfer from its locality in the poem. That is, for instance, the image of the human ancestor "hacking things out" with an ax, does not really spread to the other images of the poem, it helps move from one image to another but is not mobile as metaphor or figure for anything. The final mirror/armor image provides a focus which is also a comment on focus and gives a context for all the other shards of image the poem presents prior to it: a way and a call to see ourselves embedded in "circumstance." Correct focus for Moore, as expressed in this poem, means seeing one's reflection *and* what surrounds it, rather than the Cranian ideal of losing one's sense of focus to a different kind of resolution (that is, in the hallucinatorily small scale of a reflection in a tear). We have all the proper tools already, Moore contends, to experience the other appropriately, we just need to understand that the wish of seeing oneself in the other is simultaneously a limit on itself. The reflection we see is, this poem underscores, a *reflection*. It always bears the tarnish of its own non-self, non-other status.

John Ashbery revisits both a Moorian and Cranian sense of reflection in his "Self-Portrait in a Convex Mirror." In fact, this poem propels itself by oscillating between the two. Parmigianino's mirror portrait confronts the viewer with what appears to be an actual mirror filled with someone else's, the artist's, reflection. This uncanny replacement of the viewer is, Ashbery maintains, the single most powerful and generative effect of the painting. The viewer is fooled for a moment but then comes to his senses. The effect is stubborn and sneaky; after a period of time Ashbery forgets the uncanny replacement he has spent so much time meditating on and is surprised and unsettled anew. The feeling of being elbowed out of a frame, including one's own frame, has two parts in Ashbery's account: being deprived of a reflection and then being supplanted by a "strict otherness." For Ashbery, this "otherness," "... this / 'Not-being-us' is all there is to look at / In the mirror ..." (*Self-Portrait* 81).[21]

Many critics have read the portrait's effects, implicitly or explicitly, as the effects of Ashbery's poetry and of lyric poetry more generally.[22] Ashbery invites the analogy to his own poetry from the first line of his poem, in which he begins *in media res*, "As Parmigianino did it ...," implying that he is undertaking both a description, and an imitation, of the artist's mirror portrait. This analogy is strengthened, of course, by the shared title; Ashbery's poem is not just commentary on a painting entitled "Self-Portrait in a Convex Mirror" but is its own such "Self-Portrait." The implications about lyric poetry more generally arise from Ashbery's comments about art and representation in the poem's body and, more significantly perhaps, from Ashbery's management of lyric moments in his poem's discursive stream. To borrow a figure from his poem to describe his poem, a lyric moment in "Self-Portrait" is like "a ping-pong ball / Secure on its jet of water" (70). The poem invites us to speculate about how poetry might create, by alternating between lyric and discursive modes, a feeling of "not-being-us" in the same manner Parmigianino's mirror portrait does.

Ashbery's tension between losing oneself in a reflection and contextualizing oneself with the help of a reflection is a direct descendent of the poetic concerns over which Crane and Moore came to loggerheads. The effect of being elbowed out of one's own frame is one that Harold Bloom has identified as one that a poet must overcome in order to become a mature poet. One must upend influence in order to enter the majors, he argues. However, it seems as if Ashbery, Moore, and Crane in some of their strongest poetic moments do not struggle with the images of their predecessors for dominance, but instead struggle to surrender their image, and hence find fuel and purpose for their own reflections. In their surrendering—Moore might say—their continuing.

Chapter 5

The Magician's Advance: Late Moore

I. Ending up in the Decor

Readers of Marianne Moore's poetry can feel set adrift on a discursive stream whose currents are mysterious. Her poems begin and end, it can seem, at random points. In a 1922 review, some of Moore's first sustained critical attention, Harriet Monroe, the founder and editor of *Poetry*, suggests that each Moore poem "begins as it ends and ends as it begins—a coruscating succession of ideas, with little curve of growth or climax" (Monroe, "Symposium" 214).[1] Monroe writes that Moore's "arbitrary forms" impose themselves not just too much on "word-structure and sentence structure" but on "the more general laws of shapeliness" as well. Moore's "ideas," according to Monroe, merely follow one another rather than accruing. Calling the elements of Moore's poems "ideas" further suggests that Moore's poems do not offer the affective access and arc that Monroe thinks good poems ought; they do not reach a point of maximum tension followed by a tension reduction. "The laws of shapeliness," Monroe explains, dictate that words not be broken in half across lines for their intra-syllabic rhymes; "the more general rules of shapeliness," she implies, require that a poem's closure offers an extension, exacerbation, and resolution of a poem's opening.

Monroe's early criticism, though it gets carried away in the drifts of its own conceits, zones in on what I will argue is a central aspect and effect of Moore's poetry. John Ashbery describes the same sort of effect but from a more readerly position in his 1967 review of Moore's

Collected Poems. Ashbery characterizes reading Moore's poems as "coming up against a mastery which defies attempts to analyze it, an intelligence which plays just beyond our reach." Her poems, he continues, "start out smoothly and calmly enough ... like a ride on a roller coaster, and in no time at all one is clutching the bar with both hands, excited and dismayed at the prospect of 'ending up in the decor,' as the French say of a car that drives off the road. And not infrequently, this happens" ("Straight lines" 42). Ashbery considers Moore's disregard for shapeliness the source of her most deeply felt and visceral poetic effects. Comparing Moore's poems to roller-coaster rides counters Monroe's complaints by emphasizing thrill over destination. Furthermore, for Ashbery, driving off the road, or at least the combination of dismay and excitement that accompany the possibility of driving off the road, is no shortcoming. "Ending up in the decor" is the type of vernacular event Ashbery almost manically highlights in his own work; it insists that the reader is thrown from the poem's development unexpectedly, generating surprise and a host of other strong affects such as delight and dismay. The poem, in its apparent disregard for the reader, has more wholly involved him.

As an example of being thrown by a Moore poem Ashbery cites the last word, "it," of "The Fish," confessing contentedly, "I will never be entirely certain of what 'it' is ...." Ashbery also points to the end of Moore's "To Statecraft Embalmed," in which "you become aware that she is no longer addressing an ibis, or even you, the reader; for the last minute she has been gazing absently at something terribly important just over your left ear" (42). And, Ashbery notes, "... there are other cases in which I become aware before the end of a poem that Miss Moore and I have parted company somewhat further back. Sometimes, as in 'The Jeroba,' the author has her say and retires, leaving you in the company of some curious little rodent." This parting of company is, for Ashbery, a virtue. He is a reader who is thrilled rather than irritated by Moore's "coruscating succession of ideas"; the thrill of Moore's careening successions "tempts" him "to call her our greatest modern poet" (42).

Ashbery does not, in his rather brief but potent treatment of Moore's poetry, stray far from her early efforts, nor does he highlight the single most obvious example of a Moore poem ending up in the decor, although the title of his review, "Straight lines over rough terrain," is plucked from it. "People's Surroundings" begins by confidently asserting a connection between the spaces people live in, the decor they are surrounded by, and who they are. The poem concludes with a 12-line list of nouns. Moore announces the list with the line, "we see the exterior and the fundamental structure," a proposition the nouns that follow seem likely to illustrate or support. Thence appear six lines of occupations that name their practitioners or title-holders and begin: "captains of armies, cooks, carpenters." In one way, since these are each occupations, they offer some "exterior" and some "fundamental structure" in their position in society and their corresponding activities. However, the list offers no clue as to what is "exterior" and what is "fundamental" about each occupation. The reader might expect the relation of this list to the list that follows to provide some more help. But immediately following this list (with only the line "in their respective places—" between), the stanza descends into a list of different sorts of surroundings, "shops, prisons, brickyards and altars of churches." The place names are more various than the people names insofar as they do not all directly refer to places of work; for instance, this second list includes "dens, deserts, railway stations, [and] asylums" (*Complete Poems* 57). This difference troubles any simple matching of "exterior" to "fundamental structure." Nor, of course, does this second list provide companions to the items in the first list in any discernible, complete, or logical way. There is more than a trace of nostalgia in both lists for the time of "queens, countesses, ladies, emperors" and the places they inhabit: "castles, palaces, dining halls, theaters and imperial audience chambers." This quality of meditation bending toward daydream lightens the movement from noun to noun; delight seems the ultimate connective of all of these people and places. These last 12 lines of "People's Surroundings" are sonically delectable; the lack of any obvious motivating reason for the particularities or order of the nouns interacts with the sonic and visual orderliness of the list. Moore merges textures of both anticipation of the predictable and surprise into "an irreducible symphonic texture" (Ashbery 42).

The daydream-like indeterminacy of this poem's closure bickers with the stridency of the poem's opening: "People's Surroundings // They answer one's questions." The final list pointedly answers no questions and even makes it difficult to discern what questions one might ask given these items. This disagreement of beginning and end bucks the reader from the poem's discursivity and troubles the local connections that the confident and masterful poetic voice asserts throughout the beginning and middle of the poem.

Moore pits parataxis against discursiveness at her closure. These two modes of poetic expression, logical connection and accumulation, have crucial and rather easily accessed corollaries at the more basic level of organizing perception. Discursiveness mirrors the way a rational system connects object to object in a causal or complexly relational chain, and parataxis accumulates perceptions and provides no link between them except the inexhaustible push to accumulation. Parataxis, in organizing by the ur-principle of proximity, insists on the presence of contingency. By placing parataxis last in the poem, Moore suggests that it has the last word, and that the eye that perceives the world and makes distinctions between objects and relations between them is finally overwhelmed and humbled by their variety. This poem stages the movement of many-cylindered perception, overwhelmed by the joy of its own mastery, hopping the curb and heading into the shrubs on purpose.

The metaphoric flights of Moore's critics are generally attempts to reckon Moore's control with the recklessness John Ashbery identifies as central to her poetry. It makes sense that *he* has celebrated recklessness, saying that "most reckless things are beautiful in some way" (*Reported Sightings* 391). However, it does seem odd, considering how she has been treated critically, that Moore, as the final held note of her most famous interview, lauds Williams for his being "willing to be reckless." She concludes: "... and if you can't be that, what's the point of the whole thing?" (Interview with Donald Hall, Tomlinson 45).

In another high-profile document, her famous letter to Ezra Pound, she admits to fastidiousness and recklessness at the same time. She begins discussing how important it is that there be no "stumbling block[s]" for her readers, so that "punctuation ought to be exact." She writes, "It is as great a hardship to me to be obliged to alter punctuation as to alter words, though I will admit that at times I am heady and irresponsible" (Tomlinson 17). Interestingly, in this little paragraph Moore admits to being "heady and irresponsible" about correcting herself. Or so it seems. The "though" can torque this sentence in opposite directions. One can read this sentence as the virtuous plaint of a diligent poet; it can indicate that the "great hardship" is not a difficulty in Moore's motivation but an inevitable aspect of the pursuit of exactness. Conversely, this sentence could be the simultaneous bellyaching and self-implication of a slacker; it could indicate that it is a "hardship" in the sense of a "pain in the neck" for Moore to alter punctuation, and on top of that admission, she also, using "though" as a kind of coy further admission laced with apology, admits that sometimes she acts willfully on instinct. Moore's discussion of care and carelessness is itself carefully careless. The multivalence of this celebration/confession is complicated but not merely paradoxical; it indicates both how much affective energy Moore pours into syntax and punctuation and how aware she is that these aspects of language are themselves affectively pivotal and that they pivot.

Monroe and Ashbery are among the most eloquent voices to identify Moore's reckless break with shapeliness as crucial to her poetics. Several generations of critics, however, have proven how difficult it is to more than simply acknowledge this break. Poems, insofar as they make arguments, make them by starting somewhere and ending somewhere else. The arc between the beginning and the end of the poem is usually considered the one dependable gauge of a poem's development. Moore challenges critics and readers by frustrating the notion of beginning, the notion of ending, and/or the notion of a connection between a fixed beginning and a fixed ending. One is left to conclude that the end of a Moore poem was arrived at by means that are, to quote Ashbery, "just beyond our reach," or else that the end of a Moore poem does not conclude the whole poem but instead merely follows from the moment immediately preceding it (and that moment follows from the one preceding it, etcetera). The most common way to deal with the difficulty of discussing Moore's lyric development is to not deal with it and instead discuss her poems as if they were prose.[2]

Because Moore has often been treated as if she wrote really eloquent newspaper copy, that is, as if there were nothing enactive, or particularly, nothing erotic, about her poems, her poems are read almost exclusively by the unit of line or passage. Her critics note the movement of thought to thought in her poems, "the coruscating succession of ideas," but most often treat these linkages as if they were mere demonstrations of the poet's willfulness and intelligence rather than movements from effect to effect within the poems. It is often taken for granted that poetic movement through a Moorian stanza or across an entire poem can be properly described by investigating the movement of the thematics. Or, something that has thankfully become more rare, by counting the syllables and relating their numbers to a thematic. Moore's poetry borrows much, as Marie Boroff has brilliantly described, from promotional prose, and that makes it convenient and almost unavoidable that many critics will suggest that the clarity of the feature article or advertisement is its main readerly effect. "Thematic interest" is indeed one effect of Moore's poetry, but I want to suggest that, rather than a goal or an end point, such interest is anticipated and manipulated by Moore in order to bring about other poetic effects and with other effects, other affects. In other words, the reader is entranced by the observations Moore makes about an elephant, a ground hog, a tiger, or a town, but that trance is the launching pad of her poetic effects rather than the height of their orbit.

By concentrating on closures in her late poems, I hope to show that the "coruscating succession" is an erotic hide-and-seek in which Moore conceals and divulges her presence throughout the body of a poem only to recede or appear at the end of her poem—the final outcome breathlessly anticipated. The reader desires appearance, and suspects that an appearance, or something equally desirable (such as the surprise of the appearance of a proxy in the shape of "some curious little rodent," for instance) will be granted. As William Carlos Williams wrote in 1925: "... the quality of satisfaction gathered from reading her is that one may seek long in those exciting mazes sure of coming out the right door in the end" (Tomlinson 54). Moore's late poems, I argue, feature, most particularly, closural appearance while her earlier work leans more toward disappearance. I do not want to argue for a distinct difference between periods in Moore's work based on closures but rather illuminate the mechanics of closure in a group in which closure is the most distinctive and distinct poetic device. The late poems are more precise (in the sense of locatability, not quality of craft) about the affects and effects of the presencing or absencing of the authorial agent than Moore's early poems; they seek to create the same "quality of satisfaction" with less mazework.

My readings will highlight the way in which Moore's poems *do things*. The poems move a reader somewhere, not simply attempting to convince him or her to participate in good sense. Charles Altieri, as I discussed in my Preface, has suggested one very powerful way to distinguish these two kinds of reading: what I have been calling thematic reading and reading for the development of a poem. He has suggested that post-Enlightenment poetry has two impulses: "the impulse to lyricism" and "the impulse to lucidity" ("Motives" 656).[3] The latter corresponds to what Wallace Stevens dubbed "the pressure of reality," or as Altieri rephrases it, "the complex of social and intellectual forces leading [a poet's culture] to reject teleological thinking, to insist on scientific standards for determining the sense of linguistic expressions, and to scrutinize the ironic, self-interested and self-deluding motives in any idealistic claim or self-presentation." To read Moore as a "lyric poet" means attending to the "impulse of lyricism" in her work, that is, how her poetry performs and enacts the challenges that expressions of "the full affective life of the psyche" pose to dominant explanations and "reduction[s] of the mind's cognitive powers into analytic operations." Moore's lyric impulse is housed most often in the movement of her poems, the aspect of her poetry that seems most firmly "beyond our reach." Critical approaches that do not attempt to describe or anatomize the movement of Moore's poems place themselves not just out of examinations of her "impulse to lyricism" but out of certain basic issues of poetry as a genre, for instance, address, audience, and how a reader attaches to a poem. My readings will insist that Moore, like Emily Dickinson, "... dwell[s] in Possibility / A fairer house than Prose— / More numerous of Windows— / Superior—for Doors—" (Dickinson, "657" 327). In my readings of

Moore's poetry I hope to keep "Possibility," or in Altieri's paradigm, "lyricism," firmly in sight by attending to the decor, annotating especially the superior quality of the doors to which she shows her readers.

II. Marianne Morph

It would be impossibly complicated to begin discussing the shape of Moore's poems without first pointing out how the binary "shapely/ shapeless" has been utilized to *not* talk about Moore's poems. Discussions of the shape of Moore's poems obliquely gesture at her poetry but gesticulate wildly about her biography, her psyche, and her body. When critics remark that Moore is too angular a poet, they usually mean that she wore her hair too nattily under her famous tricorn cap, that her poems' intellectualism most certainly indicates a deep-seated repression, and only finally, that her poems look oddly sliced and diced on the page. Monroe, as the cymbal-crashing finale to the "Symposium" I quoted from above, suggests that Moore has, in a phrase poached from Moore's first published poem, a "heart of brass" that will make "every royal thing fail." Monroe is not simply suggesting that to follow the "general laws of shapeliness" one must avoid exerting too much force on words, sentences, or closures, allowing "natural" forms to take shape; she is taking Moore's poetry as evidence about Moore herself, her emotional life, and her future as a poet. This rather mundane example of poetry-as-body/body-as-poetry criticism highlights the imposition of anthropomorphized aspects of poems (intellectual = emotionless = heart of brass) into the body of the poet (it is actually Moore herself rather than her poem that has a heart of brass) and then back onto the general field of poetry (because Moore has a heart of brass she will fail at writing great poems). Moore's body is always what is at issue but never on stage; she does not mediate the appearance of her own agency in such a scheme. In fact, that is what this embodying scheme accomplishes best: reducing the distance between poet and poem to the extent that the poem no longer appears as art, but instead seems like some kind of bodily eruption. This particular tautological structure has the added aspect of transposing Moore's *own constructions* onto her body. She not only will fail in poetry but *in the same medium* and *in her very first published poem* (somehow closest to the source) she foretells her own doom.

Marion Strobel, assistant editor of *Poetry,* comments similarly about Moore's poetic efforts:

> Even a gymnast should have grace. If we find ourselves one of an audience in a side-show we prefer to see the well-muscled lady in tights stand on her

head smilingly, with a certain nonchalance, rather than grit her teeth, perspire, and make us conscious of her neck muscles. Still, we would rather not see her at all. … Just so we would rather not follow the contortions of Miss Moore's well-developed mind—she makes us so conscious of her knowledge! (Monroe 210)

Moore is not "shapely," that is, feminine, in her poetry. Her mind's strength is unseemly and disproportionate on her female body just as, Strobel implies, a masculine musculature is on a woman. She shows her neck muscles in her feats of strength. She perspires. The outrageous conceit of this passage is underwritten and overwritten by gender norms: Picturing Moore as a mannish woman performs Strobel's disdain for her mannish or "too muscular" poetry as well as her disdain for Moore's freakish, "side-show" relation to gender. The "side-show" reference is not incidental to Moore's loudly declared penchant for circuses and zoos. Strobel seems to want to include Moore in her own menagerie, similar to the way in which Monroe grafted a line of Moore's poetry back onto her body. Strobel tries to put Moore on her head right beside the animals she so often describes.

Moore, as a poet, both Strobel and Monroe agree, is in too rigid control of her subject matter to let it mean emotionally. According to Monroe, she is "… a poet too sternly controlled by a stiffly geometrical intellectuality. Miss Moore is in terror of her Pegasus; she knows of what sentimental excesses that unruly steed is capable, and so her ironic mind harnesses down his wings and her iron hand holds a stiff rein" (Ibid. 213).[4] This profile suggests that Moore does not allow her poems to "climax" in another sense. It is not only that they are not shaped with a peak but also that they do not allow emotional (read erotic) releases (or flights) for the writer or the reader. Most interesting here is the seeming contradiction Monroe invokes to describe Moore's poetry. Moore at once exerts too much control over her subjects and too little in that her poems seem to open and close whenever they like.

Strobel's suggestions that Moore has a freakish relation to sexuality and affect and ought be more feminine in her displays of technical prowess share the same terms but arrive at a quite different conclusions than the suggestions of one of Moore's more supportive contemporaries, Winnifred Bryher.[5] Bryher uses much the same conceit of a woman in male body drag, except she thinks that Moore ought adopt a masculine identity more completely.[6] Hers is made both in a critical review quoted by Monroe in her "Symposium" but also in her novel *West* in which Marianne Moore appears as a character named Anne Trollope. In Monroe's article Bryher calls Marianne Moore "a Marco Polo detained at home. It is the fretting of a wish against wish until the self is drawn, not into a world of air and adventure, but into a narrower self, patient, dutiful and precise" (209). Moore is dressed in masculine metaphoric drag, to the extent that Bryher ends her comments with an exhortation to the poet: "Only, Marco Polo, your sword is ready and your kingdoms wait. May it soon please you to leave the fireside and ride forth" (210). Strength and masculinity are what Winnifred Bryher wishes Moore would show more of.

Three years later, in her novel *West,* Bryher would develop this critique of Moore further in the shape of her heroine, Anne Trollope, a red haired poet who lives in New York with her mother. Anne is a completely transparent portrait of Marianne Moore, down to the nickname ("Dactyl") that Bryher and H. D. used to call her by in letters and, by all accounts, in person. Moore had a practice of calling her mother and Warner, her brother, by animal names, sometimes names taken from *The Wind in the Willows* (Marianne was called "Rat"), sometimes from *Ivanhoe* ("Fangs"), and sometimes borrowed from ferocious animals (Warner was "Great Turtle," "Biter," or "Gator") (Molesworth, *Moore* 20).[7] The practice of using animal nicknames was taken up by Moore's friends H. D. and Bryher, as Barbara Guest describes in her biography of H. D. "Bryher's immediate reaction to Miss Moore when she saw her with her massive golden hair like a headdress was 'It's a pterodactyl!' and "Dactyl" she became forever in their private conversation, just as H. D. was 'Cat' and Bryher was 'Fido.'" (133). "Dactyl," among poets, also can't help but mean the three-syllable foot consisting of one stressed syllable followed by two unstressed syllables. This again shows Moore's body mapped in poetic terms. In *West,* Bryher describes her main character, Nancy, who travels with a woman named Helga (H. D.), coming across Anne Trollope for the first time. "'I shall call her Dactyl, I think. She is so like a prehistoric creature, half bird and half dinosaur with her stiff head and penetrating eyes" (*West* 101).

While Nancy and Helga travel in California, they muse together on Anne's character and her choice not to travel with them and not to travel in general. Nancy tells Helga, "... she seems curiously tied up, mentally. It is all very well to be opposed to indiscriminate publication, but why is she so averse to life, any sort of life? ... She has never achieved any liberty of conscience. It may be some inherent weakness of will, but I think it is due to her education. ... I should like to cut her hair short, her wonderful hair" (101–2). Cutting Anne's hair would masculinize her, represent a liberty she has not yet achieved. When Nancy and Helga return to New York after their jaunt to California, Nancy exhorts Anne to come with them back to England. "Cut the masochism," she says, "and come with us to England" (150). It as if Anne's feminizing hair and her masochism are both aspects of her physical person with similar properties that could, but woefully, will never, be cut. After Anne's refusal of the offer to go to Europe, Nancy theorizes Anne's choice to stay with her mother in a small apartment working at a library job:

> Why did Anne carry it on, this Victorian tradition? Was it because America was in the throes of a somewhat similar period that she preferred a spirit already stamped with history. Yet it clashed with her hair, that curious bright forest colour, with her body that had the austere outline of a young scribe's form, and with the bright mosaic of her mind. Her shrinking from life was a masculine rather than a feminine gesture. It was the body's denial of himself for some misunderstood ideal. (158–9)

Anne is in such deep drag that her body is even referred to not just as masculine but even as its own entity: "himself." Further, she is so deeply masculinized that Bryher's characters exhort her to chose between two kinds of masculinity, rather than between masculinity and femininity. Anne's denial is masculine austerity gone wrong; her friends want her to shift her focus outward, toward adventures in the world, but maintain her intensity.

Anne's hair has transformed in only a few pages of Nancy's analysis from the emblem of masochism and limitation to a pennant of rebellion, freedom, and masculinity. The order and neatness of the hair evaporates leaving only the color. Nancy sums up her analysis, conflating Anne's life and her poetry in an intriguing figure: "To create meant to live. Anne had denied life so long she was afraid now to leave her barriers behind. Duty served her for emotional outlet ... hard lines from which the colour had been stripped" (ellipses in text, 159). Only a page after Anne Trollope's hair lost all its shape but retained its color for use in a metaphor, her life loses all of its color but retains its shape. It is interesting that a poet in "too rigid control" should have a body that at every slight critical breeze morphs into something pretty outlandish: a mannish gymnast, Marco Polo, a pterodactyl, a metrical foot, and a young scribe just to name a few.[8]

Moore's biography generally gets shaped according to only slightly less outlandish principles. She is constantly shifting into and out of the form of a literary text. James Fenton discusses this very effect in a recent article on Moore in which he suggests that Moore as a poet was not as rigid as her late image might make us think. He makes a plea for readers to attend to her poems with the spirit of the younger more contradictory and experimental Moore in mind. He writes, "And just as it is hard to unravel the chronology and textual history of Moore's poems, so it is easy to find oneself thinking of Marianne Moore, the famous old lady in Brooklyn, as being the definitive version—as it were, the text in its final form" (40). The largest problem with this habit of mind, as described by Fenton, is the way it diminishes the distance between an author's text and an author's body. Any comment on one seems a comment on the other. Strangely, by mixing life and literature so inextricably into one another, this tendency actually makes it impossible to note moments of muddying boundaries between life and literature. This approach squelches any discussion of erotics, since literary erotics happen at (and sometimes are) the oscillation between body and text.

Charles Molesworth states in the introduction to his *Marianne Moore: A Literary Life* (already in the title offering "literary" as the opposite of "personal" or "sexual," or just plain "life" for that matter) that the vivifying paradox of her biography is the tension between the fact that Moore seems never to have taken lovers and the impression Kenneth Burke had of her as "one of the most sexual woman he had ever met" (xxii).[9] Molesworth interprets Burke to mean that "she was fully aware of all of the dimensions of experience, physical and mental ..." and concludes his introduction with: "What follows is an account of her experience, and at least a partial explanation of the paradox." So, the crux, *the* paradox, of Marianne Moore's life, according to Molesworth, is the tension between her sexiness and the fact that her biographer can find no whiff of "actual sex" in her life. Sex is exactly, here, what "the literary" is not: Moore's "literary life" stood aside or in place of or in contradistinction to her "erotic life."[10]

The idea of erotics as what happens between two bodies, most likely of the opposite sex, but most certainly of the same species, is far too limited when considering human erotic life. Interestingly, T. S. Eliot anticipated and rebuffed Molesworth's position on Moore's relation to her poetry in his 1935 introduction to Moore's *Selected Poems*. There Eliot discusses how Moore's poetry provides erotic release, albeit a different sort than the kind of release he sees as characteristic of a "lyric." Eliot argues that in fact Moore's orgasmics exist in her subject matter; in her descriptions, he insists, she takes flight. In this discussion, Eliot suggests that most of Moore's poetry might "be classified as 'descriptive' rather than 'lyrical' or 'dramatic' " (Tomlinson 62). This distinction suggests that Moore's poems are not interested in providing a typical lyric arc, that is, a relation to beginnings, middles, and ends, as well as to propositions, turns, and reformulations performing a speaker's release from or into emotion. "Only the pedantic literalist could consider the subject-matter to be trivial; the triviality is in himself. We all have to choose whatever subject-matter allows us the most powerful and most secret release; and that is a personal affair" (63). Eliot suggests that in fact there *are* climaxes and intense attachments in Moore's poetry and that intense attachments in poetry are related to and sometimes constitute real erotic attachments and releases. These attachments simply are not arrayed in ways that uninventive readers can identify them. "The result [of the subject choices Moore makes and the way she treats them] is often something that the majority will call frigid; for feeling in one's own way, however intensely, is likely to look like frigidity to those who can only feel in accepted ways" (Ibid.).

Frigidity is the default mode for describing erotics that involve withholding. Like Strobel and Bryher, most critics who identify moments of discretion and withholding treat them as Moore's primary literary affects. She is the poet of armor and the "deepest feeling" that shows itself "not in silence, but restraint" (*Complete Poems* 91). With this premise, it makes sense that as she developed as a writer she wrote her best work in the middle and then, when her axioms overtook her talent, she edited, receded, and retreated from her own climax. Thus, in a sense, a story of Moore as nothing but a philosopher of discretion is told with a humped story line in which, after a climactic expression of Modernism, the denouement trails off into an eccentric display of repressiveness and strike throughs. This view is not impeded by the infamously laconic "Omissions are not accidents. MM," which leads up all editions of her *Complete Poems*.[11] In typical Moorian fashion, it seems, "Complete" has drifted from referring to the collection of poems and, rather, modifies each single poem in the collection.

This penchant for omission is most blatantly expressed in the amputation of all but three lines of her crowd-pleaser "Poetry" as it is reproduced in her *Complete Poems*. As much as it is noted that Moore omitted things from this volume it seems unnoticed that the book reads from poem to poem like a planned volume, composed and ordered to lead the reader through both the thematics and performances of her poems. The order of the *Complete Poems* (originally worked out with the help of Eliot) enriches each poem and is not meant as a chronological pile of works by Moore. It is very possible that she did not omit poems or lines simply out of disgust with them or a sense of reserve, though these affects may have played some part; she also chose poems to fit into a reading experience she was constructing. I point to this possibility not to pursue it here but to offer an obvious objection to certain notions of Moore as an obsessive omitter whose theory and practice of humility and reserve got out of control. The idea of a writer's radical goals subverting themselves seems to please certain critics who suppose they could better navigate in the realm of ideas and seem desperately magnanimous in their proprietorship of posterity.

Moore's career is often chopped into roughly three periods, less, it seems, out of any interesting formal concerns or themes that each group share than out of a desire to distance Moore from her late poetry, which many critics treat as an embarrassment. Sometimes a critic chops Moore's career before 1936 into three based on, say, her experiments with syllabics and quotation.[12] In a less cramped chronology, in which the large amount of material Moore wrote after her stint at *The Dial* is not utterly dismissed, the first period (to 1935) usually includes all the poetry before Moore became editor of *The Dial,* during which she took a hiatus from poetic production. The second period, in this chronology, usually includes the 1930s and 1940s when Moore's verse tended toward, as Jeanne Heuving has nominalized it, "overstatement."[13] The third often includes everything else. Critics disassemble and reassemble the boundaries of each "period" as their projects require. Periodizing can be very useful, except, as is the case with Moore's career, when it elbows whole decades of poetic effort off the time line.

With the notable exceptions of Margaret Holley, Laurence Stapleton, and Grace Schulman, critics often even suggest that the late poems, and their wateriness, caused Moore's recession from the forefront of today's inquiries into American Modernism. John M. Slatin sums up the critical response as if it were proof of something besides a critical error: "To the extent that there is a debate about Marianne Moore, the issue is whether she did her best work in the 1930s or the 1940s; there is no question at all about the work of the 1950s and 1960s, whose slightness is conceded universally" (13). Slatin, then, in a footnote, names the five critics who together constitute the universe, one of whom (Marie Boroff) concedes this slightness by omitting to mention the late poems in her critical work. The interest of Moore's late poems is definitely different from that of her earlier poems, but the absence of these poems of the 1950s and 1960s from the criticism says more about the criticism than the poetry. The "universal" concession of these poems' slightness, I hope critics begin to explore, may be a misrecognition of Moore's late and exciting experimentation.[14]

In order to give dimension to discussions of shape in Moore's poetry, I will suggest that late in her career one can trace an opposite motion in her closures from the one pursued in her earlier work. Instead of evaporating from her poems as in "The Fish," "The Jeroba," or "People's Surroundings," her presence is orgasmically distilled at the close of her late poems. When Bonnie Costello notes that "Moore's very resistance to formal closure becomes for her a means of self-revelation," her observation holds for both early and late Moore poems, but with a difference (Bloom, *Moore* 102). The "self" that is revealed early in her career has different poetic outlines than the one that appears late and the resistances that reveal her are commensurately different. The early "self," let us use this as a shorthand for poetic *agent,* is recalcitrant and receding while the late one is intensely assertive, even to the point, as we will see, of performing a showy kind of magic trick at the end of one poem.

These closural experiments do not follow ideas of lyric arc as ejaculation such as those put forward by T. S. Eliot, but lead to a reader's heightened erotic proximity to the works of the poem at its close. In these poems, the ability of a poem to involve a reader has joined the ability of objects in the world to involve perception. While in early poems the reader ended up in the decor of the poem's object world, the late poems end the reader up in the decor of their very workings. Moore, in these late poems, experiments with poetry as an environ, as, if you will, a *real* garden with imaginary toads in it. I believe it is no accident that the very popular image (real toad/imaginary garden) pointedly receded from the pages of Moore's *Complete Poems* into the notes. Moore's late products are, instead of a further recession of the author from or into her work, an orgasmic surfacing of the author's presence in the works of her poems.

III. "Love in America?"[15]

Whether we read with or against its grain, a poet's explicit commentary on erotics seems as good a place as any to start examining the subject in a poet's work. Moore treats "love" quite a bit in her poems. In fact, some of her best-received poems, most notably "The Paper Nautilus" and "Efforts of Affection," end with cymbal-crashing pronouncements about the centrality of love. In these two poems, as in almost every appearance of love in Moore, it does not just find expression through animal images and animal figures—the love expressed is felt *for animals.* While these animals are likely not be the lover or lovers Molesworth searches for in vain, they are most certainly fantastic or real players in the erotics of Moore's poems.

"Efforts of Affection" describes love as that which "can make one / bestial or make a beast a man" (*Complete Poems* 147). The "wholeness" (or "wholesomeness") of the "integration" of man and beast is the highest expression of "love" and "affection."[16] It is not negative to become a beast, in fact, it is the necessary corollary to being human. In "The Paper Nautilus," the closing stanza wraps up the content of the poem in a brilliant comparison of the rough-hewn waviness of the nautilus shell and "the mane of / a Parthenon horse." The comparison then metamorphoses from description to comment. There are suddenly human arms thrown around the stone mane, "... as if they knew love / is the only fortress / strong enough to trust to" (*Complete Poems* 122). The final nautilus shell of love of this poem is the love for a horse as expressed in the love of the sculpture of one embedded in the scale-challenging fantasy of riding a stone horse at the Parthenon. A strong sensory component clings to this highly abstracted image: warm, soft, but firmly grasping arms against cool, hard but creamily curved stone. The cohabitation of abstraction and the most feelable sensory detail, analogous to the size differential between the huge stone horse and the relatively tiny person, hits the highest note of Moore's thematics of bondage, being "hindered to succeed," and hikes the obvious relation between the "paper" of the title and the activity of the writer up from thematics and into performance. Senses are the obstacle, in that they can short out a circuit of abstract meaning, stopping thought with a tingling of the spine, but also the vehicle of poetic utterance, in that they ground abstraction and make it "graspable."

These poems show that Moore did not just love animals (however the word "love" is vectored), but that animals are central to her theories and expressions of love. Moore's poetic love is fundamentally bestial, because its structure and operations arise from meditations on and in the vocabulary of beasts. Moore's erotic thematics always oscillate between being metaphors for the operations of love and expressions of that love. This stubborn and unsettling oscillation is itself erotic. Revelation and concealment slide through Moore's poems, pointedly ungraspable, at once extraordinary and ordinary. As Eliot argued, *this,* what has so often been taken as the pathologized frigidity of Moore's poems, is an effect of an exceptional poetic intelligence rather than an expression of a stunted emotional life. Moore teases the very edge of the vocabulary of love not because she cannot treat it directly but because directness kills its linguistic/erotic charge. The single apparent exception to Moore's stubbornly bestial erotics occurs in a late poem called "Love in America?" that, though for the most part divorced from beastly vocabularies, shares the same metaphoric, discursive, and deictic slipperiness. This late poem can be seen as a radical experiment with a new formation of erotics by Moore which, by simple homology, helps reveal her bestial erotics as part of a poetic strategy, but this poem is also an experiment that takes her erotics to new heights by expanding the term "love" in her poetics to explicitly include the literary and bodily orgasm.

"Love in America?" was written in 1966 on the request of Thomas Congdon at *The Saturday Evening Post* who was producing an issue on "Love in America." The poem acts as a literal restatement and response of the request for a poem. The title is a kind of "hmm, let me see," as if the poem were a spontaneous meditation sparked by an interviewer's question. The first line, as it follows the title, suggests that Americans have a "passion" for love and also that whatever else "love" is "it's a passion." Throughout the poem, then, the discourse on love is doubled: both about the prevalence and celebration of love in America, but also about love itself. That is, the armor of this poem could be said to be the strong possibility that this poem is all about a sociological rather than an individual phenomenon. The way the poem is split down the middle tonally is important in light of its matter-of-fact discursive tone.

> LOVE IN AMERICA?
>
> Whatever it is, it's a passion—
> a benign dementia that should be
> engulfing America, fed in a way
>   the opposite of the way
> in which the Minotaur was fed.
> It's a Midas of tenderness;
>   from the heart;
> nothing else. From one with ability
> to bear being misunderstood—
>   take the blame, with "nobility
>   that is action," identifying itself with
>   pioneer unperfunctoriness
>
>   without brazenness or
>   bigness of overgrown
>   undergrown shallowness.
>
> Whatever it is, let it be without
>   affectation.
>
>   Yes, yes, yes, *yes.* (*Collected Poems* 240)

The spur of the poem, an editor asking for a poem on love in America, is constantly present. The speaker celebrates love, but questions its constitution. "Passion" and "benign dementia," after all exist in an appositive relationship in the first two lines, suggesting that the "passion" of which Moore speaks is most definitely not something describable as "heedless desire." Moore's "passion," the one she is celebrating in this poem at least, is a "benign" passion, one best characterized by its "heedfulness." This love's actions are "to bear," "take the blame," and "identify[] itself"; not the sort of heady carelessness usually associated with "a passion."

In a poem that ends with such forceful positives, it is notable that the rhetorical energy throughout is negative. Love is fed the opposite "the way the Minotaur was fed"; Midas's touch turns things soft ("tender") instead of metallic; the "pioneer" energy of love is in no hurry to be first. The concatenation of love identifying itself "without … bigness of over-grown / undergrown shallowness" doubles each adjective and then doubles its negation. After this pile up of quadrupled negatives, the poem rescinds the certainty that it could have rested on in its next humble but self-aggrandizing stanza: "Whatever it is, let it be without / affectation." From the first rhetorical gesture of offering a definition—"Whatever it is, it's a passion"—to the highly rhetorical, affected hortatory stanza where this first formulation's definitional force is undercut by its own repetition—"Whatever it is, let it be without / affectation"—this poem undertakes a program of backtracking, crossing out, restarting, and taking back.

With all this in mind, the title itself performs the same kind of offer and withdrawal as the body of the poem. The question mark in "Love in America?" signals the inquisitive tone of the poem; it is going on a search, but the question mark also signals the possibility that there is no love in America. The inquiry of the title involves at least two different specific questions: Does love exist in America? and, if it does, what does it consist of? The poem, however, goes about describing love in the subjunctive mood. Love "should be / engulfing America," and only in the very last stanza seems to answer the question of whether love exists in America at all. This answer "Yes, yes, yes, *yes*," seems to follow from the meditations on love's constitution but also departs in its uncompli-cated positive answer. The final one-line stanza seems in dialogue, on its own, with the title, as if this poem started at "Whatever it is," and ended at "Whatever it is," framed by this question and answer.

But the final yeses are also, separately, in dialogue with the "whatever" to "whatever" body of the poem. The yeses serve as an enactment of love existing without affectation, and, as such, reproduce, as I discussed above, the self-negating effect of all utterances in the body of the poem. In other words, in order to be "without affectation" one needs a poetic device that seems as gaudy on this Moore poem as does apostrophe when it appears in "Sun" with its repeated ejaculation "O Sun," or in "Granite and Steel" with its "O steel! O stone!," or the romantic, epony-mous outcry of "O to be a Dragon." This is not to say that these devices fail to achieve an integrated tone in these poems, only that, in the midst of Moore's very steady discursive drift, they stand out. I tend to think that this standing out is no defect, in fact, it is one of the brilliant uses to which Moore puts her unemphatic insistence. These are each ejaculations of appreciation, unembarrassing, and, in these poems, earned by the steadying force of the rhetorical and discursive ligature in which they are held.

The final "*yes*," then, emphatically asserts that there *is* love in America and also shows, through rhetorical performance, its constitution: an assertion despite self-negation. There are two plots in this poem, one inside the other, both of which the final ejaculatory affirmation closes. The imperative of the framed plot, "let it be without affectation," is a kind of false bottom beneath which the real stuff is found, the emphatic "yes" that is both with and without affectation. The undirected affirmative shows that Moore is willing "to bear being misunderstood." At the same time it is very strongly rhetorically placed as the answer to the eponymous question. All the traffic in the poem meets at this final stanza where regardless of the confluence, nothing is settled. There are two arcs in the poem that both touch down on the final "*yes*," but the stronger they touch down, the more the "*yes*" serves as their felt closure, the more it activates the poem's central thematic of love as that which is built on negation, or that which flourishes under the rubric of opposites.

Missing from my discussion thus far is the fact that the final four affirmations are also the cries of orgasm, offering, in one line, speaking figure, scene, rising action, and voluble climax. Margaret Holley has linked this final stanza to the conclusion of Molly Bloom's monologue in *Ulysses*. Holley sees this citation as evidence of Moore's treatment of words as part of the public domain. "The unique thing about verbal arts," Holley writes, "is that its materials belong freely to everyone and to many people at once" (191). Holley does not take anything but the staidly literary relation of Molly's orgasmic "yes" seriously in relation to Moore. If this is borrowed from the scandalously indiscreet Molly, it also must borrow its sexiness, which Holley does not pursue. I am not convinced that four yeses an exclusive reference to *Ulysses* make (particularly because *Ulysses* does not take place in *America*). Regardless of their intertextuality, these affirmations are obviously orgasmic and not only literary citations.

Further, Marianne Moore, whose urge to clarity and exactness, who lines before went to the rather extraordinary effort to define a "brazenness or / bigness of overgrown / undergrown shallowness," has *let her poem's meanings go*. The utterance stands as signifier of passion, as release, and as willingness to be misunderstood. The discursive tone of the poem is aggressively shattered and any attempt to place the "yeses," say as Molly Bloom's, must only be one of uncontainable multitudes of interpretations. Most importantly perhaps, this orgasm is a *break from discursivity.* This poem challenges the idea of the lyric as an utterance whose beginning, middle, and end chart a tension development and release. Here, the climax is a self-contained performance. It is a flight from what lead to it, and this final line constitutes its own rhetorical and tonal plot that charts the movement (introducing to developing to concluding) of a scene separate from all those that came before (excuse the pun).

IV. Moore as Lyric Poet

To decide what shape Moore's poems take or resist, we must first attempt to place Moore *as* a lyric poet, as vexed and slippery as that definition process may prove. To start, it must be said that the category "lyric" is hardly an exclusive club. The term "lyric" does not entail, at least in attempts thus far to define it, an explicit shape. Northrop Frye, as I noted in the Preface, even suggests the "practicable approach … that a lyric is anything you can reasonably get uncut into an anthology" ("Approaching" 31). Thus, it may seem that Monroe's complaints about Moore's early verses occur on different terminological grounds, that is, she does not seem to be questioning Moore's poems' genre, only her execution of genre; but as I will explore in T. S. Eliot's musings on the lyric, a sense of shapeliness *is* embedded in the term "lyric," even while this falls out of more general critical projects of genre definition. That is, Monroe activates questions of lyric by using the specter of the lyric as the ideal shape that Moore fails to realize.

Eliot discusses Moore's poems as challenging the category of the lyric in his introduction to her *Selected Poems* (1935), in which he writes that "Miss Moore's poetry, or most of it, might be classified as 'descriptive' rather than 'lyrical' or 'dramatic'" (Tomlinson 62). The "descriptive" apparently takes its meditational dynamics and cues from the objects upon which it meditates while the "lyrical" or "dramatic" poem takes its shape, its point of departure and its point of arrival from the dynamics of address.

In an essay written almost 20 years later, Eliot is clearer in his definitions of "lyric" and "dramatic" poems (*On Poets* 96). At that time, 1953, there is no discussion of "descriptive" poetry, and Eliot identifies only three voices of poetry: lyric, dramatic, and poetry addressed to an audience "large or small." What he had described as "descriptive" verse in 1935 would probably later come under the rubric of the "lyric" voice.

Somehow, however, the material referent, the thing that a Moore poem describes, allows her poems slack. Her poems are difficult in that the speaker is half, or completely, hidden behind the object she is describing, but perfectly lucid in that the object, or some object, is always in clear sight. These "descriptive" poems are, as it were, moored but drifting.[17]

Eliot's tentative 1935 suggestion that Moore's poems belonged to an entirely new genre of poem points to a particularity of Moore's verse that, though it is not perhaps best named by its distinction from "the lyric" as indicated most clearly in Eliot's retreat from a genre of "descriptive" poetry, is still worth attempting to name. William Carlos Williams offered something similar, if more hyperbolic, when he wrote in his 1925 review of Moore in *The Dial:* "All things are inescapably caught in the beauty of Miss Moore's passage through them. ... This too is a quality that greatly pleases me: definite objects which give a clear contour to her force. Is it a flight, a symphony, a ghost, a mathematic? The usual evasion is to call them poems" (Tomlinson 57). If it is an evasion to call them poems, it is even more of an evasion to call them lyrics, but in the strain that the terms suffer in their application there are fingerholds for critical description. These poems can shift from focus on one object to focus on another object, but never lose the aspect of a gaze as it shifts, lingers, jolts, jumps, or wanders. I think it is important to keep the activity of Eliot's distinction in mind, that the "descriptive" poem is different from lyric in shape but similar in voice, even if this definition is inexact.

In *Anatomy of Criticism,* Northrop Frye defines the lyric with a slightly finer brush than in the statement I quoted above; here he calls the lyric "preeminently the utterance that is overheard" (249). In contrast, dubbing Moore's poems "descriptive poems" suggests that the poet is addressing her audience without the fiction of turning her back to them but also without the consistent attention to the audience's balance within the poem. Eliot suggests that the center of gravity of these poems is the object that the poet describes, that that is the constant most present aspect of the poem. The poet's speaking position, the audience's invitation or exclusion, and even the entire contract of address, whereby one consistent voice addresses one consistent listener are all at the mercy of the poem's maintaining proximity to the object that it describes. This "descriptive" nature of many of Moore's poems, whereby the object described gets first dibs on the direction of the poem, is certainly important to note, but it seems an important aspect of Moore's lyrics, an important location of lyric effects, and not the cornerstone of a whole new generic distinction.

I think that Eliot also called Moore's poems "descriptive" because he had a notion of the lyric as discharge that Moore's poems did not fit. In his essay "The Three Voices of Poetry," he describes the "lyric voice" as that of the poet "talking to himself—or to nobody" (*On Poets* 96). This poet discovers an "obscure impulse" for which he does not a have a mode of expression. When he has found the words to express this impulse, the impulse itself disappears and is replaced by the poem (106–7). The poet "is oppressed by a burden which he must bring to birth in order to obtain relief. Or, to change the figure of speech, he is haunted by a demon . . . and the words, the poem he makes, are a kind of . . . exorcism of this demon" (107). Eliot goes to lengths to be clear that he means that a lyric poem is an ejaculation resulting from masturbation; he revises and revises his figures until they are no longer impulse or demon, each metaphor is too burdened by its figurative baggage, but describe exactly a certain kind of masculine orgasmics. "In other words again," he delivers his final stroke,

> . . . he [the poet] is going to all that trouble, not in order to communicate with anyone, but to gain relief from acute discomfort; and when the words are finally arranged in the right way—or in what he comes to accept as the best arrangement he can find—he may experience a moment of exhaustion, of appeasement, of absolution, and of something very near annihilation, which is in itself indescribable. And then he can say to the poem: "Go away! Find a place for yourself in a book—and don't expect *me* to take any further interest in you." (Ibid.)

Post-orgasm, the poet tosses the tissue of words that now holds his "obscure impulse" under the bed. Eliot offers this definition of the lyric to encourage readers to have patience with poems, and to expect that if a poet is "obscure," he may be trying "to put something into words which could not be said in any other way" (111). There are two aspects of Eliot's orgasmics: the writing process whereby a poem passes from an inchoate state inside the poet to an actualized state outside and the reader's sympathetic vibration with that process. The reader must, according to Eliot, identify the lyric process as one of orgasm before he may himself experience the orgasmic passage into lexical actuality that the poet felt and meant to reproduce.

With his poetics of discharge in mind, it makes perfect sense that T. S. Eliot had trouble identifying Marianne Moore's poems as "lyrics." They do not seem discharges in the way he describes, either in their composition, that is, it doesn't seem that they were once impulses and became poems, nor in their relation to readers, that is, they do not offer the reader the single poetic climax that Eliot suggests comes at the height of a poem's pitch. In Moore's poetry, I will argue, ejaculation is not the figure for the lyric utterance. Instead, the poetics of ejaculation are one among a number of poetic effects active in her poems, deployed locally instead of globally used as an axiom of lyricality.

V. "Tippoo's Tiger"

One of Moore's last poems, "Tippoo's Tiger" (1967), is named, as Moore states in her notes, after a "vast toy, a curious automaton" that Tipu, ruler of Mysore, India, had constructed (*Complete Poems* 241). Moore also points out in the notes that "Tippoo is the original form of the name used in the eighteenth century; 'Tipu' is the accepted modern form" (297). The "toy" is, as Patricia Willis describes it,

> ... a wooden construction nearly six feet long and two and a half feet high which depicts a prostrate European being savaged by a Bengal tiger. Inside is a wooden pipe organ operated by a handle. ... When the handle is cranked, the victim's forearm waves and the organ emits sounds "very much like the growling cough of the Bengal tiger at its kill." (99)

Moore's poem celebrates Tipu, for whom the first line declares, "The tiger was his prototype" (*MCP* 241). Interestingly, the title of the poem and the first line clash in terms of their subject. The title proclaims that this poem will be about Tippoo's tiger, spelled in the "original" way, while the first line starts right in about Tipu himself, in the modern transliterated form of his name. The overlap is no mistake; this is a poem about the overlap between the ruler and his emblem, between ferocious action and its symbol.

The poem's first two stanzas delight in Tipu's tiger themed throne and costumes of his infantry and palace guards, borrowing an image of a nine-times-kissed emerald carpet from Keats' "The Cap and Bells, or The Jealousies" (*Complete Poems* 376). The "Man-Tiger-Organ" makes an appearance in Keats' poem as a favorite toy of his poem's Emperor. The Emperor's servant, Eban, "... feared less / A dose of senna-tea or nightmare Gorgon / Than the Emperor when he play'd on his Man-Tiger-Organ." The "Man-Tiger-Organ" playing is a sign of its player's "moody bitterness." Nothing could be further from Moore's tone as she almost gleefully narrates and celebrates Tipu's accomplishments, but mostly his relation to tigers and to toy tigers.

> Tipu owned sixteen hunting-cats to course the antelope
> until his one great polecat ferret with exciting tail

escaped through its unlatched hut-door along a plank
above a ditch; paused, drank, and disappeared—
precursor of its master's fate.

His weapons were engraved with tiger claws and teeth
in spiral characters that said the conqueror is God.
The infidel claimed Tipu's helmet and cuirasse
and a vast toy, a curious automaton—
a man killed by a tiger; with organ pipes inside
from which blood-curdling cries merged with inhuman groans.
The tiger moved its tail as the man moved his arm.

This ballad still awaits a tiger-hearted bard.
Great losses for the enemy
cannot make one's own loss less hard. (*Complete Poems* [1967] 241)[18]

Moore sticks fairly close to the description of "Tippoo's Tiger" she had
in a Victoria & Albert Museum monograph written by Mildred Archer
(Willis 98). The monograph tells how the toy commemorates the slay-
ing of the son of Tipu's enemy, Sir Hector Munro, by a tiger. The major
addition Moore has made to the image of this toy is to merge "blood-
curdling cries" with "inhuman groans." The toy itself, according to the
monograph's account, "emits sounds, as noted above, 'very much like
the growling cough of the Bengal tiger at its kill' " (quoted in Willis 99).
Moore's frank, riveted fascination shows most in the final line of the
fourth stanza in which the most gruesome aspect of the toy is zoomed
in on and served up as a balanced syntactic treat: "The tiger moved its
tail as the man moved his arm." The equivalence of the predator and the
prey's movements eerily underlines the participation of both in the scene
the automaton partially reanimates.

Once this violence, the screams and the mechanical wriggling and
wagging, is brought to the surface of the poem Moore steps an indentation back and declares that this is not the occasion of any more than a
schematic presentation of the tale of Tipu and his tiger. She leaves her
reader to wonder whose "ballad" will be sung when a "tiger-hearted
bard" finally takes to the task of singing it. Critics have explained that
the final two lines are about the "great losses" of both Tipu and the
British, for which this toy stands as double emblem.[19] However, Moore
eagerly anticipates a "tiger-hearted bard." She makes a call for *identifying with the tiger* of the toy, of which she shows the petticoat by adding
"blood-curdling screams" to the toy's effects.

The third stanza, the only real-time narration—"paused, drank, and
disappeared"—breaks from the other object-oriented descriptions of

Tipu's identification with the tiger in order to display its sympathies with the living beast, whose "exciting tail" prefigures the toy tiger whose tail moves in feeding frenzy. This prefiguration occurs in a stanza whose dominant rhetorical trope uses the whole tiger, who disappears, as a "precursor of its master's fate." The tail, in a kind of ripple effect of this very dramatic poetic synecdoche, serves as a "precursor of" *its* "master's fate," but its master is the tiger who will become a toy tiger whose only moving part is his tail.

This poem highlights and muddies the relationship between emblem and prototype. The relation the emperor has to the tiger turns out to be similar to the relationship the tiger has to the toy tiger. And at a metapoetic level, just as the tiger is the emperor's prototype so is his toy this poem's prototype. It is a machine to elicit identification with the tiger it represents. The sketchy ending, like the gruesome toy's crank, powers the motor that makes it groan, scream, and writhe. Like the toy, the poem turns a one-time climax into something which can be reenacted time and time again. The combination of putting off the ballad and splaying the identificatory wire ends rotates identifications: The great losses could be the European father's, they could also be Tipu's loss to "the infidel," his loss of his toy, they could stand for all these losses of human life, or they could be the loss of the human lives that produced, in their murderous concatenation, the loss of animators for this operating emblem of the tiger. Finally, the losses could be the loss of the tiger to the past, this toy making the reader or poet wish that the actual tiger were present. This poem is not, in other words, the ballad that completes a circuit of historicized or mythologized human action. Instead, the play of the interpretive and identificatory contradictions that arise from human action (a son's death, an emperor's being deposed, a museum collecting a big toy) is the generator that keeps open the possibility of "a tiger-hearted bard."

"The enemy" is entirely mobile. This final tercet, in Moore's "I am uttering a truth" tone, is a trap. The tone of the last two lines belie that which they express; the certainty of the hard-landing end rhyme, an effect held in abeyance until this final stanza, occurs at the site of greatest interpretive difficulty. Who has lost, what they have lost, and who their enemy is are all uncertain, although there are a number of viable options present in the poem.

Moore's earlier poem "Voracities and Verities Sometimes are Interacting" celebrates "a tiger-book I am reading" in a way similar to her celebration of Tipu's toy. This poem begins by comparing diamonds to emeralds, the latter favored for their "unobtrusiveness" that dazzles. The second stanza of "Voracities" tells "poets" not to "make a fuss" about themselves just because they write—the elephant itself writes with its trumpet. Animals can stand for themselves, just as the tiger in "The Monkeys" so eloquently elaborates. But also, the viciousness of the tiger is something that Moore relishes and for which she insists that she may "be pardoned." "One may be pardoned, yes I know / one may, for love undying" (*Complete Poems* 148).

In case the reader did not know to which tiger-book she was "under obligation," or inspired by, a note at the foot of the page (which is unusual, most notes gather at the end of the book) explains: "Tiger-book: Major James Corbett's *Man-Eaters of Kumaon*" (Ibid.). Patricia Willis points out that the tiger-book in question was a gift from Louise Crane, to whom Moore's *Complete Poems* is dedicated (64). Regardless of other possible meanings of the "love undying" in the final couplet of this poem, two unclosed possibilities are that Moore is forgiving the tiger its hunger for its grotesquely phrased "love undying" of human flesh, or that Moore herself is inventing forgiveness for her own love of "man-eaters" regardless, or quite possibly because of, their voracity. Finally, and perhaps most compellingly, Moore could be expressing her love for Crane by expressing her love of the "man-eaters" represented in a gift from Crane. Attention-grasping violence and stories of its control or uncontrollability might be the perfect "unhackneyed" medium for passionate affection.

The knot of elements: Legend, man-eating tigers, intimate knowingness, obligation, pardon, and love are all also present at the close of "Tippoo's Tiger." Concomitant with all of these associations is the notion of writing, in the early poem, "Voracities," achieved by the direct address of "Poets" and in the latter by an invocation of a possible future "tiger-hearted bard." In "Voracities" the second stanza indicates that writing is not such a big deal, even elephants do it. The other side of this "verity" is that writing is a huge deal, though not one to make a particular fuss about, because every creature does it in its own way. In this associative train, then, the tiger writes on bodies and is written in legend by its ferocity.

IV. "The Magician's Retreat"

The last poem Moore published, entitled "The Magician's Retreat" (1970), is interested in the very focused effect of presencing an absence as closure. In other words, the very absence of an element in the close of this poem, as I will show, completes it. Darlene Erickson, and other critics, have made a big deal about this being Moore's last poem and about showing the house that is represented in this poem as Moore herself. The poem, whether or not Moore knew it would be her last, has interest beyond the biographical card tricks one can perform with it. As I have shown in two other late Moore poems, during this period of Moore's production, so often overlooked or categorized as "slight," she experiments with poetics through closure in highly interesting and rich ways. These experiments revolve around how the mechanics of a lyric can rearrange its orgasmics. Eliot's idea is that for poet and reader an actualization of an internal and inchoate need to utter is the goal. Once an utterance is ejaculated by a poet, he need no longer concern himself with it. The reader on the other hand returns to the poet's product again and again in order to experience the shape of meaning forming, peaking, and closing. For Moore, as I have been suggesting, however she imagines the poet's experience of writing the poem, the result does not read like the transcript or performance of a single poetic ejaculation. Instead, she manipulates her closures to accommodate other types of readerly pleasures and pleasurings. This accommodation has the reader's expectation of lyrics providing orderly and single climaxes in mind. Sometimes, as is best illustrated in "Love in America?" she provides the orgasm but descenes it. Or, as in "Tippoo's Tiger," she hits her bardic peak and most viciously celebratory stride while suggesting she is not the singer of the tiger's ballad, and then splays the most strongly engaged terms and energies in the poem in a wild, willful fray of polysemy.

The title of Moore's last poem is linked to two representations of two separate buildings in the "Notes." The central image in the poem is Réné Magritte's "Domain of Lights," a painting of a house under a canopy of trees: The sky is filled with daylight, but under the trees a lamppost before the house appears illuminated as it would in the dark of night. Two windows glow orange on the left side of the house, and the sky-defying brightness of both lamp and windows is reflected in dark water immediately in front of the house. The source of Moore's title, but a less obviously present referent for the poem, is a work by "visionary architect" Jean-Jacques Lequeu, "Repaire de magiciens," which Moore had seen on the cover of *Arts Magazine*'s December/January 1967–68 issue.[20] This is a haunting, ornate, blocky structure with elephant-head gargoyles at its eaves and a stone sorcerer and a female figure each in its two first floor windows "above tondos inscribed 'Mortals, never forget that you are all equal,' and 'Virtue alone distinguishes men.' A wrought-iron gate bars the door, and there is no apparent means of opening it" (Lemagny 184).

The fact that Moore borrowed her title from Jean-Jacques Lequeu (1757–1825?) is both testament to the lexical flexibility of the title, able to be at once a place and a performance, and also to the poet's desire to have this architect present in her poem; he appears with his dates and the location of a reproduction of his drawing in Moore's "Notes." In the article Moore refers her readers to in *Arts Magazine,* Lequeu is discussed in conjunction with Boullée and Ledoux, who are from the same period and are also considered "visionary architects" but whose plans were a little more establishment friendly and less outrageously fantastic than Lequeu's. Though Lequeu's career started with a bang, his life ended mostly in "poverty and solitude." Especially attractive to Moore was probably the honest, uncompromising eccentricity of Lequeu's biography. But also, digging deeper into Lequeu's oeuvre, Moore probably adored his plans for a "Cow's Stable" that was a stable in the shape of a huge cow with an urn on its head and a rug on its back, or his drawing of "The Prince's Hunting Gate" that features animal heads on obelisks, which reminds a contemporary viewer more of a Joseph Cornell box than anything. Furthermore, the descriptions of Lequeu's drawings, especially of what is considered his masterpiece, "Meeting Place of Bellevue," sound hauntingly like descriptions of Moore's poems. J.-C. Lemagny writes: "The strange structure is completely asymmetrical, yet harmonious, and juxtaposes the most varied styles: a Renaissance tower topped by a Greek temple, a turret surmounted by an observatory, a Gothic door, and assorted windows and apertures. Despite his assembling of heterogeneous parts, Lequeu succeeded in giving coherence to his composition" (*Visionary Architects* 179). Moore's use of Lequeu's title seems both a mark of appreciation and artistic kinship, but also indicates that Moore's poem might have structural analogies to Lequeu's impossible but gorgeous designs.

Instead of suggesting that in this poem Moore imagines herself as a building, as Erickson does, based on these intertexts, it seems possible to identify figural concerns Moore borrowed from each image and attempted to reproduce in her poem. Lequeu's visionary drawing is most intriguing insofar as it offers an imaginable exterior to an unimaginable interior. This "magician's retreat" is meant as nearly an advertisement for mysteries unplumbable, activating the binary obvious/secret (and its most basic distillation: present/absent). The oscillation between these two makes the discrete lines and rather unornate exterior of Lequeu's building seem like purposeful restraint meant to exacerbate the imaginations of onlookers rather than restraint meant to quell curiosity. Magritte's painting even more stubbornly adheres to a binary, simply light/dark and insists that its operations are contextual. As representations of buildings, both works feature the trope of enclosure, but utilize enclosure to achieve different effects. Lequeu's picture uses the binary inside/outside to suggest a deep interior, whose cool one can almost feel in the blacked-out windows. The fascination of Magritte's picture on the other hand, while still firmly pivoting on the inside/outside binary, is the foregrounding of the everyday magic of context. "L'empire des lumières" or "The Domain of Lights" represents a possibly real, precisely recorded event of light and space. Lequeu's enclosure gestures to a deeper absence while Magritte's more frank enclosure (of light outside a house rather than of magic within a house) is its own present marvel and mystery.

Moore's poem uses its own title as its first line, and while Moore often treated her titles metonymically, in this poem, as was the case in "Love in America?" the title's separateness from the body of the poem and subsequent mobility within the poem serves as a crucial site for structural innovation.

> ### THE MAGICIAN'S RETREAT
>
> of moderate height,
> (I have seen it)
> cloudy but bright inside
> like a moonstone,
> while a yellow glow
> from a shutter-crack shone,
> and a blue glow from the lamppost
> close to the front door.
> It left nothing of which to complain,
> nothing more to obtain,
> consummately plain.
>
> A black tree mass rose at the back
> almost touching the eaves
> with the definiteness of Magritte,
> was above all discreet. (*Complete Poems* 246)

Though the central image of the poem hails directly from Magritte's painting, Moore never introduces that painting's most salient feature: the contrast between a noon-bright sky and a midnight-dimmed facade. "The definiteness of Magritte" seems to gesture to "The Domain of Lights" 's near photo-realism, buoyed up by the incredibly sharp line of contrast driven through its middle. For Moore, as she explores in her poem, the contrast between night and day has transferred to the contrast between the mysteriousness and secretness of a magician's retreat and its "consummate" plainness. That this retreat leaves "nothing more to obtain" seems pointedly odd considering that it is the subject of a fascinated exegesis.

In another Moore poem, the testimonial parentheses of the second line would appear simply as another (unparenthetical) line. Many of her poems begin with her situation in relation to her poetic subjects, the most famous example being "I, too, dislike it" from "Poetry" (*Complete Poems* 36). A much earlier poem, "Critics and Connoisseurs," offers the most similarly situated remark to "I have seen it" as part of the main current of the poem rather than pooled in a parenthetical eddy. "I have seen this swan and / I have seen you; I have seen ambition without / understanding in a variety of forms" (38). Elsewhere, Moore's parentheses are used to amend descriptions, "(I'm referring / to Henry James and Beatrix Potter's Tailor)" (231), ejaculate good-naturedly, "(what a bear!)" (109), admire the characters in her poems, "(Note too that over-worked Bach was not irked)" (209), and demarcate very stagy stage whispers.

Here, in "The Magician's Retreat," the aside nature of the assertion, "(I have seen it)," prepares the reader for a kind of elevated, fablelike tone and separates the voice that speaks the poem from the site of the house that it describes. It prepares us to suspend some disbelief, because the poet is warning that what she has seen is either improbable or rarely seen, or both. While of "moderate height," the parenthetical remark implies, this building is special in that it is so fabulous you may not believe the description and perhaps only a few have seen it and even then only once. The three color-based images—moonstone-like interior, yellow glow from a shutter, and blue-glowing lamppost—that describe the house at the beginning of the first stanza are balanced by the triple, entirely abstract, rhyme at the close of the first stanza. These abstractions offer a site for readerly identification, that is, some judgments are being made implying an agent, but they do not proffer hints as to what kind of agent would make such judgments. This triplet is resoundingly artful (three rhymes are often heard by readers as one rhyme too many), but so reserved in its content that the rhymes seem as unobtrusive as the punctuation that ends the lines containing them.

The two threes, three images and three rhymes, cry out for a "consummate" third. However, the final stanza seems instead to add a third detail, the "black tree mass," and the final two lines crash into one another. The final line, "was above all discreet," has to reach three lines up in the stanza and three prepositional phrases back in the sentence to find its subject. Then, even, how the mass of trees that are almost touching the house's eaves with the "definiteness of Magritte" are defined by this proximity to the house "above all" seems unsure. However, if "discreet" carries with it its dyslexic twin "discrete," one starts to feel a charge running through the close of the poem. The separateness of the trees from the house is an act of prudence, apparently, raising specters of a tree-punishing wizard inside. "Discrete" is the first of the lexical ghosts that haunt the close of this poem.

Still, even after locating a plausible subject for the final line, it dangles limply since it is attached to the thematically uncertain tree mass. The triple rhyme that occurred in the first stanza, moreover, finds a pale reflection in the second in which the only way a triple rhyme exists includes the weak "eaves" with the strongly linked and rhymed "Magritte/discreet." Further, the sentence that begins with the black tree mass seems to run out of momentum at "with the definiteness of Magritte." The pause between the penultimate and the ultimate lines is befuddling and sends the reader up even further in the poem than "the black tree mass" for answers. And there, in bold face, flying like a pennant over the poem, is the single most plausible subject for this decapitated line. "The Magician's Retreat" rushes down to squeeze between the last lines, snugly fitting the final statement in relation to the thematics of the poem. The entire first stanza was *about* the discreteness of the house and the second about its discretion. The comma after "Magritte" torques into a kind of apostrophe and the stanzas take shape around their punning dual aspects of the house. The title acts both as a ghost line and as enactive evidence of the retreat's discreteness: It is way up there at the head of the poem separated from the body but acting on it everywhere. Again paradox enters: This discreteness is exactly indiscreteness mirroring the way that the house's discretion is indiscretion.

V. Conclusion

These three late poems show a very different movement at their closures than the "ending up in the decor" John Ashbery described in Moore's earlier poems. However, as I have suggested, they still end up in the decor, just a different decor. Instead of in the poems' object world these poems end up in the mechanics of the poet's agency. Moore's late poems make the business of poems into a decor of its own. As an agent she appears at the close of each of these poems to see the reader out. While she splinters Eliot's notion of lyric-as-orgasm, she does provide lyric climaxes, though they are more stubbornly local and various than Eliot suggested. For instance, in "Love in America?" the very obvious orgasm Moore provides happens in one willful line with rhetorical links to the rest of the poem but a self-contained erotic plot line that both enables and resists those linkages. An extradiscursive voice intercedes to conclude the poem, gesturing to an extrapoetic agent. "Tippoo's Tiger," at its close, features an explosion of identification that acts as an orgasmic appearance of an authorial agent, willful in her refusal to chose a particular sympathy or identificatory position. The explosion is sponsored by polyvalence that proliferates even violently opposite meanings but provides no tension reduction. "The Magician's Retreat" then reaches climax based on something Whitehead might have called lyric action at a distance. The mechanics of readerly attachment and understanding are based on invisible principles and a principle of invisibility. This almost telepathic movement of meaning has its source in the obvious patterning of Moore's poem but surpasses its visible patterns. The invisible force that moves meaning around inside this poem makes Moore's presence almost palpable. She is the most available possible ghost in this machine.

In the process of reading these poems I hope to have shown a lively poetic intelligence at work and a sustained attention to particularly lyric, and more generally, to have teased out some of the literary and metaliterary erotics in Moore's late poems. I have paid special attention to the movement of Moore's poems, what has often fallen under the shabby lean-to of the binary shapely/shapeless and is often disregarded in considerations of "form" in her poems. The willfulness in her late poems more fully embodies her in her poems, and as embodiment and disembodiment oscillate erotically throughout her oeuvre, more fully involves her readers. In one of Jarrell's jaunty and brilliant essays on Moore, he writes what I will treat as my own closure, in honor of Moore's own formal concerns in critical essays *and* poems:

Miss Moore's forms have the lacy, mathematical extravagance of snowflakes, seem as arbitrary as the prohibitions in fairy tales; but they work as those work—disregard them and everything goes to pieces. Her forms, tricks and all, are like the aria of the Queen of the Night: the intricate and artificial elaboration not only does not conflict with the emotion but is its vehicle. And her machinery ... fits both form and final content of her poems as precisely as if all three were pieces of some extraordinary puzzle. (*Poetry* 163)

Chapter 6

Danced Undone: Performances of Exhaustion and Resignation in Crane's Lyrics

I. Exhaustion's Register

In the chapters that precede this one, I have discussed closure as a site of heightened poetic agency. In my examination of John Ashbery's poetry, I examined how he offers his closures as a model of living in meaning specific to homosexual subjects. He utilizes poetic materials, especially closure, to explore ecstasy that arises from and occurs simultaneously with a spoiled identity. In Chapter 4 I showed how Moore changed Crane's poem "The Wine Menagerie," particularly its closure, in order to change the valence of its commentary on ecstasy. In Chapter 5, I discussed how Moore quite calculatingly built the closures of her late poems in such a way as to provide her reader with a heightened proximity to the agent of the poem. Moore's late poems explore closure as a site of ecstatic presence, rather than, as in her earlier poems, a site of meandering absence. The end of a poem, I have been arguing, exhibits a moment of poetic choice more clearly than other sites of the poem, more even than the beginning, because closure is a site where the poet either does or pointedly does not complete the patterns developed in the body of a poem.

The close of a poem can also exhibit a giving up. A poem's closure can perform forfeit. This is different from the effect of the poet receding at the end of her creation as Moore does in some of her early poems, leaving us with a little rodent, as John Ashbery so memorably noted, or actually having us "end up in the decor." Moore never stages resignation or exhaustion as the close of her poems; energy still flows through the channels of the poem but shifts to pointedly underground routes. She does not declare the limit of the reach of her poems, but instead nudges forward the possibility that they might engage even beyond the bounds of her particular poem. Ashbery himself is present in the stubborn polysemy of his closures and always seems slyly peeking around a corner back at the reader's progress.

Crane's experiments with staging exhaustion are different from Moore and Ashbery's experiments with polysemous closures because, first and foremost, these poems take exhaustion *as their subject*. It requires thematic support for a poem to quit and not just appear incomplete. The Crane poems I will examine do not appear unfinished, but close by proposing their own very definite limits. Closure serves as an intrapoetic completion that indexes the poem or poet's inability to reach beyond the poem, or beyond his own subjectivity. The poet in these poems crests the apex of his agency as he declares the limits of his realm of activity or influence.

I take the title of this chapter from "To Portapovitch (du Ballet Russe)," an eight-line poem Crane composed between 1917 and 1919. This period more or less coincides with the period of Crane's friendship with Stanislaw Portapovitch and his wife, Anna.[1] In 1917, when Crane first arrived in New York City, he befriended Stanislaw Portapovitch who had danced in Diaghilev's Ballet Russe; they were close for about two years until Crane lost interest.[2] "To Portapovitch" depicts a dance performance with springing, imperative lines. The first quatrain describes what appears to be a performance by Portapovitch while mimicking his rhythmically arranged leaps: Each line is discrete, touching down at each line break to pause and then, with the next line, spring anew. With each new line, the poem offers a different image to describe the dance. It formulates and reformulates an interpretation; these attempts accrue in variety, richness, and dimension.

> Vault on the opal carpet of the sun,
> Barbaric Prince Igor:—or, blind Pierrot,
> Despair until the moon by tears be won:—
> Or, Daphnis, move among the bees with Chloe. (*Complete Poems* 147)[3]

"Or" twice assures a swift movement from descriptive attempt to descriptive attempt, each character torn from a separate narrative danced by the Ballet Russe: Prince Igor, Pierrot, and Daphnis. Prince

Igor, Pierrot, in the form of Petrouchka, and Daphnis were most famously danced by Vaslav Nijinsky, whose queer legacy is traced in recent critical studies by Michael Moon and Kevin Kopelson. Nijinsky left his indelible mark on these characters as well as on the faun in "L'Après-midi d'un faun," the performance of which he concluded with a scandalous, masturbatory gesture. Equally remarkable was Nijinsky's Golden Slave in "Schéhérazade," in which, as Moon explains, Nijinsky appeared as "[b]oth subhuman and superhuman, he is simultaneously perceived as an effeminate cat and a tremendous stud, but not as 'masculine' in any ordinary sense" ("Flaming Closets" 28).

Crane's unpublished poem "OF AN EVENING PULLING OFF A LITTLE EXPERIENCE (with the English Language)" (1923) performs the same scandalous gesture Nijinsky does as the Faun in "L'Après-midi d'un faun." Crane stages a performance of masturbation at the end of this poem directly referencing Nijinsky's performance as the Faun (with the difference that Crane signals masturbation with punctuation and innuendo, a dash signifying orgasm).[4] The poem announces itself as a poem written by "EEEEEECCCUUUMMMMMMIIINNNGGGSSS (for short)" and utilizes the typographical devices for which cummings, a friend of Crane's, became well known. Cummings's name itself, from the start, by its further defamiliarization, enters the fray of polysemy Crane kicks up around the topic of masturbation. Crane's poem begins "wrists web rhythms," wends through showy tricks that figure the male genitals, and ends:

> blundering fumbiguts gather accu
> rate little, O-SO masturbations in/
>
>   to
> fractions of heaven. Hold tight bless
> worms trilling rimple flock to
> sad iron
>
>   goats of
>   love-
>   semi-colon
>   piping (dash) (*Complete Poems* 180)

The "goat[] of / love-" is clearly Nijinsky's Faun and shows that Crane's interest in Nijinsky was not a single-poem, nor solemn, affair.

Nijinsky's scent was still in the air in America, but especially in New York, when Crane conceived "To Portapovitch." Crane arrived in New York just months after Nijinsky had finished a two season run. After the New York seasons, Nijinsky set off across America on what would prove a terribly exhausting tour, ending in February 1917.[5] As we have seen in "The Wine Menagerie," Nijinsky would continue to figure strongly throughout Crane's career. In "The Wine Menagerie" (1926), Petrushka and characters from Wilde's *Salomé* people Crane's unmoored hallucinations. In "To Portapovitch (du Ballet Russe)," Crane channels his fantasies about Nijinsky, whom he never saw perform, through his friend, who becomes an easy signifier for Nijinsky by having performed in the same ballet company.

The frenetic movement from line to line of the first stanza of "To Portapovitch" both indicates the plasticity of the dance performance and suggests the delight that such plasticity elicits in the poet. The sun/moon figure serves to connect each mythic persona to an atmospheric transformation born of sadness. The tears of the characters, in a grand figural move, turn the sun's surface into the cool surface of the moon. The sun/moon transformation also helps describe the dance that starts out hardly touching the ground, figured as the surface of the sun, and then descends more and more as the surface cools and the spring of despair is exhausted. The end of the dance comes when tears have transformed the surface of the sun to the surface of the moon, offering the suggestion that despair stops when it has transformed the world by its effects but not in its image. The operations of despair, that is, the feelings that accompany the world's hostility or unamenability, become materialized in tears and change the physical world into a more amenable place, a place where one can rest on the ground without being burned. This slant paradox charts the operations of exhaustion, which, the poem suggests, is not the absence of affect but is an affect all its own with a different relation to the world than its ostensible cause, here, despair. Exhaustion, this poem suggests, happens when affect transforms the world into a place in which exhaustion can be felt and physically embodied as a presence, rather than an absence, of feeling.

The second, and final, stanza is both a comment on the movement of the first stanza as well as being its own performance of release and return to the material ground of the scene.

> Release,—dismiss the passion from your arms.
> More real than life, the gestures you have spun
> Haunt the blank stage with lingering alarms,
> Though silent as your sandals, danced undone. (147)

This stanza begins by employing the imperative, but an imperative muted by correction. The crisp commands to "vault," "despair," and "move" in the first stanza are sure footed, while "Release,—dismiss" emphasizes the presence of the poet who is issuing the commands rather than foregrounding the performance of those commands. This amplification and greater specification of the verb diminishes the verbal springing. "Release" smears into "dismiss," as if we were watching the poet find just the right word, and from this quaver until the end of the poem the pulsion from line to line slows, hitting the water barrels of a description that is no longer imperative at all. While the first stanza featured dancerly and poetic vaulting, each line springing anew from the descriptive default position, the second drops out of the present and into the past. In the first stanza it seems almost as if the poet's imperatives animate the dance while describing it, while the second recedes to the safe and less strange position of straightforward poetic description. The smallest parts of the dance in the first stanza were the tableaus the dance created, while in the second, the dance is made of less mythic stuff, "gestures," and occurs on a "stage" rather than among imagined "bees."

The poem starts springing and settles into the graceful and slow flow of the final three lines into one another. The movement of this two-stanza poem enacts the movement of the dancer but also suggests that the only physical remainder from the performance is the untied sandals, whose undoing, in one sense, was the activity of the performance. The dance left nothing but "lingering alarms" on a "blank stage." The evidence of completion in one register, the dance, is incompletion in another, the sandals. While the sandals were instrumental to the dance, whose ephemerality is marked in the jump from descriptive attempt to descriptive attempt in the first stanza, they are the material image that holds the memory of what has passed. In the poem, too, the sandals are a distillate, the most striking verbal concatenation.

The sandals, however, are also something for the reader to trip over. What danseur could or did perform in shoes that come undone? I offer this as a rhetorical question in the spirit of Paul deMan's famous meditation on the subject of the rhetorical question. DeMan writes:

[A]sked by his wife whether he wants to have his bowling shoes laced over or laced under, Archie Bunker answers with the question: 'What's the difference?' Being a reader of sublime simplicity, his wife replies by patiently explaining the difference between lacing over and lacing under, whatever this may be, but provokes only ire. ... The grammatical model of the question becomes rhetorical not when we have, on the one hand, a literal meaning and on the other hand a figural meaning, but when it is impossible to decide by grammatical or other linguistic devices which of the two meanings (that can be entirely incompatible) prevails. Rhetoric radically suspends logic and opens up vertiginous possibilities of referential aberration. (*Allegories* 10)

Bunker's laces lead deMan to the ultimate Modernist rhetorical question posed by Yeats in "Among School Children": "How can we know the dancer from the dance?" (qtd. in *Allegories* 11–12). Both forms of deMan's meditations on rhetoric, telling the figural from the literal and telling the dancer from the dance, come into play when considering Crane's sandals. We must ask whether Crane is writing about a dance Portapovitch performed at all or is instead writing by means of metaphoric slippage about Nijinsky, and in either case, why the dancer sports such improbable footwear. However, while we must ask, we may not answer.

In a sense, Crane's sandals are the element of this poem above all others that "opens up vertiginous possibilities of referential aberration." The gestures the poem spins are "more real than life" by depending on a figure with little or no connection to the reality of its context, ballet, as well as on a dancer who is more the unnamed Nijinsky than the eponymous Portapovitch. One possible referent for the loose-laced sandals are the sandal-like shoes Nijinsky wore for his performance of The Faun in *L'Après-midi d'un Faune,* however, even then, ballet shoes must, by the nature of their use, undergo the stress of strenuous activity and not come undone. The literal meaning of the sandals, that is, their unlikeliness, does not settle with their figurative meaning (the poem depends on this figure for a firm-footed closure). The conflict gestures to the split of the real subject of the poem between Portapovitch and Nijinsky but also to the split between dance and lyric poetry. Dance is the figurative but not literal subject of the poem. Lyric poetry is the figuratively constructed literal subject: It, not dance, requires an exhausted remainder that then gets transferred onto dance.

This poem suggests that the identifications forged in art (identifications here with Prince Igor, Pierrot, and Daphnis) leave a physical remainder in another register. The most moving identifications, by which I mean to imply motion as well as emotional content, outreach their original medium whereby success in maintaining their traces requires a kind of mnemonic and affective shift from the identifications at hand to the material mechanisms of those identifications. This material remainder does not hold the identifications but becomes an emblem of their possibility, of their ephemeral passage, but also of their repeatability.

In "To Portapovitch" Crane's linguistic performances attempt to mime the physical dance performance, even using the imperative to indicate that the poem comes before *and causes* the dance performance. The poem jumps when the dancer jumps and settles and finishes with him. This imbrication is more than a poetic gimmick; it creates an analogy between dance performances and lyric performances, unsettling the notions that lyric performances occur out of real time and that all moments of a lyric are available in the same way on the page at any moment of reading. It is true that the material of a lyric is available after a performance in a way that a dance is not, but Crane invites us to speculate that what remains of identifications in a lyric performance may be just as evanescent as the pirouettes of Portapovitch/Nijinsky. We, as readers of a poem, may be left solely with some poetic version of untied sandals as an index of our identifications within a particular reading of a poem.

Sandals for the dancer, in Crane's forthrightly figural use of ballet, are like present-tense reports from the senses for Crane in his poems. These reports of primary vision and hearing are a particular device for the lyric poet. To say "I hear" or "I see" or "she hears" and "she sees" in a poem declares the poet's or persona's body and holds it in a position of attentiveness. Such statements both develop a map of a material world but also hold the witness in a place where he is subject to it. This is different from the notably more interior "I remember/he remembers" or "I dream/he dreams," from the more distant past tense "I heard/he heard" or "I saw/he saw," or from any less announced witnessing in which the witness's body is more mysteriously present as, for instance, in the move into the subjunctive or self-reflexive. The analogy is strongest if we consider the undoing of such reports. At the end of a lyric performance, just as at the end of Portapovitch's dance, these devices may have been jarred to a state of undoneness. The poet/persona might for instance still be able to hear and see, but cannot use these abilities to the same ends they have been employed throughout the poem.

In the poems I examine, these processes, hearing and vision, fail to break the boundaries between subjectivities but stand as the remainders of momentary felt breeches in their immiscibility.[6] These are local limitations, or failures, folded into the Crane's larger poetics, not, I will maintain, "a poetics of failure" in the way that many critics have defined Crane's project.

II. Failure

The discourses of "failure" that swirl around Crane criticism are bewildering in their variousness and scope. "Failure" is used to describe Crane's life, his alcoholism, suicide, sexuality, and career, as well as single poems, groups of poems, his poetics, his execution of those poetics, and his cosmology. Mostly, I wish to note how in the poems I examine the "failure," which most critics define generally as relating to Crane's poetics, consists of, more specifically, sites of staged "exhaustion," "undoneness," and "resignation." The stagedness of these moments, the fact that these poems perform "failure" poetically, inserts a voluntarity into the mix that bucks the term "failure," and the affective content of these moments is not one of shortfall or frustration, but rather one of respect for wholly other subjectivities. These "failures" are constructed by Crane as poetic effects that perform and invite the affects accompanying the deep experience of bounded subjectivity; their "failures" are evidence of their success as lyrics.

R. W. Butterfield enlists Crane's own comments about his intentions to indict Crane's biography, poetics, and poetic projects in one broad stroke.

> [I]n any terms, but chiefly in his own, Crane's is indisputably a record of failure, both as a man and as an artist. He was a philosophical optimist who collapsed into a violent and desperate alcoholism and committed suicide at the age of thirty-two; he was a man who at the age of thirty had so lost belief in the long poem he had begun almost seven years previously that he could complete it only under publisher's pressure; he was a poet who during the last four years of a brief life produced little but fragments. (v)

Crane was optimistic but fell into despair, gave up on his longest work, had to be goaded to complete it, and dithered into incomplete poems toward the end of his life. Butterfield does, to his credit, chalk Crane's failure up to his "refusal to be satisfied with limited ambitions," but he has opened a Pandora's box, and even the brokenness featured in his book's title, *The Broken Arc: A Study of Hart Crane,* succinctly illuminates a sloppy double movement of Crane's poetics into his biography and his biography into his poetics. The "broken arc" of Crane's "The Bridge" becomes also the "broken arc" of his life narrative.

R. P. Blackmur seems to have started the party with the famous concluding sentence of his influential 1954 essay, "New Thresholds, New Anatomies: Notes on a Text of Hart Crane," in which he makes a call for readers not to "give up" on Crane. He writes, "... there is about him ... —such were his gifts for the hearts of words, such the vitality of his intelligence—the distraught but exciting splendor of a great failure" (Trachtenberg 64).[7] "Failure" here is something that happens despite Crane's ability as a poet. This failure is encapsulated easily by a witness to it, but was out of Crane's reach. It stands for a crisis in his being that is given a strange independence from his other characteristics: That strange independence is what critics dwell on most. "Failure" stands, in these accounts, for something Crane could not control or account for. It was beyond him. He fell short.

The optics of Crane's failure are steadied and organized by the rigid one-way mirror of retrospect. During his life, without the closure of his suicide, his trials and difficulties as well as despairs and ecstasies were not failures or successes. Each experience, mood, or condition helped or hindered the creation of a failed or successful poem, afternoon, love affair, or friendship. All the critics of Crane's "failure" indicate that he wanted to go further than he did, that he wished to transcend or pass over to another place. That is, critics suggest that poetic transcendence and bodily transcendence are the same thing. Anyone who has been transported by a poem while sitting firmly in an armchair knows that while these two are mysteriously related, they are unmistakably different from one another.

The uncomplicated conflation of poetic and lived transcendent moments undergirds the conflation of lived teleology and biographical teleology. Since "failure" has to do with the goals of the person involved, any discussion of it must include some treatment or attempted reconstruction of those goals. Otherwise, all lives are potentially failed because they end in death. As such, the global use of the term "failure" seems flawed from the beginning, because it seems a rare person who imagines himself as a seamlessly biographical subject and has the same goals posterity's contexts will rig up for him. Further, with a poet's rich and varied work, goals seem one of the very least interesting approaches. For instance, Federico Garcia Lorca started many projects and never finished a large percentage of them. This might tell us that he had quite a few goals that went unmet, that he fell short of, or it might tell us something about his creative process that has little to do with his fortitude or success as a poet. It might tell us that, instead of a failure, he was a genius.

Joseph Riddel, at the very beginning of his influential essay, "Hart Crane's Poetics of Failure," announces the "wisdom" of conflating Crane's biography and poetics. He writes: "Hart Crane's last poem, 'The Broken Tower,' is so confused with the sensational events of his last days that it is hard to consider the poem apart from the man. On the whole, it seems wise not to, for this is a poem which dramatizes, once and for all in our time, the pathetic gesture of a man dying into his work" (473). This introduction does more than suggest that Crane's final poem has a strong presence in Crane's last days, and vice versa. Suicide and artistic crisis coincide at the very defined point of "The Broken Tower," and this single point of overlap then allows access to Crane's "poetics," forcefully driving home Riddel's central claim that failure was an aspect of both Crane's poetics and life.

Joseph Riddel sees Crane as failing doubly. The first failure in Crane is an intentional part of his poetics. Like Poe, Riddel suggests, the poet, as a part of his poetic project, "is to be destroyed with his vision" (476). Riddel sees Crane's as an impossible poetics, because it requires limitless enthusiasms and energies. When the energy wanes, so does the ability to throw his vision into words and ultimately, but according to plan, fail. The poet in Riddel's overbearing formulation has to pick himself up after each inevitable failure and try again hoping that he will at some point transform into the process itself. He writes, "The end for Crane's poems, it seems, was to justify the need for further poems, in which, ultimately, self and world might become one" (478). Crane's poems, thus, affirm "alienation as a prelude to transcendence." Riddel theorizes exhaustion as something outside of Crane's poetics, something that happens to him based on them but that is not accounted for or dealt with in them. Exhaustion, for Riddel, is something that *happens to* rather than *is performed in* Crane's poems.

Further, Riddel maintains, Crane fails even within the terms of the "poetics of failure." "The consequences of Crane's vision are as obvious in his life as in his style. The method arrives at an impasse, condemning the poet to a repetition that can only be sustained by an heroic expenditure of energy upon intense and forced moments" (492). Crane fails to maintain the level of expenditure that might finally and resolutely break the transcendent cycle Riddel puts forward. He becomes exhausted. Thus, his failure in poems and thus, his suicide. The unbelievably rigid and one-size-fits-all nature of Riddel's case about Crane's basic poetics has not kept his account from becoming critical currency. The most outrageous aspect of Riddel's account is how teleology outranks performance. Of course transcendence writ large always fails. That has been the motivation of, rather than the defeat of, artistic production for as long as it has been understood that the evidence of transcending language, or any medium, would be, by its nature, impossible to present in that medium.

This theorization of Crane's poetics is itself an impasse: it takes the legs out from under any activities a poem might engage in besides questing for transcendence. Crane, and by extension the reader of Crane's poems, are not allowed to speculate on exhaustion as an affect within his poems. Exhaustion is what happens to a poet in Riddel's account without the poet being able to grasp it or treat it as poetic material. With nothing else to go on, of course every poem is a failure: It is impossible to present evidence of surpassing the evidentiary.

In Riddel's formulation, the ballet performance that Crane witnessed is also a failure. The sandals only stand as evidence of the inability of the dancer to surpass himself and become motion. "What is left," of Crane's poetics, as I am suggesting might also be applicable to Portapovitch/ Nijinsky, "displays enough of the corruption, and of the purity, to remind us of his heroic pathos" (496). The dancer would then have to pick himself up and perform again, at a great expense of energy. The only affect those sandals would stand as trace of would be the "heroic pathos" of the dancer. This is a tepid effect for dance or poetry, indicating a great distance of the audience or auditor from the affects and identifications forged in the artistic work. The memory of the identifications made during the dance would be subsumed in this consideration of the artist and his attempts to break the barrier of his medium. Such a summation of the artistic enterprise and its reception offers little to explain the motivation of a reader or audience.

Allen Grossman, in his essay "Hart Crane and Poetry: A Consideration of Crane's Intense Poetics with Reference to 'The Return,'" pulls the rug out from under Riddel's simple conflation. Grossman explains how any consideration of Crane's poetics will require a consideration of his life, but that the most interesting observations arise from keeping these two terms active while making precise distinctions between them. Grossman seeks to "… consider whether the harrowing cooperation of the authentic powers which Hart Crane brought to his art—he was beyond doubt a poet— with the enormous need which as a person he addressed in it, does not indicate … some boundary at once of poetry and human hope—whether, in short, what you cannot have or be, you also cannot in well-formed poems say" (842). Crane himself, as Grossman points out, was interested in the distinction and conflation of life and poetry. It was a part of his poetics. Exhaustion, where it occurs, is not just a reminder of an "heroic pathos" but evokes powerful and deep insights and emotions about the very state of being a person.

That Crane's life was a failure, as it is probably already abundantly clear, is a presumption I am not willing to make. Above and beyond all of its inaccuracies and bluntnesses about Crane's life particularly, it suggests things about a successful life that seem suspect. To die sighing sad but loving wishes to a circle of relatives at a ripe old age with a shelf full of books does not seem to me "success," it seems merely a very particular way to die. "Failure" is so mobile a term that it can describe any botched task or frustrated aim; it is so sloppy a term that it threatens to mean nothing. Nonetheless, it appears as the pennant above so many critical studies that to study "failure" in Modernist American Poetry is tantamount to studying Hart Crane.

William H. Pritchard makes the interesting observation that "Usually we do not bother to assert that a short lyric is a failure, but wheel the term out only in the case of longer poems; so it might be well to ask ourselves just what sort of unified or coherent poem would satisfy us in this century ..." (256). Pritchard suggests that Crane's *The Bridge,* the usual object of the discourse around "failure," is no more "conspicuously" a failure than other celebrated long poems such as William Carlos Williams's *Paterson,* Pound's *Cantos,* and Eliot's *Four Quartets.* His comments problematize the term "failure" and help situate Crane's amid other attempts to write long poems.[8] Pritchard's comments also help show how, like his suicide, Crane's long poem is used as a touchstone from which to make generalizations about the rest of his work. Lyrics are not usually described as failures, but in the critical commentary on Crane, it is near impossible to wrench his lyrics away from the critical apparatus that is "wheeled out" to describe his foray into the long poem. Crane himself theorized failure within his lyric poetry and explicitly located poetic closure as the site of heightened effects around failure.[9] Closure is, to begin with, a natural place to discuss failures. The last words of a poem offer the last chance for that poem to do what it set out to. If it fails to perform its self-appointed task, it is safe to call it a failure after having reached the end. On the other hand, in a "successful," that is, not failed, poem, closure must happen at the point exactly before the poem would fail by trailing itself off into insignificance. This discussion is on the level of the relation of thematics to linguistic performance. There are also, as Barbara Herrnstein Smith has pointed out in her study of closures, sonic, rhythmic, and other formal patterns that give the reader a feeling of closure. A version I discussed in the first chapter is Alan Williamson's suggestion that John Ashbery's poems end with sonic patterns that give the feeling of completion while the thematics are by no means closed down or finished.

III. Undone: "Reply"

The experiment with ending a short lyric "undone" in "To Portapovitch (du Ballet Russe)," an early poem by Crane, is refigured in "Reply," a late one. This poem shows Crane turning rhetorical and thematic "undoneness" to account, specifically against homophobic readers. This poem considers time on a larger scale than "To Portapovitch." Here, the poet imagines, like Whitman in "Recorders Ages Hence," a time after his death; the "reply" of the title is the poem itself as a text, but is also, more importantly, the poet's imagined legacy. Crane suggests that his fame will be the precipitate of his scandalous performances and that his fame will be increased by homophobic attacks. In the course of Crane's transformation from a living poet to a dead but famous poet, his "shame" will come "undone."

In "To Portapovitch" Crane discovered how undoneness could serve as a powerful index for emotions and performances, and here he is putting that discovery to self-preserving use by projecting it through time into the imagined future.

REPLY

Thou canst read nothing except through appetite
And here we join eyes in that sanctity
Where brother passes brother without sight,
But finally knows conviviality …

Go then, unto thy turning and thy blame,
Seek bliss then, brother, in my moment's shame.
All this that balks delivery through words
Shall come to you through wounds prescribed by swords:

That hate is but the vengeance of a long caress,
And fame is pivotal to shame with every sun
That rises on eternity's long willingness …
So sleep, dear brother, in my fame, my shame undone.
(*Complete Poems [1958]* 193)

Crane theorizes that all reading is based on "appetite" in grand, archaically arch language, which, as the poem moves forward, melts into both a more vernacular and a more forgiving tone. The poet declares that, contrary to what this hostile "brother," like Yvor Winters, might think, the poetic contact is made of mutual desire: The poet desires the reader in his text, and the reader desires the poet. "Here," at the site of the poem, the brothers of reader and writer "know conviviality" without seeing each other. This makes of poetry a site of abandonment that works, in the face of drawn swords, to inevitably point those very swords back at the aggressor. The homophobe who "blames" will find that the violence he directs at the gay poet will be turned against him and, in a further twist, his hate will turn to "a long caress." In other words, sustained vitriol turns over time to love, because love is, first and foremost, attention. The poet will become more famous as he attracts attention over time, and the shame that spurred the fame will dilute itself with the presence of more and more brothers, some, or many, undoubtedly not homophobic.[10]

The more vicious the attacks on Crane, this formula goes, the more tenacious his legacy. Shame leads to fame that undoes shame. The greater the shame, the greater the fame. This may not be a historically accurate picture of every interaction of homophobia and artistic fame, but if we look to Wilde and Nijinsky, two of Crane's queer exemplars, it holds some water. This poem is a direct precursor to John Ashbery's similarly three-quatrained poem, "The Grapevine," in which homophobic interest in finding gays unwittingly provides a situation in which gay men can find one another. Furthermore, Crane's poem works best, like Ashbery's, as an enactive fantasy. To a certain extent, saying it does make it so. That is, in each case the reception of the poem as a meaningful act is predicated upon the mechanics of readership the poems discuss. Each poem provides access, by calling into being in fantasy, a homosexual continuance across time. Creating a legacy and creating a community are the engines of a queer genealogy, and both these poets see shame and homophobia as the fuel.

In Crane's poetics, this fantasy derives directly from retooling and refiguring undoneness as a crucial category in his poetics. Crane's figural economies here, as elsewhere, illustrate and enact one pattern dissolving as another takes sway.

IV. "The Idiot": Vision's Limit

Each of the estimations of Crane's "failure" dwell exclusively on Crane's attitude about and relation to his own position as a poet. He butts his head against a seemingly possible transcendence. However, if the emphasis is shifted from Crane and his own position, I will argue, the failures of his lyrics show him wrestling with the difficulty of the subjectivity of others, and with the further difficulty of how to present them as inviolable but at the same time available. The poet is a trespasser but trespassing is a necessary misdemeanor to begin to imagine an other as whole but not wholly available to vision. Crane addresses just this double bind in "The Idiot," one of his thematically accessible poems in the *Key West: An Island Sheaf* group. Located on the Isle of Pines where Crane spent some time, the poem's four first-person quatrains describe the idiot's reception by other children, his joyfully absurd behavior, his song, and finally, the poet's uneasy identification with him.

The poem begins with the poet figure avoiding "the idiot," going out of his way not to see the boy who is "it's likely / fumbling his sex." Because of "the idiot's" fumblings, other children "laughed // In such infernal circles round his door / Once when he shouted, stretched in ghastly shape." The poet "hurried by" to avoid the embarrassment of such a scene but also ostensibly to avoid either witnessing or driving deeper the cruelty of the sneering children. Though he generally goes out of his way to avoid the boy, one day, on the way "back from the hot shore," the poet happens upon him and witnesses an entirely different and fascinating version of the boy's "idiocy."

> ... He was alone, agape;

> One hand dealt out a kite string, a tin can
> The other tilted, peeled end clamped to eye.
> That kite aloft—you should have watched him scan
> Its course, though he'd clamped midnight to noon sky!
> (*Complete Poems* 118)

The boy stares through the closed off, failed telescopic device of a can, rapt. In the final stanza the poet again goes out of his way to avoid the idiot boy, but for new reasons. The final stanza suggests that hearing without seeing the boy chastens the poet's vision.

> And since, through these hot barricades of green,
> *A Dios gracias, grac*—I've heard his song
> Above all reason lifting, halt serene—
> My trespass vision shrinks to face his wrong.

The "And since" that starts this final stanza means both that the poet has not seen the boy "since" chancing upon the kite scene, but also, that *because* the poet has heard the song he averts his eyes in order to respect the boy's verbal expression by disconnecting it from his visible abjection. The boy's song chastens the poet's vision. This avoidance of the idiot boy is unlike the avoidance in the very first line of the poem: "Sheer over to the other side,—for see—/the boy straggling under those mimosas..." (118). At the end of the poem, the poet doesn't have to see the boy to avoid him. The poet, after seeing the boy with the kite and the unpeeled can clapped to eye, has affirmed the limit of their relations, and now suggests that they are based on a complicated respect rather than on mere curiosity and embarrassment.

The poet refurbishes the boundary between himself and the boy. He makes it more sturdy by suggesting that his own curiosity sullies the idiot's beauty. Without looking at a boy who is "likely fumbling his sex," only hearing his voice lifted in song, the poet can respect the boy as a singer of songs, but also, by stating himself a trespasser, the poet affirms that the boy inhabits a subjectivity. The boy's stigmatized subject position is not, as is the usual action of stigma, vacated. The song somehow endows him with an interior and therefore a personal exterior. This is more than a version of "good fences make good neighbors" though. The poem ends by transferring the shame that initially seemed to belong to the boy to the portrait artist himself. Early versions of this poem were entitled, "The Idiot Boy," and the removal of specification in the later version gently suggests that the poet may be "the idiot" figure, that term given a more vernacular pitch.

The poem ends because the thematics of the poem declare it necessary. The first line directs the reader's gaze "—for see—" and the final line breaks the speaker's sight line. However, the reader who has been directed to see is still loose in the scene, and the closure marks a separation of speaker/pointer and listener/watcher. The time line of the poem creates some difficulty for the reader. The poem started out in the present, the reader being shown the subject of the poem from a distance. The speaker then, with that scene in mind and perhaps in the visual field, tells about two scenes where he saw the boy, one being laughed at and the other alone playing with a kite. Finally, the speaker tells how, since hearing the boy sing, he cannot stare at him. However, while the poet cannot look at the boy without feeling like he is trespassing, he has just pointed the boy out to his companion/the reader as they moved to avoid the boy "straggling under those mimosas."

One could imagine this set up as a clever "My Last Duchess" moment, in which the speaker gives something away about himself, but I think, considering the thematics, it is not the mere assertion of a vexed or untrustworthy monologist. Instead, the distance between the speaker and the listener reenacts the boundary making between the speaker and the boy. The speaker does not wholly conscript the reader to his shadow's glow. The reader does not occupy the same position as the speaker, though they share a place in time. When the speaker looks away, it does not enforce a looking away for the reader. Paradoxically, the speaker must present what he has decided to look away from to his interlocutor in order that he or she may come to a similar ethical stance. The poem suggests that witnessing, and even more, that being a model witness, a guide, is ethically vexed.

The closure of this poem, which is in fact the close of an aperture, is laden with complex considerations of subjectivity and closure. In order to respect the difference of the idiot boy, the speaker declares that he must listen but must not look. However, his walking companion and interlocutor must himself trespass in order to come to a similar ethical stance. Trespassing is not indicted outright. It is, this poem suggests, a necessary step toward the constitution of other subjectivities as special, respected, and self-determined.

V. "Moment Fugue": Sound's Limit

One almost schematic example of Crane's use of resolved and unresolved patterns to explore thematics of disconnected- and unfinishedness is the late poem "Moment Fugue," which was posthumously included in the

Key West group of poems. The poem was, in its time, and probably still is considered too difficult to make full-blown sense of. Crane, having sent this poem to Jessica North at *Poetry,* received a note from her saying that she could not paraphrase let alone diagram the poem's sentences; to be utterly clear, she included her humorous attempts with her flat rejection of the poem. The very title of this poem, however, hints at the charged intersection of bifurcated meanings that do not tidily line up. Interestingly, for a poem that is about immiscibles coexisting, this poem has two *diametrically opposed* versions that are available. The first appearance of "Moment Fugue" was in *transition* in 1929, where the final line read "Beyond the roses that the flesh can pass," but the version found in the folder from which the *Key West* poems were taken after Crane's death, and that appears in Marc Simon's version of the *Complete Poems,* reads "Beyond the roses that no flesh can pass." I will utilize the second version because it is the later one, but also, as I will show, it is more successful in completing the poem's sonic patterns as well as developing the poem's thematics.

The poem engages two meanings of "fugue": one the musical term describing a polyphonic composition and the other a psychiatric term meaning a state of psychological amnesia during which a patient seems to act rationally and consciously, but when the fugue ends the patient remembers nothing. The poem describes the fugue of a syphilitic "selling violets" with a *fugue,* various voices (in the musical sense), coming and going. This structure works by dragging meaning and sound across the apparently impenetrable borders of the unit of the sentence.

MOMENT FUGUE

The syphilitic selling violets calmly
        and daisies
By the subway news-stand knows
        how hyacinths

This April morning offers
        hurriedly
In bunches sorted freshly—
        and bestows
On every purchaser
           (of heaven perhaps)
His eyes—
        like crutches hurtled against glass
Fall mute and sudden (dealing change
for lilies)

Beyond the roses that no flesh can pass.
(*Complete Poems* 129)[11]

The first stanza reads jerkily but has a subject, the syphilitic, and a lan-
guorously posing harem of verbs and objects: selling violets and daisies,
knows how hyacinths. ... This is a stanza posed as a sentence fragment
gone poetic; its colloquial counterpart might read: "The syphilitic
who is calmly selling daisies and violets by the subway knows how
hyacinths ..." The next moment, when what the syphilitic knows will be
revealed, is held off by a stanza break that seems like a clever setup for
the loud, dropping hammer of wisdom.

It is not difficult for a reader who has understood the first stanza's
convolutions to make sense of "how hyacinths / This April morning ..."
will do something. However, the verb "offers" sends the plural subject,
hyacinths, hurtling off these syntactical tracks. The subject is suddenly,
again, the syphilitic. It is he that this April morning offers. Or—it is he
that knows that, and perhaps what, "this April morning" offers. Either
way, there is a strange displacement of the agency of the subject. That
is, either the syntax holds off reporting the identity of the subject or
the speaker enacts the fuguing subject's own displacement of self into his
temporal location. Uncannily, then, the fuguing man knows how the
morning offers flowers through his own *person* though he as a *personality* is absent. This dual possibility creates dissonance beyond the mere
jerkiness of the lines. Within either, or both, of the above possibilities
the stanza shift jerks the reader back to the syphilitic, drives him as the
subject through the stanza, and then lets the poem's mind wander off
even to the edges of heaven. Let us drift as deep as parentheses and as
far away as the tab key allows.

Then with the shift from second to third stanza, again a verb is
snatched from our expectations. Between the first and second we had
the subject of a verb kidnapped and now, between the second and third,
the object goes from the expected flowers to the eyes of the syphilitic.
Finally, a shift occurs from his eyes as object of what the syphilitic
bestows to the eyes as subject of the verb "fall" and as the only travelers
who can pass beyond the roses. The poem occurs all in one sentence,
but utilizes the reader's expectation of the stanza as sentence to fracture
syntax breathtakingly.

The effect of this constant break for correction places the reader inside
and outside the poem at the same time. Thus, these different voices, or
rather, more correctly, strands that take up stanza to stanza in different
registers, serve to enact the fugue on/in the reader. The apparent sense

of the poem is strung on the madness of the subject's body that always reasserts itself as the axis of any sense the poem's syntax might make. First and most simply the syphilitic asserts himself as the subject of most of the verbs. The syphilitic is the fractured subject of "knows," "offers," and "bestows." But more powerfully, his is the voice of the disjuncture the reader struggles to follow, until the poem stops at the mystery of the syphilitic's vision. The sick man travels in his thoughts marvelously, or madly, and the undisjunct, the reader whose body and flesh most of the time may pass as deeply interconnected, cannot pass with the syphilitic's vision. The final and most touching moment of this poem is its respect and awe of the bifurcated, of that which the poem imitates but does not claim to be. This imitation as effect thus becomes a respectful approach to another person, one suffering in a certain way, and the results are small but palpable disturbances on the tissue of meaning and not that fire blanket of understanding so often uselessly thrown on the gloriously burning. The syntactical disruption makes the reading of this poem a feat of familiarity. One gets used to the breaks, becomes fond of the breaks, melts at the breaks. They become both the desire to include the syphilitic in the compassionate poetic vision but also define the boundaries of such a vision.

The sonic effects of the first two stanzas, repeating insistently slanted internal rhymes, do thematic work while also setting up a pattern against which the final stanza's short, sharp shock of an end, the impassable glass/pass rhyme, is set as counterpoint.[12] At a different level of patterning, the sonic and syntactic serve as two voices of a fugue for this poem. The sonic wending its way at times in alignment with the syntactic and at times playing against it, but finally coming into utter accord to end the fugue.

In the first version of this poem, the one published in *transition,* the final line suggests that "the flesh" can pass "the roses" but the eyes and spirit cannot. Roses register as actual flowers as well as emblems for syphilis. These roses, the implication is, the flesh can pass. Conversely, the syphilitic roses are impassable: They are themselves the flesh. Also, the idea that the passersby are flesh and the vendor is all eyes or all spirit and desire during his fugue serves as an effective final touch to the scene, if the relation between syphilitic and public is a distant one. The latter version, "that no flesh can pass," is sonically better; it does not have the flaccid "the" modifying "flesh" and clogging the line. Thematically, this version suggests a reach of vision that the flesh cannot share. Vision, whether actual, because the vendor is paralyzed in place, or metaphorical, that his imagination travels to magnificent but close-by beyonds that are immaterial, exceeds the syphilitic's physical agency.

VI. Heeding the Negative: "Havana Rose"

In "Moment Fugue," Crane shows vision and sound colliding to forcibly cauterize a closure, just as in "The Idiot" sound, most particularly singing, interrogates, and at the close, shuts down the act of looking at the idiot boy. "The Idiot" presents a largely thematic treatment of the relation between the two while "Moment Fugue"'s thematic of the relation between sight and sound are mostly submerged in the syntactic and unannounced sonic activities of the poem.

The close of each poem serves as the mimetic closure of a subjectivity: The syphilitic passes no further, and the poet is shamed out of further looking or "trespassing." Each lyric is closed off in the relation of its elements just as the subjectivities it considers are closed off. Such carefully wrapped lyrics, ending in the immorality or impossibility of further interrogation of a subjectivity, succeed better the more spectacularly they fail. Their cumulative effect is that of resignation in the face of impassable borders, but a resignation that is tightly controlled and a forfeit that is not lightly conceded. The craft of each poem is making the resignation significant; the more significant the more respectful to the subject of the lyric.

A late and incomplete prose poem, "Havana Rose," distills Crane's theorizing on the limits of "pattern's mastery" over other subjectivities in a virtuoso stream of consciousness. He also furthers the consideration of the rose as a figure for the passages and blockages between flesh and spirit featured at the close of "Moment Fugue." The poem begins with the poet at his desk, "Let us strip the desk for action—" and descends through all the swirling details of a "night in Vera Cruz" in an attempt to fully present the statement made by an American doctor to the poet "during the wait over dinner." The poem ends in a quotation, a method of closure we examined with "The Wine Menagerie," but here the quotation is firmly held in place by the scenic details, and its utterer, the doctor, is fully, if fitfully, introduced. Similar to "The Wine Menagerie," this final quotation introduces new and central terms to the poem as well as offering a glimpse of the farthest reach of those terms. Crane suggests that the doctor is a "rare poet" in his relation to typhus.

> Poets may not be doctors, but doctors are rare
> poets when roses leap like rats—and too,
> when rats make rose nozzles of pink death around
> white teeth ...

The system of symbols that is illness and its mobility makes the doctor a master of metaphor. Having given the doctor's credentials,

Crane reports the advice he himself was given by this other "poet" of the flesh.

> And during the wait over dinner at La Diana,
> the Doctor had said—who was American also—
> "You cannot heed the negative—, so might go on
> to undeserved doom ... must therefore loose yourself
> within a pattern's mastery that you can conceive, that
> you can yield to—by which also you
> win and gain that mastery and happiness which
> is your own from birth." (*Complete Poems* 201)

This advice seems almost inscrutable without heeding the comparison between doctor and poet that Crane proposes in the stanza/paragraph before this one.

A critic with a simple take on the relation of Crane's death to his poetics, best illustrated by Joseph Riddel's collapse of exhaustion from the poetic into the biographical register, might read this poem as the advice Crane understood but could not take. He failed to "heed the negative" in the proper way, seeking to foreground its operations in an attempt at transcendence and thus sending himself to an "undeserved doom." I propose however, that the advice presented by Crane as the jewel in the crown of this poem, as *the* "Havana Rose," is precisely what Crane did heed in his poetics, avoiding a different "undeserved doom" than his suicide. The doom this doctor/poet thematizes has everything to do with the contagion he studies and has been a victim of which had "engaged / him once before to death's beyond and back again / —antagonistic wills—into immunity" (200). Undergoing typhus, the doctor had won immunity, but his advice is to avoid such operations when the contagion is not well understood. Mysteriously, and with an edgy causality, "Tact, / horsemanship, courage were germicides to him."

"Those metaphysics which are typhoid plus" entail contracting a disease to escape it. The "plus" stands for "more than typhoid" but also for "the presence of typhoid." This metaphysics suggests that there is a way into immunity through contagion; however, the doctor advises against such a path in favor of "loos[ing] yourself / within a pattern's mastery that you can conceive, that / you can yield to ..."(201). The doctor suggests that his experience with typhoid is a warning rather that a model. A pattern that one "can yield to" is a pattern that does not utilize absolute negation, that is, death, as its horizon. Instead, the doctor suggests that the poet use another horizon to stand in for this one. This poem is all about the mobility and contagion of metaphor: The rose of typhus turns to the rose of rats' mouths, which turn to the blooming rose of advice. As I have been suggesting in the readings of poems above, for Crane that horizon is the subjectivity of others, not his own obliteration. In both "The Idiot" and "Moment Fugue," Crane yields to the limits of his witnessing.

VII. Unlaced: "Enrich My Resignation"

In the poems I have discussed so far, Crane exposes the limits of witnessing the subjectivities of others as this witnessing intersects, interacts, and interlaces with poetic closure. In a poem composed in the fall of 1929 and considered a fragment by some and a finished poem by others, Crane confronts the limits of witnessing his own subjectivity.[13] "Enrich My Resignation" begins with the eponymous undirected command: "Enrich my resignation as I usurp those far / Feints of control—" (*Complete Poems [1958]* 148). This line seems to be a command requesting or demanding that some powerful being give meaning to a moment of resignation. This could be "*prophet's pledge / Prayer of pariah [or] lover's cry,*" but the first stanza very quickly moves from any plausible scene in which the command is issued to a dissociated, uninhabitable landscape with full audio.

> Enrich my resignation as I usurp those far
> Feints of control—hear rifles blown out on the stag
> Below the aeroplane—and see the fox's brush
> Whisk silently beneath the red hill's crag,
> Extinction stirred on either side
> Because love wonders, keeps a certain mirth.—

The voice of command present in "enrich" transfers to "hear" and "see." The poem seems to be exhorting a witness to "enrich a resignation" by being a witness. However, the relation of the command of the first two lines, the scene of the third, fourth, and fifth, and the final line's summation is not transparent. The witness, whether the poet himself or a companion, is never given a firm foothold in the poem. The commands "hear" and "see" indicate a position but the poem does not provide anything to define that position relationally or spatially.

The rifle and aeroplane scene sets up a number of relationships: hunters to stag, rifle noise to aeroplane noise, sight of whisking brush and sound of whisking brush, and, finally, a mysterious relation between two different kinds of extinction in "Extinction stirred on either side." Also, a very distinct chiasmus arises: An axis of above (plane) and below (hunting scene) crosses an axis created by the fired rifle, in front (stag) and behind (hunter).

The second, and final, stanza begins with another command except this time it is aimed at "centuries," ("Die, oh, centuries, die ...") and then shifts to a declarative statement of presence, a declaration of "now," ("It is the moment, now, when ..."). This poem is difficult because there is no immediately available central strand around which other strands can twine themselves. It is missing a manifest organizing principle or schema that would provide a before and after or a here and elsewhere. Because of this, each shift of tone seems only to accrue haphazardly, offering no reason for the shifts and no principle of sequentiality. The tone shifts from command, to description, to comment, to command, to comment. Each shift of scene, though this happens increasingly less discretely and less often in the poem, has the same disconnecting effect. The poem begins unmoored to place, offers a scene as an example or effect, then shifts with the second stanza to an interior scene of contemplation and interior alteration.

> Die, oh, centuries, die, as Dionysus said,
> Yet live in all my resignation.
> It is the moment, now, when all
> The heartstrings spring, unlaced—
> Here is the peace of the fathers.

The call for the death of centuries likely stems from Nietzsche's exploration of the categories of artistic production he calls Dionysian and Apollonian in his *The Birth of Tragedy.* Crane discusses his view of Nietzsche in a short 1918 essay entitled, "The Case Against Nietzsche," published in *The Pagan,* in which he defends Nietzsche against charges of "Prussianism." The reference is loose however and seems most to tap the chaotic energy of the figure of Dionysus as a figure for self-shattering and order-shattering in general. This self-shattering is large enough to feel as if it is taking history, or centuries, with it in its dissolution. However, the second line of this stanza suggests that that dissolution will index the centuries which have dissolved with it and thus make the centuries live on, though transformed.

Crane explores a similar transformation, frankly based on anal sex, in the third section of his famous six-sectioned poem, "Voyages" (1923). The first section of this poem, originally entitled "Poster," warns its intrapoetic "kids" playing on the beach that the sea, while apparently offering a playground similar to its sandy rim, accoutered with "shells and sticks," is crueler than it appears. "The bottom of the sea is cruel," this section closes, declaring at once Crane's interest in the deep ambivalence of the sea's power but also in "bottoms," the unseen depths where violence and transformation lurk. The second section of "Voyages" declares that, despite the ocean's violence, it is the best figure for presenting "the wrapt inflections of our love" (*Complete Poems* 35). "Our love" here points to a particular love between the poet and a specific beloved, but also, in the presence of so much figural grandness, to gay male love in general. The sea's "rimless floods [and] unfettered leewardings" spell "dark confessions" that are perfectly in tune with the secrecy and excess that Crane attributes to gay bonds and sex. The poet notes how the sea's "turning shoulders wind the hours," and how "sleep, death, desire, / Close round one instant in one floating flower." "Turning shoulders" is a motion quite possibly preceding anal sex. "Floating flower," then, concatenates the spectral (unlocalizable because unseen) effects and actual appearance of the anus. Both of these images show the poet trying his hand at describing homosexual love and sex in the figural language of the sea. These figures take so firmly that, in the next section, anal sex becomes the figure through which the sea is described.

The third section of "Voyages," thus prepared for, turns more toward the frank utilization of the figure of the sea to express the poet's love. The sea has "tendered" the theme of the lover to him, that is, both is the tender, or imagistic currency, through which the exchange of affection occurs, but also, the sea's terms make the love attachment tender, in the sense a bruise is tender but also in the sense that a loving touch is tender. One of the most impressive effects of this poem, throughout, as seen here in the splash of the verb "tendered," is its expansiveness of meaning, and I do not mean to flatten its difficult effects. As Thomas Yingling has noted, "Voyages" is "perhaps the most insistently difficult text in a difficult corpus" (*Crane* 93). My reading does not seek to bring its full breadth and heft into account, but instead, to bring out the specific ways in which this poem parallels and prefigures "Enrich My Resignation" in its treatment of anal sex. The most lucid and extended treatment happens in the second stanza of this third section:

> And so, admitted through black swollen gates
> That must arrest all distance otherwise,—
> Past whirling pillars and lithe pediments,
> Light wrestling there incessantly with light,
> Star kissing star through wave on wave unto
> Your body rocking!
>   and where death, if shed,
> Presumes no carnage, but this single change,—

> Upon the steep floor flung from dawn to dawn
> The silken skilled transmemberment of song;
>
> Permit me voyage, love, into your hands ... (36)

The "black swollen gates," "whirling pillars" and "lithe pediments," as Thomas Yingling notes, figure the anus as a cosmological threshold. He writes: "The threshold image, surely subterranean and supernatural, an anal rather than a vaginal harbor for masculine desire, turns the lover's body into a cosmos ... Here the homosexual body becomes a trope for the ordered universe, for identity ... and—perhaps most significantly— for immortality ..." (97). Here, as I will explore in "Enrich My Resignation," anal sex offers a site for the passage through death, in which death is "shed" and "presumes no carnage." The orgasm is well known as a "little death," but even more cogently, the loosening of con- striction through rocking, itself, independent of orgasm, offers a pro- gressively greater breach in the anally penetrated subject. This death is the death of the subject as contained in a cosmology becoming instead a cosmology all its own with a "steep floor flung from dawn to dawn."

This shift of subject embedded in a world to a world embedded in a subject mimes a felt moment of anal penetration. An outward radiation of waves and kissing of stars goes a long way in describing the flush of anal involvement spreading to include, and perhaps, occlude, the entire body. A breach of bodily boundary, through anal penetration, can lead to two changes in bodily state: what might be called an anal orgasm, which transforms and rearranges the feeling body, and the better-known and more often-described genital orgasm.

With the doubly breached anal cosmology of "Voyages" in mind, we can ground "Enrich My Resignation" in a scene by reading "resignation" as the dropping of bodily resistance against both bodily and fantasmatic penetration. The speaker's resignation, or experience of anal penetration, is supplemented or enriched by orgasm, a second kind of self-shattering or bodily breach. The scene that follows the initial self-command or what can now be read as a kind of playful plea to a partner takes place on two sides of a "red hill," with an interaction between closeness and farness. *This* side of the body, the genital, and *that* side, the anal.

The fantasmatics of the body in this poem depend on the unplace- able nature of the scenic material. The rifles are loud, as is the aeroplane, but the "fox's brush" is silent, problematizing the position of the witness in the poem. Where would one have to be to hear the rifles and the aero- plane and see but not hear the fox's brush whisk? The witness, he who is calling out for enrichment in this fantasized scene, could be in the "aeroplane" hearing the rifle shots and seeing the brush whisk in the scene unfolding far below or on the ground, but too far away from the stag's fall to hear the brush whisk. It is impossible to tell which, and that is a centrally important effect of the poem. The witness has evaporated into the scene of phallic thrust, plane and discharging rifle, and wounds, crags, and dead stags.

After setting out this scene in which the witness is unplaceable, Crane makes a point of emphasizing the either/or element of the scene. The "either side" of the commentary on the scene of aeroplane, rifle, and stag, on a literal level, refers to the fact that the sound and size of the aeroplane outdoes and drowns out, "tops" if you will, the rifle, and the rifle subordinates the stag. But the "either side" does not stick very well to that shifty scene, because there are several sides, not just two, as well as ups and downs; this undecidability leads the "either sidedness" to shunt back to the body of the speaker, to either side of his body, a scene more easily imagined and closer to home. The "extinction stirred on either side" can then be the orgasms that occur on either side of the "red hill's crag." "Love's mirth" refers back to the initial command, indicating the strangeness of the situation in which the more a bottom resigns, lets go, or loosens up, the more control he has over the outcome, as it were, of the process.

At the end of the second stanza, the yearning of the first two lines of the poem has transformed to a tonal and thematic completion. One way of, so to speak, lacing up this poem is to work with its meaning backwards, since it declares that it comes to a point, to a "now" and a "here" at its close. Some complete motion has taken place in the poem; it has gotten from a there to a here, from tension to tension-release, from a diffuse to a very, very exact sense of space and time, and from motion to stillness. The "now" is offered by the placement of a moment of displacement, or "unlac[ing]," and the "here" is offered somehow in consequence. Being penetrated offers the emotional and somatic disorder that marks a moment by difference: Now I am unlaced; further, the orgasm that follows from the completeness of that displacement replaces the self in a "here." The space and time that were unraveled figurally, by the blockage of a witnessable stance, and thematically, by calling for the dissolution of history, return by a different route.

The 1929 figure of "heartstrings ... unlaced" recalls Portapovitch's decade-earlier "sandals, danced undone" and the more contemporary "undone" shame of "Reply." I have discussed how in "To Portapovitch (of the Ballet Russe)" these undone sandals index the dance performance that undid them, suggesting by poetic mimesis that lyric performances can undo themselves to completion. The sandals are the final image and the final paradoxical movement of the poem. In "Enrich My Resignation," Crane suggests that the undoing of dance, lyric, and here, sexual performances, can close not merely by leaving a remainder of their own ephemerality, but can also react to that remainder within their own borders. The scene of anal sex offers a new way to figure incompletion, exhaustion, and resignation as closure. In this poem, closure is split in two in two different registers: anal and genital and temporal and spatial. Both registers are up for grabs throughout the body of the poem and the body of the speaker. Tension reduction, "the peace of the fathers," no less, can follow the "peace" of exhaustion. Crane splits the moment and spatiality of the sandals and shows how physical condensation can accompany a temporal condensation.

"The peace of the fathers" gestures to a transhistorical sense of completion that in its reference to "the fathers" suggests a calm in reproductive continuation. There is a barb, or ironic upshot, in the linkage of "the fathers" to an orgasm following anal penetration by which Crane suggests that this feeling following orgasm during penetration was well known throughout history, even by "the fathers." More powerful, however, in this image, is the contradiction of the urge to kill "centuries" that lead up the stanza. The pre-orgasmic, still tied-up heartstrings yearn for the unraveling of history while the post-orgasmic, untied heartstrings are content with revivifying the feeling, "the peace," of the ancestors. This marks the motion of dead centuries "liv[ing] on in all my resignation" and is indeed the enrichment of the resignation staged in the penultimate lines of the poem.

This poem stages transcendence, the term so often invoked to depict Crane a failure, within its own borders. The poem fulfills its own ambitions by staging two dissolutions of the self, two different sorts of shatterings, that follow one upon the other, the second surpassing the first, and accrue past dissolution to placement in time, in space, and in an ancestral chain. The final, orgasmic dissolution dissolves the self into a fantasmatic history of feeling, showing exhaustion to be a place of its own, not simply an absence of life force or enthusiasm. The self, twice jostled by way of anal and genital orgasm, relaxes finally into "peace" that places the speaker in a barely specified but powerfully referential genealogy.

For Crane, as for each of the poets I have discussed, closure acts as an aperture: opening up ways of inhabiting subject positions, sites of authorial presence, and as a queer conduit through which influence and genealogy flow.[14] Endings are the preludes to absence but as such reinvigorate notions of presence, and when taken in hand poetically, can dialectically take a reader through absence, to not simply notions, but to felt realities, of revitalization and resurrection.

Chapter 7

⌒

The End of the Line: Spicer in Love

I. A Difficult Poet

John Ashbery and Jack Spicer were born in 1927 and 1925 respectively. They were contemporaries associated with opposite coasts: Ashbery with the New York School and Spicer with the San Francisco Renaissance. Spicer was contemptuous of Ashbery; he called Ashbery a "faggot poet" and pronounced the title of Ashbery's first book, *Some Trees,* "Thumb twees" (Ellingham and Killian 65).[1] Robin Blaser remarked that, "Jack made Ashbery's work symbolic of everything he disliked…" (75). Spicer's contempt is a complicated mix of jealousy, homophobia, and political critique. Spicer was a different, less effete brand of homosexual and more out than Ashbery in his poetic persona. But, as I will argue below, Spicer's dislike of Ashbery may have more to do with their similarities than their differences.

I treat Spicer after Ashbery because, although he died in 1965, Spicer's national career only really got started in 1975 with the posthumous publication of his *Collected Books.* However, I do not treat Spicer as post-Ashbery in any way; further, it is unlikely that Ashbery read very much Spicer during Spicer's lifetime. Spicer made a point of printing little and keeping what he did print within the confines of California. Both poets did appear in Donald Allen's influential anthology, *The New American Poetry 1945–1960,* but seem to have no other real connection beside this proximity.

Spicer is a difficult poet on several counts, only a few of which intersect with Ashbery's difficulty. Spicer was, first of all, a difficult person. He was needy, lonely, unkempt, drunk, and at times extraordinarily cruel. He insisted on absolute loyalty from his friends and followers and when he didn't get it, or felt he didn't, as in the famous case of Robert Duncan, the offending party was banished from the Spicer circle.[2] Spicer's personal difficulty translates into a number of other difficulties that impact the dissemination and reception of his poetry directly. He made no attempt to court the larger poetry world; rather, he seized opportunities to alienate important poets in public settings. At a reading Duncan arranged in Mill Valley in honor of Denise Levertov and Helen Adam, Spicer read the poem "For Joe," from *Admonitions,* which is, at the very least, complicated in its relation to misogyny.[3] The poem begins, "People who don't like the smell of faggot vomit / Will never understand why men don't like women ..." (*Collected Books* 62). The poem shortly after shrilly proclaims: "The female genital organ is hideous ...." Immediately then, the harsh tone softens. There is a change from aggression to conciliatoriness: "Forgive us. Give us / A single example of the fact that nature is imperfect." The poem is not misogynist in any uncomplicated way: It ascribes both perfection and hideousness to the female genital organ. Clearly, however, the sarcastic or sincere (or both) plea for forgiveness for the statement and the ensuing complicating paradox (perfection as hideous) were, at the reading in Mill Valley, and perhaps are in any reading, lost in the shock of the attention-grabbing misogynist outburst. Both women in whose honor the event was being held, and many others present, were offended.[4]

Spicer's attitude about the larger poetry world, it must be said, was not just crankiness. He had real complaints about the poetry that the national magazines were printing and about the goals of contemporary poets. "Today," he writes in 1949, "we would rather publish poetry in a little magazine than read it in a large hall" (*One Night Stand* 92). He wanted poetry to be less precious and polite and thought that it had lost its audience because it no longer cared about gripping or entertaining. The fallout from Spicer's reading of "For Joe" proves very revealing about the polite mood of the poetry scene. No one shouted Spicer down or even chided him. Levertov did however write a powerful poem, "Hypocrite Women," in response to Spicer's reading. I do not wish to excuse Spicer's bad politics as poetic incitement, but in this case his outburst did work as such.

In an interview many years later Levertov complicates things further. She recalls that the Mill Valley reading, "was ... my first exposure to homosexual males as a group—I had, & have continued to have, individual homosexual friends but I find homosexual males & lesbians uncongenial in groups, when they reinforce each other's sexism towards heterosexuals" (Ellingham and Killian 126). Homosexual males may have showed badly that day in Mill Valley, but the added homophobic snipe about *lesbians* in groups is unrelated; it is also, well, misogynist.

No matter how complicated the Mill Valley event was, Spicer showed up as an offensive troublemaker and otherwise congenially inclined poets such as James Broughton avoided Spicer because of just such unpredictable behavior and random acts of verbal cruelty (127). Spicer's orneriness affected his publishing career in some more obvious and close to home ways. In one case, he treated people at the Auerhahn Press so badly that they "printed two copies of *The Heads of the Town Up to the Aether* on the pink sheets that divide reams of paper, without title, colophon or illustrations."[5] This was, according to Andrew Hoyem, " 'in revenge against Spicer's bitchiness' " (Hazelwood 47).[6] So, due to his principals, bad behavior, and bad reputation, Spicer's poetry, until at least 1975, was difficult to find at all.

Once found, Spicer helps make it difficult to take a critical stance on any of his individual poems. He disowned his work written before *After Lorca* (1957) because, before this book, he treated poems as single objects without relation to other poems. In a letter to Blaser that Spicer included in his 1958 collection *Admonitions,* he writes: "There is really no single poem .... That is why all my stuff from the past ... looks foul to me. The poems belong nowhere. They are one night stands filled (the best of them) with their own emotions, but pointing nowhere, as meaningless as sex in a Turkish bath" (*Collected Books* 61). A paragraph later he writes: "Poems should echo and reecho against each other. They should create resonances. They cannot live alone any more than we can." Critics have snatched this morsel out of Spicer's oeuvre as evidence that one ought not "close read" Spicer's work. The tidbit supports claims that his work is about the serial poem or about the immediate community he was building while reading his poetry aloud or discussing it in North Beach bars.

However, I see no reason to interpret sex in a Turkish bath, or a one-night stand, as meaningless, nor as evidence of aloneness. In fact, for some gay men acts of anonymous sex seem exemplary episodes in resonant series, creating concurrently a sense of community. Spicer treats being part of the San Francisco gay sex scene as "being alone," in contradistinction to being "in a relationship with one other person." These are not the only two options; Spicer's own practice of creating tight circles of friends proves this.[7] Friendship can mitigate aloneness without inspiring or creating couples. Similarly, sex has often served as the glue that holds certain gay communities together. A Turkish bath seems a strong figure for the resonance of poems (individuals) within a "serial poem" (communal space/community).

Poets, literary history has shown, can produce amazing poetry based on shaky theories. Spicer himself, in a 1955 letter to Robert Duncan, made a distinction between William Carlos Williams's poetic products and Williams's theories of poetry. Spicer writes that Williams's theory of poetic language is wrong, but that the poetry he produces using the theory is quite good. "... [T]he stress patterns of the spoken language ... are simply not the patterns of any poem in it, never have been, and never will be. This is why Williams' theory, as I understand it, is wrong. He tries to take as a unit what is a unit in conversation but *isn't* in poetry. The results are marvelous, but the theory stinks" (*Acts* 18).

Another difficulty Spicer experienced, which translates into the slow surfacing of his poetry, was that he was very openly gay. When Donald Allen introduces *One Night Stand & Other Poems,* a collection of Spicer's early work, he immediately, and slightly awkwardly, writes, "From the first [they met in 1948] he struck me as being the most vividly original gay man I'd ever encountered anywhere" (xxix). It must be recalled that the poetry scene around this time was hostile to declarations of homosexuality. In 1944, Robert Duncan came out in the magazine *Politics,* which spurred John Crowe Ransom to reject an already accepted poem from the *Kenyon Review.* From the beginning of his career Spicer did not hold back. He celebrated being a citizen of Sodom in one poem (1955), published a prose poem featuring a section entitled "Homosexuality and Marxism" (1963?),[8] and wrote another prose poem addressing Walt Whitman, telling him, "Forgive me, Walt Whitman, you whose fine mouth has sucked the cock of the heart of the country for fifty years ... You are sucking the cock of a heart that has the clap" (undated) (*One Night Stand* 65; 81–2; 88). Each of these poems, as these brief notices suggest, includes a very open consideration of the politics of nationality and homosexuality.

Nor did Spicer shy away from homosexual themes in his first large-scale public appearance. He published a poem in the influential Donald Allen anthology *The New American Poetry, 1945–1960,* "Imaginary Elegies I–IV," which concludes with a homoerotic rewriting of the eleventh section of "Song of Myself," where boys' groins are lovingly imagined pressing into the warm cement around a pool (*One Night Stand* 146). This poem was favorably reviewed by Marianne Moore, who included her review in *A Marianne Moore Reader* and "thus at least two lines of Jack's work sneaked their way into unsuspecting library shelves all over the country" (Ellingham and Killian 148).[9]

The political act that had the most immediate material consequences in Spicer's life, however, was his refusal to sign "an oath of loyalty to the constitution with specific anticommunist provisions" that the Regents

of the University of California were requiring faculty to sign in 1950
(32).[10] Spicer was a researcher for the Linguistics Department at
Berkeley, which was an important center of gravity for Spicer's early
poetic community. It provided him a place to hold workshops—until
the English Department determined that the poetry workshops in
Wheeler Hall were too gay—and, equally crucial, his affiliation with
Berkeley provided him with library privileges. Spicer's refusal to sign the
Loyalty Oath amounted to "professional suicide" and "expulsion from
his Berkeley paradise." He moved to Minneapolis for a job at the
University of Minnesota where no Loyalty Oath was required and spent
two miserable years there "long[ing] to return to California" (33; 38).

In terms of Spicer's place in gay politics and history, it is important
to mention that he was an early member of the Mattachine Society,
one of the earliest political organizations focused on homosexual rights
(46). Robin Blaser reports, "Jack really did a great deal with the
Mattachine ... attending meetings, organizing them and so on, for well
over a year. He took an activist position in it. As far as I know, he never
hid that aspect of himself" (49).

However more "out" Spicer was in his poetic persona than Ashbery—
always addressing very clearly defined male beloveds, and describing
male beauty with obvious sexual intent—his homosexuality is still part
of his difficulty. Homosexual meaning does not have to be teased out of
his poems, but being homosexual itself creates difficulties in meaning
making. The main difficulty is being cut off from the general, or as some
poets and critics would have it, "the universal," or "wisdom," which in
heteronormative culture are the elected officials of a tradition based on
reproduction as transcendence. Spicer did not fit into a great list of
"begats." He would beget no one—his poetry had to beget for him—
and it was equally crucial to know who begat his poetry.

This accounts for Spicer's preoccupation with poetry as subject matter. Poetry is the place where his continuity and connection to larger systems of meaning happens. Thus, his first book is in dialogue with the
dead Lorca, his second attempts to create poetic community by addressing his living friends individually in poems "for" each one of them,
his third consists of lyrics to music that has not been composed, and
his fourth is a long love poem to Billy the Kid. Each of these books is
centered on the search for interlocution and starts by declaring its
impossibility. Even the poems to living friends are "admonitions," or
disciplinary statements attempting to correct what friends have done or
gotten wrong. By naming them such, and by having so many of them,
Spicer takes the gale wind out of the sail of any particular advice or
admonitions he might voice. He writes a "Fake Novel about Arthur

Rimbaud," and his last book, *Book of Magazine Verse,* consists of poems written for venues that Spicer assumes (rightly) would not accept them. All of these missed connections are meant to bring missed connection to the fore. Spicer must forge new kinds of connections, across the line between life and death and between dephysicalized poets as they exist on the page; thus, his preoccupation with mediumistic writing and his (sometimes literal) love affair with the apocryphal. Spicer's poems are attempts to dwell in the impossible since connection with a tradition modeled on biological reproduction is barred him.

Spicer wrote that he saw being homosexual as "essentially being alone" (*One Night Stand* 88). For him, aloneness is at the center of both poetry and sex as well as at their intersection. In his "Fake Novel about the Life of Arthur Rimbaud," the middle of the three-sectioned *The Heads of the Town,* Spicer asks Rimbaud, " 'What is the reason for this novel? Why does it go on so long? Why doesn't it give me even a lover?' / 'On the page,' Rimbaud said" (*Collected Books* 163–4). Poetry, for Spicer, is essentially, "how we dead men write to each other" (*Collected Books* 34). "Dead" here means physically dead in some cases (Rimbaud, Lorca, Whitman, Crane, and those who speak through the poet in the process of dictation), but more to the point, dead means absolutely absent in time and place.

The poet must be dead to be a poet, that is, must accept utter alienation from real people, including his own real self, in order for his poetry to be pure.[11] "Loneliness," Spicer writes to the dead Lorca, "is necessary for pure poetry" (*Collected Books* 48). I do not wish to harp on Spicer's various theories of poetry, because, as I suggest above, although they always prove interesting, they never quite take as a complete system. In fact, they are *about* incompletion and not taking. Spicer's poetry, for all it discusses poetry, is poetry first and poetics only second. One can easily see how a poetry that performs missed connections cannot always be relied on for statements about its own activities. His poems enlist the words with which we discuss poetry and make points about language and its functioning. However, they are not important for their always contentious content; they are important for their performances as poems.

Spicer puts it best when he argues about the inclusion of the language of criticism in poetry in the form of a letter to Joe Dunn on the first page of *Admonitions.*[12] Spicer says that at one point he thought that including "notes on particular poems" in books was a "confession that the poems were totally inadequate ... the terrestrial mechanics of criticism belong[ing] to the garage or stable rather than to the Muse" (*Collected Books* 55). However, he came to the conclusion that the Muses "are not afraid to dirty their hands with explications," but that explications are only secondary.

The Muses "are patient with truth and commentary as long as it doesn't get into the poem ... they whisper (if you let yourself really hear them), 'Talk all you want, baby, but *then* let's go to bed.' " Poetry has to do with effects, erotics, and magic, not theories of language, though theories of language, he suggests, are not unwelcome.

All of Spicer's talk about rejecting the single poem is important to take into consideration, but does not, as most critics of his work have let it, prohibit the treatment of single poems as they act on the reader. That is, Spicer's critical notions have gotten in the way of reading the effects of his poems because critics feel chastened (or some of them self-righteously reassured), by Spicer's own critical commentary within his poems. A critic as astute as Peter Gizzi comments that:

> Thinking and writing about Jack Spicer is not unlike a Grail search. His statements are mercurial, and his lines refuse to be pinned down into a stable system of meaning. His poems repeatedly disrupt even their own procedures by jamming the frequencies of meaning they set up. All these conditions make their discovery and placement in critical terms not impossible but beside the point. Like the Grail, what Spicer's work accomplishes is not any declared goal but the assembling of a community of peers for a specific and unified purpose. (xxiv)

While I do agree that community is an important term in Spicer's work, I *strongly* disagree that Spicer's work ought not be treated as words on a page, open to a community beyond the one that he worked so assiduously to gather around him during his lifetime. Gizzi, along with the otherwise astute critic Michael Davidson, would, I think, cheat Spicer's technique, jamming or jibing, of the close attention it deserves.

The living poems, as they were spoken by Spicer in bars in North Beach, are gone. We have no access to them except through tales told by his peers and friends. I, for one, prefer the poems on the page to the biography, the tales of bar talk, and the histories of alliances and fallings out, which more often then not impose a more oppressive teleology on Spicer's work than any critical apparatus could. Sometimes friends speculate what Spicer was thinking about Duncan, or the war, or his "impending" doom, as if they knew what his motives were and as if he knew when he was going to die. Spicer's poems are both verbal performances and written texts. And since we have them as written texts we must treat them as such.

Without single poems, or units, to analyze in their development and performances, critics end up discussing Spicer's theory of language or poetry. These are indeed a *part* of Spicer's poetry and effects. He invites the reader to think categorically about what happens in his poems and in poems in general, in his language and in language in general, but this theorizing is not the *only* thing that makes his poetry vibrant. Spicer's theories, for me, pale in comparison to the linguistic performances of his individual poems, let alone his resonant groups of poems. I prefer him in bed rather than in the garage. In the rest of this chapter, I will read poems for their effect as units before I read them as resonating within series. The effects of single units, as I will show, are crucial to the development of larger movements in Spicer's poetry.

II. No One Listens to Poetry

Throughout his career, Spicer uses closural techniques similar to those I have already discussed in Ashbery's work, but the two poets seem to have come across these techniques independently—on opposite coasts and in very different poetic environs. Ashbery's open closures, as I have described them, occur on the level of deictics, address and tonal shifts, and innuendo, while Spicer's are consistently based on puns and the malleability of line breaks. These two poets, sharing a common genealogy of American poets: Whitman, Crane, and Moore, particularly, wound up with similar closural innovations at the center of their very different poetics and poetry.

The leading, untitled poem of Spicer's book *Language* (1964) concludes with the ubiquitously quoted sentence, "... No / One listens to poetry" (*Collected Books* 217). The poem, consisting of a single stanza, heads "Thing Language," the first of seven sections, and seems to act as an introduction to the book as a whole. It begins:

> This ocean, humiliating in its disguises
> Tougher than anything.
> No one listens to poetry. The ocean
> Does not mean to be listened to....

The ocean and poetry are held in uneasy proximity. The initial deictic, "this," indicates either that the speaker is in the actual (presumably Pacific) ocean's presence at the inception of the poem and/or that the "ocean" is standing in for language or poetry. The poem never wholly separates the "real" ocean from the ocean as metaphorical figure. From the very first word, the reader faces the slipperiness of things in proximity. Dyads fuse into single items and then just as quickly and mysteriously split in two again.

The first line break—following "This ocean, humiliating in its disguises"—due to the absence of a verb in the second line, "Tougher than anything," retroactively takes on the quality of a bold-faced colon. The break marks a thoughtful decisiveness. This first line break and fragmentary sentence sets the tone for the rest of the poem in which punctuation, syntactical units, and line breaks are plastic. In the next line, the poem stridently proclaims that the ocean's crashing or ebbing is meaningless:[13]

> … A drop
> Or crash of water. It means
> Nothing.
> It
> Is bread and butter
> Pepper and salt. The death
> That young men hope for …

The ocean, containing both "drop" and "crash," is double in its constitution like "bread and butter" or "pepper and salt." The noise of the ocean—constant, deafening—produces its own reception. So many signals at such volume can only be received as meaningless. A fourth, internally doubled, term: "The death / That young men hope for," completes the list of doubled things—after salt and pepper and bread and butter—that go together constitutionally. These nouns, joined by "and," are conventional couples. The death that young men hope for is then a combination of separate items that are incomplete without one another. Heroism, the height of individual expression and life, and death, the end of individual expression, go together like these other pairs of *things*. By making drop and crash, bread and butter, salt and pepper, and the death that young men hope for into a series, Spicer suggests that doubleness—importance and irrelevance—reside inside heroism. Moreover, this doubleness suggests that poetry, the ostensible subject of the poem, is also at once important and irrelevant.

This completion of the series of couples is followed by a return to the ocean:

> … Aimlessly
> It pounds the shore. White and aimless signals. No
> One listens to poetry.

The final sentence, as a repetition of an unbroken sentence in the third line, calls attention to itself. It is unceasingly quoted by critics to show

Spicer's despair at the state of the reception of his poetry. The repetition nails the point, and its attendant despair, home.

However, I read the final line differently. Instead of just being "white and aimless signals," the line breaks in this poem produce progressively more resistant enjambments.[14] The meaning of the final lines entirely changes when they are read, repeating the heavy line break that precedes it ("Aimlessly / It pounds…"), with a strong break between "No" and "One listens to poetry." "No one listens to poetry," becomes "No. One *listens* to poetry." The final line break holds the mood and aim of this poem in the balance. It is another dyad that peels apart and sticks together. This resembles Ashbery's experiments with the doubling of meaning at a closure to contain fully activated contradictions. It also resembles Ashbery's closural technique as I have treated it in "The Grapevine," "Fairies' Song," and "Or in My Throat," by being *at once* cry of despair and defiant assertion of viability. The poem, if the last line break is left doubled, transforms the third line's: "No one listens to poetry." The poem has made the reader "listen to poetry," because the change in the last line break only fully grips if the reader follows the patterns (the progressive peeling apart of dyads and the progressively stiff enjambments) that lead up to it.

Elsewhere, Spicer uses the same sort of line break after "no" to insert purposeful and controlled ambiguity into a poem. "For Russ," in *Admonitions,* is clearly a love poem to Russell Fitzgerald, but a love poem that has two distinct vectors. "For Russ" begins by declaring exasperation in the face of the complexities of love:

> Christ
> You'd think it would all be
> Pretty simple
> This tree will never grow. This bush
> Has no branches. No
> I love you. Yet. (*Collected Books* 57)

Even though the tree never grows and the bush has no branches and there is not a declaration of love, an "I love you," the poem continues, concluding, "… Yet. / I wonder how our mouths will look in twenty five [sic] years / When we say yet." On its drill-through-to-the-end reading, "For Russ" makes sense as a love poem that suggests that although nothing seems to be flourishing in the way that it ought to around love—there has not been an "I love you" spoken yet—the amorous connection between the author and his beloved will last twenty-five years. The poet is so in love that he loves even the idea of waiting for a declaration of love.

Alternately, the line break after "No" might be read as having a full stop, like the full unpunctuated stop at the line break two lines before between "Pretty simple" and "This tree will never grow...." The polyvalence of the line break after "No" serves as a pivot. If the lines are read "No. I love you," the valence of the "yets" changes dramatically. If "I love you" is a proclamation by the speaker rather than some phrase that does not get uttered by the beloved, the "Yet" that follows it qualifies the declaration rather than qualifying the lack of declaration.

This love poem has two very different love poems in it. One proclaims that even without all the obvious markers of love, the poet will love his beloved into the conditional future with a measure of wistfulness. The other love poem says that even though there are not outward declarations of their love, the poet continues to hope for them and will continue hoping for even a quarter of a century. The first version celebrates love's ability to overcome adverse conditions; the second highlights the conditions imposed on love's celebration.

III. The Deep Leaves

Spicer's book *Language* begins and ends with poems that use the same closural technique. I have already discussed how the first poem in the book uses its final line break to torque the lines "No / One listens to poetry" into polyvalence. Similarly, the final poem creates an unresolvable contradiction at its closure utilizing the, by mid-century, conventional plasticity of the line break in lyric poetry. The prominent placement of this effect indicates that line breaks and closure are highly charged locations of resonating meaning both within single poems and between poems in *Language*. However, if we are prevented from reading Spicer's poetry as it operates on the level of *lyric units,* these resonances would be damped. The critical notions swirling around Spicer's work that argue against treating his poems as lyric units might be distilled to three particularly strong trends. I categorize them as the "series over lyric," the "poetry as *communitas*," and the "rejection of closure" arguments. The first argument is adopted by almost all critics of Spicer. They quote his "there is no single poem" letter to Blaser from *Admonitions,* which I quoted above, and the case is closed. A reader, according to this argument, is misguided in seeking the effects of single poems, because right there in one of his books of poetry Spicer tells us that he is only interested in larger chunks of meaning. The second trend, which I have already discussed as most evident in the criticism of Peter Gizzi and Michael Davidson, undervalues Spicer's poetry as it lives on the page and overvalues it as it was used by Spicer to create a community. The idea that Spicer used poetry to create community is important, but not exclusive. Spicer had his eyes on his forbears and his future readers, I contend, as much as he did on his friends sitting in front of him at Gino & Carlo's.

The final approach, what I am calling the "rejection of closure" argument, borrows its name from Lyn Hejinien's influential essay, "The Rejection of Closure." This approach, most evident in the critical works of poet/critics associated with the Language School, suggests that poetic closure has to do with a poem's closedness to the "vast and overwhelming" world. Closure is exemplified by "the coercive, epiphanic mode . . . with its pretension to universality and its tendency to cast the poet as guardian to Truth" (41). A poem ought be open, Hejinien argues, because "each moment [is] under enormous vertical and horizontal pressure of information, potent with ambiguity, meaning-full, unfixed, and certainly incomplete." She gives the example of a poem that is open: A poet winds up a watch and starts writing a poem that is complete when the watch stops. Even if I wished to read someone's fourteen (or however many) hour ramble, I would describe the product as a meditative poem, not a lyric. This objection is second to another more pressing objection: Where the poet stops may be random in the process of composition, but will inevitably be read as a way to organize what came before it. Thus, meditative poem or lyric, the stopwatch experiment produces closure without the poet's consent. This experiment may reveal something interesting about contingency in poetry, but does not challenge the fact that a reader will give special significance to the end of a poem in her piecing together of its patterns.

Lyric closure is a formal aspect of any lyric, and as such, I argue, it can be resisted, thwarted, played with, but not rejected. A lyric poem cannot, just as an abstract painting cannot, preclude a reader or viewer's response to it *as a unit.* The end of a lyric effects what comes before it and, as soon as the end provides a starting point for the reader's backward hypothesizing about the poem as a whole, there is closure. Closure is indeed a function of the lyric's boundedness; however, it does not hold off ambiguity or the pressures of a chaotic world. In fact, I've argued that for a genealogy of poets that begins with Whitman, closure is precisely the entry point for chaos, ambiguity, and the "pressure of the world." Closure is not something to embrace or reject, it is constitutive of the lyric; it is that which produces the lyric as a *unit.*[15]

Each one of the critical approaches I treat above would prevent the very resonance across the series that all of the positions claim central to Spicer's poetics. As I have been reading the poems, some of the strongest effects in Spicer's work are the way he creates stubborn polyvalence at his closures; without lyric units there would be no closure and with no closure, no polyvalence.[16]

Language's final poem closes with a polyvalent gesture recognizable from the first poem in the book. The poem ends:

> The earth quakes. John F. Kennedy is assassinated. The dark forest of
>   words lets in some light from its branches. Mocking them, the deep leaves
> The time leaves us
> Words, loves. (*Collected Books* 243)

On the most cursory reading, the final lines parse: "time leaves us words and loves," that is, time offers us these two spheres of activity, whatever else it takes away. However, if the "deep leaves" are read not as nouns that mean the leaves of the trees but rather as "terrible abandonments," the final two lines read as a series of *things* that are *the* deep abandonments that mock the little spurts of light flitting through the branches above us. With these meanings in play, the final lines might parse: "Mocking the light that sometimes makes it through the canopy of dark, time leaves us, words leave us, and love leaves us." This reading is certainly more in line with Spicer's general views on the betrayal of words and love. As he puts it elsewhere: "words / turn mysteriously against those who use them," and "[h]omosexuality is essentially being alone" (*Collected Books* 125; *One Night Stand* 88). Still, the initial and easiest way to read the last lines of *Language* linger in any meaning we can bring to the lines. A syntax remains in which hope is appropriate.

This poem, number 10 in the section entitled "Graphemics," begins "Love is not mocked whatever use you put to it. Words are also not mocked" (*Collected Books* 243). The poem goes on to claim that the "soup of real turtles"—not, one supposes, that of "mock turtles"—flows through the poet's veins. This poem ends with the "deep leaves" (as I've been reading it: "heartbreaking abandonments") that mock the realness of an earthquake or a political assassination. The poem itself suggests that the spaciousness of the diphthong in the word "poet" causes both earthquake and assassination.

> Being a [poet] a disyllable in a world of monosyllables. Awakened by the
>   distance between the [o] and the [e]
> The earth quakes. John F. Kennedy is assassinated. The dark forest of
>   words lets in some light from its branches.
> (*Collected Books* 243; brackets in original)

The earthquake and assassination are real world events brought on by the absence of sound between an "o" and an "e" in the word "poet." This is the sort of significant absence I have been highlighting at Spicer's line breaks. Headline reality is mocked by Spicer's magico-poetic causality. The real world, represented by two major events, is both correspondent to nothing because language is a system of represented absences, but also, the losses that occur in this "real world" leave us with the losses that then make language possible and necessary. Time, loves, and words leave us. They abandon us, but their absence also leaves us in a third, arboritory sense: They cover us and feed us.

Throughout the book *Language,* Spicer makes declaratory statements about John F. Kennedy's assassination. Toward the beginning of the sequence, a section of "Thing Language" concludes with the frank: "This is a poem about the death of John F. Kennedy" (221). Later in the sequence, "Shot / In the back by an arrow, President Kennedy seemed to stiffen for a moment before he assumed his place in history" (229). Further on, at the end of a poem that seems more about Halloween than JFK, the poet insists that "This / Is another poem about the death of John F. Kennedy" (239). These final lines are meant to be hypothesized backward, an activity spurred by closures in general. However, there is simply no way to make the bulk of this or any of the other poems I've quoted fit the slim theme of John F. Kennedy's assassination.

The assertiveness of the assassination as a theme without any content to shore it up is so glaring that it must either be enjoyed and then dismissed as a prank or taken seriously as a comment on the notion of thematics itself. These two options are of course not mutually exclusive, as little is in Spicer. Spicer's feints, jokes, and difficulty are precisely the material that critical terms might serve to illumine. The mention of John F. Kennedy's assassination throughout *Language* is the kind of jamming that Peter Gizzi discussed as not benefiting from exegesis, but I see these assertions as inviting, in fact, *insisting* on exegetical work. *Because* they are not true, or rather, because no case can be made that they are *particularly* true, these statements must be incitements. Incitements to listen closer, to bristle, or possibly, to respond. Spicer, a poet whose poems are constantly preoccupied with poetics, and whose theories critics can't spend enough time discussing, without ever discussing the fact that the poetics are disclosed as poetry, is playing with the very notion of intention and thematics. This game might trouble critics who take each of Spicer's utterances about poetry, in poem, letter, or lecture form, at face value. If nothing else, the not-being-about-JFK's-assassination strand of the book *Language* is a challenge to Spicer's readers *not* to listen to him. This is the sort of technique that I discussed in Whitman's "Calamus" poems, in which the poet dismisses the reader, only to continue his poem, assuming that the reader is still reading. Spicer challenges his reader *not* to listen. Don't listen *to* the poetry. Instead, perhaps, let the poetry act. But, of course, in order to let the poetry act one must listen quite closely. Similar to the reuse of the "No"–line break combination, Spicer utilizes a pun–line break combination to produce effects of doubling a closure against itself in a much earlier poem. Spicer's early, long poem, "Imaginary Elegies," is one of the only poems he wished saved from his pre-*After Lorca* period. The six-part poem is a meditation on God, the imagination, the place of the poet, and the problem of closure. The first four sections of "Imaginary Elegies" were written over a five-year period and proved to Spicer, as he repeats three times in Section IV, that, "In these five years in what I spent and earned: / Time does not finish a poem" (*One Night Stand* 50).

In 1959, the last two sections, V and VI, were appended. Section IV, occupied throughout with closure, concludes with the question: "But does it end?" It answers: "The birds are still in flight. Believe the birds" (51). The poet ought trust that the poem remains suspended in time as the birds are suspended in flight. Five years later, however, Spicer believes differently. In Section V, the birds he was telling himself to believe are ripping out Prometheus's liver. Spicer stagily enunciates the fire thief's name as "Pro-me-thee-us." He was pro, or for, the progression from me to thee to us. The birds, though they proved a correct figure for poetic closure because the poem remained suspended for five years after its ostensible completion, are hell when they land. Rather than being satisfied with the flight of birds as a figure for suspension in poetry, the final two sections of this poem suggest that any figure the poet musters can turn on him. The tight metaphorical relation of landscape to poetry has given way as the elements of the metaphor grow beaks, eyes, and a taste for liver.

In the sixth and final section of "Imaginary Elegies," a suddenly appearing Alice from *Alice in Wonderland* has drunk the potion that told her to drink it and has grown "27 feet tall." She can no longer escape through the "little window" through which she entered the room. The poem goes on to liken Alice's situation to that of the poet who is offered a poem that says: "Drink me. I'll find a substitute / For all your long- / Ing" (54). The potion makes good on its promise, but only by making any fulfillment of longing physically impossible. Alice (and the poet) cannot get out of the room/poem. The poet is stuck, and thus his longing has been substituted by tragedy or a sense of fate. The poem then closes:

> And that little door with all those wheels in it
> Be-
> > Leave in it
> Like God.

The commands "Be / like God" and "Believe the birds" that close sections III and IV have combined to become "Be- / Leave in it / Like God." The poet's final command has changed from a more-or-less straightforward piece of advice to a doubled simile doubled by a pun. The two similes are that the reader ought "believe" in this door that leads to the outside of the poem like one believes in God and that the reader ought to concurrently "be" and "leave" in one's situation like God is in His situation. The similes are each doubled by the pun on "believe." Neither sonic "Believe" nor graphic "Be-Leave" take the fore; they are equally active and indicate ambivalence at the center of both belief and being.

This poem ends in a knot that cannot be untied, or, as Spicer writes elsewhere, the poem ends with "The grand concord of what / Does not stoop to definition" (*Collected Books* 69). The splay of meaning takes the reader to the heart of a territory of puzzlement. In a sense, we are "27 feet tall" and stuck in the poem, like Alice. There isn't a way out, even though we are at the "end" of the poem. While this closure does not provide a "substitute for all [our] long- / Ing" it does provide a structure by which we can stave off definition and achieve concord without longing for a single definitive meaning to close the poem (*One Night Stand* 54).

The combination of being and leaving is also the state of the ghost. Ghosts haunt all of Spicer's poetry. Either the immaterial becomes material, as in his theory of dictation in which he receives poems from spirits, or the material becomes immaterial, as when the poet turns into text or the reader becomes "involved" in poetry ("the reader of this novel is a ghost. Involved" (*Collected Books* 167). These are deeply Whitmanic concerns. The content of the "Be-Leave" knot is more attuned to "Calamus" than to the poetry of Ashbery; while the knot itself suggests that Ashbery and Spicer were in the same scout troop. While Ashbery and Spicer share the technique by which their closures splay to a number of discrete strands, Spicer and Whitman share the desire to have poetry muddy the line between the material and immaterial and the living and dead.

IV. It Walks In

Earlier I discussed how Spicer and the critics who follow his lead make it difficult to write about individual poems as lyric poems rather than pieces of larger, serial poems. However, in the serial poem "A Textbook of Poetry," Spicer explicitly insists we read one particular section as a lyric. "A Textbook of Poetry" is the final piece of Spicer's impressive three-part book *The Heads of the Town Up to the Aether* (1960–61). "A Textbook" is entirely written in prose paragraphs, except for Section 17, whose final one-line stanza commands, "Imagine this as lyric poetry" (*Collected Books* 177). This line insists that the reader consider Section 17 itself as a lyric poem but also as illuminative of lyric poetry in general. The poem itself consists of six stanzas, three in lines and three in prose. The first stanza reads:

> —A human love object is untrue.
> Screw you.
> —A divine love object is unfair
> Define the air
> It walks in.

The dashes heading the first and third lines of this stanza indicate spokenness; in addition, the second dash seems to indicate the shift to a new speaker. The tonal shift between the first two lines indicates an address shift and presents two speakers in conflict. After this clear-cut conflict, though, it becomes unclear which line is spoken by which speaker. The difficulty of the poem is largely figuring out how to assign the lines to the voices.

The first stanza can be read as the beginning of an argument between a human and a divine subject. The divine subject starts the poem and then is rebuffed and called unfair by the human subject. After which, the divine subject challenges the human subject to define unfairness in a divine context. The implication of the last two lines of the first stanza, spoken by the divine interlocutor, is that a human cannot define the air the divine object walks in, let alone whether its actions are fair or unfair. All of this, of course, can be figured as the relation of a lover to his beloved—the lover being the human party and the beloved, the divine.

Another reading of this poem pays closer attention to the end punctuation, so that any period marks the end of a speech by a particular voice. The first two lines would remain as I have read them above, but the material after the second dash would all be spoken by the human subject, or lover. The command to define the air would then be an unanswerable challenge to the divine speaking subject. The divine love object is unfair, the human voice complains, because it does not follow human rules. The qualities "untrueness" and "unfairness" are perfectly lined up with the human and the divine. The human can only be false to its past or words while the divine has the power to bend the rules. Neither of the readings I've offered is entirely satisfactory. This first stanza requires material from further along in the poem to provide the patterns and context with which to read them satisfyingly.

The poem continues with two prose stanzas:

> The old human argument goes on with the rhymes to show that it still goes on. A stiffening in time as puns are a stiffening in meaning.

> The old human argument that goes ahead with our clothes off or our clothes on. Even when we are talking of ghosts.

The argument in the first stanza then is not an argument with gods or God in the mythical or Biblical senses, it is "the old human argument." The voice that intrudes with "Screw you" is that of a beloved accused of being unfaithful. The speaker of this prose is very familiar from the rest of the prose in "The Textbook." He is at once personable, pedagogic, and vatic.

The third stanza—"clothes off or on"—locates and dislocates the argument of the first stanza of the poem. The arguing voices belong to specific lovers, in and out of bed, talking about this and that; however, along with the "we" of "when we are talking of ghosts," the "we" is also humans in general. The third stanza also carries the slight suggestion that the lovers might be ghosts. "Even when we are talking of ghosts" the "old human argument goes on." That is, even when we are talking about love affairs with ghosts, the affairs adhere to the rules of human love affairs. The general or particular lovers in the first stanza could one or both be ghosts. We can be talking, this stanza argues, about sexual relations with or between ghosts and remain within the context and discourse of a "human" love relationship.

The poem then amplifies this slight rumble about ghosts by demonstrating how one can have sexual, or other material, relations with immaterial beings. The next two stanzas are in lines again and are largely a repetition of the first stanza split apart and bereft of a period. The rest of the poem reads:

> —A human love object is untrue.
> Screw you
>
> —A divine love object is unfair
> Define the air
> It walks in.
>
> Imagine this as lyric poetry.

The rhymes (untrue/you; unfair/air) in this repetition are stiffer than in the first stanza. The mention of rhymes stiffening time in the first prose paragraph (second stanza of the poem) makes the reader notice the containing effect of end rhymes, and thus accentuates the effect in the stanzas that follow. This stiffness leads to firm couplets, which then leaves the third line of the penultimate stanza—"It walks in"—dangling off on its own. In these stanzas, unlike in the first stanza of the poem, final punctuation does not hold one voice from the next. The absence of a period after "Screw you" means that, in this reiteration, line breaks can do the work of keeping one voice from another. Line breaks are, as I've remarked, stiffer.

The lines "—A human love object is untrue. / Screw you" here read much the same as the accusation and response they repeat from the beginning of the poem. The lines that follow these, however, change due to the stiffer breaks and the introduction of a "ghost" thematic. Instead of two voices in argument, or one voice making a statement and then issuing a challenge, this stanza can be read as a statement, a command, and then the report of an event. That is, a voice complains that "A divine love object is unfair"; it is instructed to "Define the air"; and consequently, the divine love object "walks in." The poem has materialized a ghost by defining "the air / It walks in."

The final line of the poem, in the voice of the pedagogue of the textbook, "Imagine this as lyric poetry," is powerful if the reader experiences the change "Define the air / It walks in" has undergone in the course of the poem. Lyric poetry is, in the language of this poem, "defining the air" and having the divine love object walk in. Magical materialization of a divine love object is the sign of a lyric's success. This is fundamentally a literary effect, but exceeds the literary. Somehow a ghost got into the machine. The ghost is there and is not. We can only maintain the ghost's presence as long as we "Be-Leave." The effect is fragile, and the ghost is whisked away by explanations like the one I've provided, but, strangely, the effect is very resilient; the ghost can be reinvoked whenever the lyric works as a lyric. When the undecidability of the penultimate stanza of this poem exists, the ghost exists. To materialize the ghost we need to decide not to decide on a single meaning.

Whitman's materialization of ghosts can be much more straightforward. In Section 11 of "Song of Myself," for instance, a young widow watches "Twenty-eight young men bathe by the shore" from behind the blinds of her "fine house by the rise of the bank" (*Leaves of Grass* 197). She is lonely and imagines herself into the midst of the young men. "Where are you off to, lady? for I see you, / You splash in the water there, yet stay stock still in your room." The bathers do not notice their new playmate, nor do they notice as "An unseen hand also pass'd over their bodies, / It descended tremblingly from their temples and ribs" (198). The horny widow "seizes fast" to the young bathers. Whitman ends the poem by foregrounding the perception of the young men; we are told what it is that they do not see. This final negation helps insert the widow deeper into the scene than she could insert herself through imaginary projection. Section 11 closes, "They do not know who puffs and declines with pendant and bending arch, / They do not think whom they souse with spray."

The young widow is similar to the divine love object. The surrounding, or air, around her is described, and suddenly, there she is. The poet uses his ability to rotate the optics of the poem in order to offer the young widow a space in the young men's company, although it is a space carved out by negatives. The reader, taken by reverie, and the gentleness with which the river scene is drawn, is taken down to the river in the words of the poem and has his shoulders turned back up toward the house by Whitman's sympathetic hands. The widow is in the river, grasping onto the young men, being splashed by them, while we are being grasped and turned by the poet. The young men do not see a ghost, only the reader and Whitman, those involved in the literary spell of presencing absences, do.

V. In Love

The "walking in" of the divine love object in Spicer's poem looks quite similar to Whitman's ghostly projection of the young widow. Elsewhere, however, Spicer makes it quite explicit that he would like to project *himself* through space and time. Such projection is "being like God" for Spicer.

Spicer's first significant book, *After Lorca,* orbits around the gravity and excellence of his translation of Lorca's "Ode to Walt Whitman." Lorca's poem deals mostly with his ambivalence about homosexual life in the real New York City in relation to the pastoral vision of gay life Whitman offered of it. Eric Keenaghan sees Spicer's translation of "Ode to Walt Whitman" as "assiduously reclaim[ing]" Whitman "as a contributor to a gay literary tradition" (283). Throughout the criticism of Spicer, it is often wondered whether Spicer was for or against Whitman's poetics or politics.[17] This is the wrong way to inquire into the relation between two intensely performance-oriented poets. Spicer was so involved in Whitman's poetry, historical position, and persona that there is no question of him holding a simple position in relation to "Whitman," the man, the ghost, the myth, the philosophy, the poet, the poetics, or the poetry.

Spicer makes this clear in a prose piece called, "Some Notes on Whitman for Allen Joyce" (*One Night Stand* 81). Here, he notes that he can still remember the "sweet and painful" world that Whitman "was reaching for . . . ." Spicer writes,

> . . . in his world roads go somewhere and you walk with someone whose hand you can hold. I remember. In my world roads only go up and down and you are lucky if you can hold on to the road or even know it is there.

Spicer is suggesting a very complicated relation with Whitman. Spicer had a glimpse of Whitman's "world" but "cruelty . . . severed your world from me, fouled your moon and ocean, threw me out of your bearded paradise. The comrade you are walking with suddenly twists your hand off." This is certainly not the acceptance or rejection of a poetics or a politics; Spicer is involved with Whitman's world in the same way that we as readers are "involved" in Rimbaud's life while reading a "fake novel" about it. Spicer has been thrown out of the paradise of "Calamus" where "you walk with someone's hand you can hold." Spicer concludes his brilliant rant:

> So when I dreamed of Calamus, as I often did when I touched you or put my hand upon your hand, it was not as of a possible world, but as a lost paradise. A land my father Adam drove me out of with the whip of shadow. In the last sense of the word—a fairy story. That is what I think about Calamus. That is what I think about your damned Calamus.

Whitman is an important forbear for Spicer. Spicer longs for company, a comrade in real life, but also, and as importantly, a genealogy in poetry. The problem with Calamus is that it is a fairy land where the poet, a fairy, cannot live. That is not to say that it cannot be visited. In fact, Spicer puts his hand on Whitman's, and Whitman is still active "sucking the cock" of a gonorrheal America. The vituperation of the last sentence is loaded with sadness, and loss, but all these minor chords are undertoned by a triumphant major insofar as this rant is *addressed to Whitman*. Further, Spicer puts his hand on Whitman's. Whitman is a present conversant of Spicer's even as Spicer is thrown out of Whitman's paradise. Or, perhaps, Whitman is a conversant of Spicer's *only as* he is being thrown out of Whitman's paradise.

The conversation with Whitman spans Spicer's career. Spicer performs the trick of the young widow of "Song of Myself" at the end of

Section III of "Imaginary Elegies." He writes himself into the presence of boys sunbathing.

> The boys above the swimming pool receive the sun.
> Their groins are pressed against the warm cement.
> They look as if they dream. As if their bodies dream.
> Rescue their bodies from the poisoned sun,
> Shelter the dreamers. They're like lobsters now
> Hot red and private as they dream.
> They dream about themselves.
> They dream of dreams about themselves.
> They dream they dream of dreams about themselves.
> Splash them with twilight like a wet bat.
> Unbind the dreamers.
> > > > Poet,
> Be like God.
> (*One Night Stand* 50)

Spicer gets into the scene by folding dreams into dreams. The boys dream about being dreamed about. Spicer imagines that he can use the landscape to "splash them with twilight" rather than have them "souse [him] with spray." If the poet can at once "rescue," "shelter," *and* "unbind" the dreamers, he can be like God. The lusty poet must maintain the erotic charge of the boys' privacy while removing them to his own imagined landscape. He wants, in a Promethean effort, to smuggle the spark of life into his poetry. As Spicer writes in a letter to Lorca:

> How easy it is in erotic musings or in the truer imagination of a dream to invent a beautiful boy. How difficult to take a boy in a blue bathing suit . . . and make him visible in a poem as a tree is visible, not as an image or picture but as something alive—caught forever in the structure of words. Live moons, live lemons, live boys in bathing suits. (*Collected Books* 34)

This materialization of something other than the poet in the poem is a step further than Whitman went in "Calamus." Spicer wants to materialize not just his own hand or his own presence for the reader, he wants to be able to conjure things that he, the poet, wants to touch. It is as if Keats's "living hand" that reaches out of his famous fragment were not waiting to be grabbed by the reader, but instead was doing the grabbing. In other words, Spicer doesn't just want his own real hands in his poems, he wants real hands he can hold as well. Whitman and Keats both settled for materializing themselves to the reader. Spicer yearns to materialize himself within the world in his poems, but acknowledges this longing to be impossible to satisfy. It can, however, be answered by substitution, as the "drink me" section at the end of "Imaginary Elegies" suggests. Spicer's central poetic insight is that impossibility is vulnerable to substitution, or shifts of register. Substitution gives Spicer a way not to satisfy, but to slake, his desire for *company*: specifically, the company of poets, a dead poets' society. It is as in Moore's poem "Marriage," in which Eve says: " '*I* should like to be alone.' " To this, "the visitor replies, / 'I should like to be alone; why not be alone together?' " (Moore, *Complete Poems* 62). Spicer's loneliness is not solved, but is doubled, and thus changed: Poets can be alone together.

He makes the point in the "Intermissions" section of *Language* that if a poet "dare" write poetry without the "taste of acid on his tongue" and "carries his dreams on his back like a packet," that

> Ghosts of other poets send him shame
> He will be alive (as they are dead)
> At the final picking. (*Collected Books* 231)

This conclusion to the last of three "Intermissions" suggests that a poet must first of all have pain or the memory of pain in order to write poetry without being shamed by poets past. Interestingly, though, the punishment for writing poetry untouched by pain is to be *alive* "At the final picking." This suggests that writing "real" poetry makes one dead: Further, it suggests that for a poet *qua* poet it is shameful *not to be dead.*

Maria Damon hints at what I am suggesting when she writes: "Spicer partakes of the gay tradition of bridging words, of revealing connection of the physical and the spiritual, and of constituting in his poetry, a gay community based on the work of gay forbears (Whitman, Lorca, Rimbaud, etc.) and a primarily gay readership comprised of his own friends and fellow poets" (*Dark End* 173).[18] Spicer's forbears are not only the basis of his real gay community; these dead poets *are* to a very large extent Spicer's queer community. *The poetry on the page* is the site of a connection of the physical and the spiritual. Rimbaud's reply to Spicer's complaints that his poetry does not even get him a lover—"on the page"—is instructive, not least because Spicer is being instructed by a dead poet on where to find a lover.

That poetry, like love, is something you can be "in" is a theme delicately explored in the poem "Ghost Song" in which Spicer plays incessantly with the in-ness of love and the in-ness of his ability to love. This translates to "The in /   ability to love" in which the "ability to love" is appositive to, as well as something cancelled by, "The in" (*Collected Books* 73). There's an in to love: It is about entrances but also about negations. Later in the poem, the point is driven home by repetition: "In love. In love. In love. The / In- /   ability . . . ." The hyphen here shows that the "in / ability" of the first line's "in /   ability to love" was not one word, but two. One must have the ability to be in to be in love. But if one has the ability to be in, paradoxically, the word "ability" flips over and negates itself. An inability in love is ability to love and ability, in love, is inability. Love, this poem argues, is only as powerful and present as its own negation.

GHOST SONG

The in
        ability to love
The inability
        to love
In love
        (like all the small animals went up the hill into the underbrush to
        escape from the goat and the bad tiger)
The inability
Inability
        (tell me why no white flame comes up from the earth when
        lightning strikes the twigs and the dry branches)
In love. In love. In love. The
In-
        ability
        (as if there were nothing left on the mountains but what nobody
        wanted to escape from)
(*Collected Books* 73)

The poem has three parentheticals that punctuate the different formations of in, ability, and love and that chart a diminishment of negation. The first parenthetical has animals running up a hill "to escape from the goat and the bad tiger," which represent the power of fear and repulsion—the negative—to motivate motion or emotion. The second parenthesis finds that lightning striking dry twigs and branches does not start a fire anymore and the third paints a mood- and landscape in which it is "as if there were nothing left on the mountains but what nobody wanted to escape from." This progression implies that the desire to escape is what makes being "in" of value. This poem is entitled "Ghost Song" because love, as Spicer explores it here, is particularly suited to ghosts. A ghost has an in-ability to love because it can have volition, "in love," but no action, "inability to love." A ghost cannot be "in" anything, it is immaterial and thus forever "out" of body. This inability is the ability to yearn as only those who are absolutely unable to have can. Those who want most, in both senses of want, are those who have nothing. This is a Barthesian or Proustian theory of desire: The beloved always evaporates in the approaching heat of the lover's adoration. Here however, the negative charge necessary for intense longing wears off as the lover approaches the delightful beloved and takes the fire and ire out of desire. The beloved, by this logic, is always immaterial. As Spicer writes elsewhere, "Nothingness is alive in the eyes of the beloved. He wears the clothes wherein he walks naked. He is fame.... He is what he is because he is never where he is" (*Collected Books* 172).

This state of affairs means that the beloved is most appropriate when dead or absolutely unavailable. However, Spicer understands that love ought to mitigate loneliness. This is why he likes to hang out, as a dead man, in the company of the dead. Spicer is always in proximity, as Damon suggests, to queer forbears. In fact, I would suggest that these queer forbears are always one sense in which we must read the ever present/absent figure of the beloved in Spicer's poems. The presence of these ghosts mitigates, but does not ameliorate, the "loneliness" that pervades Spicer's works, and actually makes his poetry, while sad, a body of love poetry to queer history.

VI. Love Poems

I will conclude by reading the "Love Poems" section of *Language* as directed at Spicer's queer predecessors, particularly Whitman. "Love Poems" has nine numbered sections that I will read as a developing series. That is, I will read the series as having an arc. The series starts at one place and gets to another. The closures I have examined to this point have utilized lyric mechanics to both assert a deep-felt loneliness and concurrently the possibility of mitigating that loneliness by literary means. The poems in "Love Poems" make specific connections of love, words, abandonment, presence, and a queer literary genealogy.

"Love Poems" begins by announcing the impossibility of "The touch / of your hands on my back." (*Collected Books* 225). Section 1 closes saying that "The Giants / Winning 93 games / Is as impossible / In spirit / As the grass we might walk on." This despairing swipe at Whitman's *Leaves of Grass* fits with Section 1's general mood of impossibility. "Calamus"-like love is impossible in reality. Reality, the grass we might walk on, is too real to be included in the poem. As Spicer examined in his letters to Lorca, real lemons, if they could be put into poems, would rot the way real lemons do. Similarly, real boys put into poems would age. The transference either way, from literary lovers to real lovers, or vice versa, is blocked.

Section 5 starts *in media res:*

> Which explains poetry. Distances
> Impossible to be measured or walked over. A band of faggots (fasces)
>   cannot be built into a log cabin in which all Western Civilization
>   can cower. And look at stars, and books, and other people's magic
>   diligently. (227)

The first line does not really attach to the section that precedes it. But "Which explains poetry" is repeated from the last line of the third section. In a sense, this section's first line signals that it is picking up the thought that concluded Section 3 and from which the speaker digressed in Section 4. Poetry is about distances and bands of faggots that cannot be constructed into a shelter for Western Culture. Instead, these faggots must find some different way to organize themselves besides as a useful building. Spicer quotes Einstein as saying that "Distance ... goes around in circles," and then comments that the "band of faggots" deal with the distance in some way that "is the opposite of a party or a social gathering." Distances bite their own tail. Thus, the distance in time and space between one queer poet and another queer poet is bridgeable, but exactly how this bridge looks is not clear. This model, Spicer complains, "does not give me much to go on."

Section 7 follows with an obsessive repetition of the words "heart" and "deer" in an almost nonsensical riff. It begins with the poet's statement that "I do not know where my heart is," but then states that his "heart" is in the mountains hunting a "deer" (228). Deer is simple code for "Hart" in the proximity of so many mentions of "hearts." In the sequence immediately preceding "Love Poems" Spicer describes himself as "Chaplinesque / As the fellow says" (224). "The fellow" is Hart Crane, who coined the term "Chaplinesque" in his poem of the same name (Crane, *Complete Poems* 11). Section 7 is a spell to summon Hart with words about a heart hunting a hart.

Section 8 explains, in Moorian cadence, that:

> There is real pain in not having you just as there is real pain in not having
>   poetry

Not totally in either case as solace, solution, end to all the minor tragedies
But, in either case (poetry or you)
As a bed-partner. (228)

Here it seems that the conjured Hart might be the "you." But the "you" is also a living person, the sight of whose "locked lips" sends the poet home "sweating." The "you" addressed in each section of "Love Poems" is clearly "the beloved," but the poet is making it clear that "the beloved" is a category that might fit a real, live person, or a dead Hart Crane, but which is most heavily a category of being. Having the real live beloved, or having poetry, as bed-partner would only be a temporary satisfaction.

"The beloved" does however firm up in the very last line of the last section. The final line reads:

I gave you my imaginary hand and you give me your imaginary hand and
    we walk together (in imagination) over the earthly ground. (229)

The poet has achieved a shift from the ground that he might walk on with his beloved being impossible, as it was in the first section, to it being "earthly" in the final section. I want to explain this transformation by the progressive coupling of the real beloved and the poetic beloved who come together in the figure of Walt Whitman. This final line is a direct reference to the final line of Hart Crane's "Cape Hatteras" section of *The Bridge*. "Cape Hatteras" ends with the spine-tingling presencing of Whitman:

>   yes, Walt,
> Afoot again, and onward without halt,—
> Not soon, nor suddenly,—no, never to let go
>   My hand
>   in yours,
>   Walt Whitman—
>
>   so—
>   (Crane, *Complete Poems* 84)

The summoned Crane summons Whitman. Spicer's closure stages his own dematerialization and the materialization, then dematerialization, of Whitman by reference to Crane. But these are not the only poetic presences haunting this closure. Marianne Moore presides over the proceedings with what is perhaps her most famous image, from the poem "Poetry," in which she writes that poems are "imaginary gardens with real toads in them." Spicer has reversed the imaginary/real axis of Moore's ideal poem and made the earth real and its inhabitants imaginary. In his first "Vancouver lecture," he suggests that one must complicate the "imaginary garden with real toads in it" definition of poetry. Poetry is, he says,

> about a lot more things than that. It's about the whole business of being able to go by the imagination into whatever other worlds there are, where the real toads can't eat the flies of the imaginary garden, and the imaginary garden doesn't even feel the step of the real toad. (Spicer, *Lectures* 31)

"Love Poems" closes by suggesting that Walt Whitman becomes, in the course of the series, *the* beloved behind the conventional "you" to whom the series, and the book *Language,* is addressed. The book begins with a poem ending with the active "No / One listens to poetry" and closes with the "deep leaves / That time leaves us / Words, loves." It is centrally concerned with how to bridge distances between both actual and literary lovers. The lovers are entirely "in" Spicer's "ability" to conjure a world and are most alive in the impassable closures of his poems in which their impossible possibility thrives in literary performances. The power of these "words" and "loves" comes from forbears who are only really listening while they are really being listened to. And, of course, vice versa.

Notes

Chapter 1   Snags and Gags: Cruising the Difficult

1. Vernon Shetley cleverly utilizes Steiner's typology to illuminate the resistance to and academicization of modernist difficulty in the introduction to his *After the Death of Poetry: Poet and Audience in Contemporary America* (7–10).
2. Mark Jarman's "The Curse of Discursiveness," a review of *Flow Chart* and several other books by other authors, is a stark example of the way what is perceived as tactical difficulty shifts critical weight from charging a poet with insincerity to charging his appreciative audience with being dupes. Jarman muses about what "must be going through an honest reader's mind" as he makes his way through *Flow Chart*. He then qualifies: "I say honest reader, because Ashbery has many dishonest readers. They are his admirers. They include anyone who claims that a poem like *Flow Chart* is not boring, not devoid of any subject except its own composition, and not finally unrereadable. By unrereadable I mean that, having read it once, I hope never to read it again. How can a poem do this to a reader, except by being bad?" (Jarman 158). The willful stupidity of Jarman's prose allows him to place himself as the pivot of "unreadability;" a belly flop from the particular to the general. Jarman ends his consideration of Ashbery by suggesting that it is a joke played on his "admirers," a word, here, inflected with homophobia. "I think that, unlike his admirers, Emperor Ashbery knows he is naked" (Ibid.).

Chapter 2   Rhetorical Suspense, Sexuality, and Death in Whitman's "Calamus" Poems

1. Hershel Parker takes issue with Helms's construction of "Live Oak" ("The Real" 145–60) and has printed what he maintains is the original "Live Oak, with Moss" in the *Norton Anthology of American Literature,* 4th ed. He upbraids Helms for reconstructing "Live Oak" from poems published later in "Calamus" and suggests that the real "Live Oak," the one that he repeatedly (almost obsessively) insists has no comma in its title and consists of earlier versions of "Calamus" poems. Even though textual evidence seems to be on Parker's side, his conclusions are even more suspect, and far more hasty, than Helms's. Instead of a tale of sadness, Parker reads the original "Live Oak" as a joy-bringing "manifesto." He writes: "It may have been through

sheer textual haplessness that [Helms] took a sequence that should have been liberating and explicated it as a sequence about victimization and oppression" (157). Parker reaches the shrill heights of accusing Helms of buckling under to current discourses of "victimhood," and actually harming gay youth by publishing his version of "Live Oak." "The text of 'Live Oak, with Moss' matters," Parker writes, "because so many Americans (and so many readers worldwide) look to Whitman not only for aesthetic pleasure but for guidance in living a sane and hopeful life" (159). The notion that the "right" version of "Live Oak" has some unequivocal relation to sanity and hope is at best strained. To his credit, Helms's eloquent response to Parker ("Commentary" 413–5) soundly defends his interpretive work as part of an ongoing project of criticism. Both critics, however, treat "Live Oak" as having a single affective upshot, as well as constituting a single narrative, each of which seems inappropriate to a sequence of poems. As I argue in my reading of the "Calamus" sequence, such a sequence cannot be boiled down to its narrative parts without losing its most characteristic qualities and effects.

2. Sedgwick uses "Walt Whitman as a figure to stand for the transition to our crystallized homosexual/homophobic world—not Whitman as he writes in America, but Whitman as he is read in England" (202). She observes: "photographs of Whitman, gifts of Whitman's books, specimens of his handwriting, news of Whitman, admiring references to 'Whitman' which seem to have functioned as badges of homosexual recognition, were the currency of a new community that saw itself created in Whitman's image" (206).

3. I am indebted to Judith Butler's discussion of "trouble" in her preface to *Gender Trouble* (ix–xi).

4. Yingling links the movement from imagining ages hence to a present touch to Crane's "Cape Hatteras," where the final stanza declares: "Recorders ages hence, they shall hear / In their own veins uncancelled thy sure tread" and proceeds to fantasize about walking hand in hand with Whitman himself: "My hand / in yours, / Walt Whitman— / so—" (*Hart Crane* 84). Yingling reads this, convincingly, as Crane's "literary coming out … no one had before claimed *Calamus* (and its 'Recorders Ages Hence,' alluded to above) as his master text" (211). This moment in Crane, and its connection to Whitman, is central to my treatment of Jack Spicer in Chapter 7.

5. My discussion of the comforting effects of "Calamus" must be considered in light of Michael Moon's discussions of the "corrosive rather than therapeutic" effects of Whitman's "Leaves," succinctly expressed in the double sense of "blades" as knife blades and blades of grass (*Disseminating* 166–7). This powerful ambivalence that runs throughout "Calamus" can be understood, I contend, as a constitutive feature of an overarching project to comfort. Whitman's comment that his poems will not "do good only, they will do as much evil, perhaps more" illuminates the way he imagines the import of his poems as of a higher order than good and evil (271). In a similar gesture, his poems will not *comfort only, they will do as much discomforting* on their way to a higher register of comfort, one that includes discomfort. That is, comfort in the face of death requires unpleasantness to be effective.

Unpleasantness and discomfort are crucial ingredients in Whitman's medicinal preparation.

An interesting treatment of Whitman's homosexuality and his relation to medicine, especially to the hospitals in the Civil War, can be found in Robert Davis's *Whitman and the Romance of Medicine*, where Davis argues that Civil War hospitals offered a place for the specularization, love, and care of male bodies that was impossible in a less liminal space. He makes the important observation that it was at this site that much of Whitman's poetics around the body, democracy, and homosexuality found literal and figural purchase.

6. Warner provides an apt phrase for this, "cultivated perversity on the metadiscursive level," which he illustrates with "Song for Occupations," in which Whitman's speaker "references the speech situation itself in a way that is manifestly wrong" (42). In "Whoever You Are," the speech situation per se is not wrong, or disjunct, but the relation between the speaker's command and his ensuing actions is wrong.

7. Yingling links Whitman's thematics and poetics of cruising to his text's continued "ability to seduce" and notes that Whitman, in writing about homosexuality at the time, is "not just writing what cannot be politely written of, but what in some sense cannot be written of at all because it does not yet exist." "His text continues to seduce," Yingling claims, "precisely by virtue of its namelessness, its uncertainty, its ability to entertain meanings not dependent upon fixed semiotic practices. Whitman's text demonstrates an uncanny homosexual ability to ... cruise its reader skillfully" ("Homosexuality" 143).

Chapter 3   Reports of Looting and Insane Buggery behind Altars: John Ashbery's Queer Poetics

1. Two examples that consider Ashbery as a love poet writing to a male lover but do not figure homophobia or the particularity of homosexual desire into their discussions are John Keeling's "The Moment Unravels" and Charles Altieri's "Ashbery as Love Poet." Altieri claims that in love poetry, "Demonstrating one's seriousness as a poet becomes inseparable from demonstrating a seriousness as a lover responsive to the ways in which the beloved leads the imagination beyond particulars" (31). While this may be a real concern with connecting to an audience, it squashes the particularity of gay desire into the particularity of the beloved. These particulars are not particular in the same way: While a poet may avoid merely describing the beloved in order to invite readers into his poem and make himself serious as a poet, we must note, for instance, that Ashbery as a love poet never proposes marriage or seeks to define or reflect his love through reproduction. These are cogent, central, and manifest particulars that cannot be brought "beyond particulars." Altieri proposes a fine way to teach Ashbery's poetry, and his approach is not hobbled by its lack of specificity, but more attention to just such particularities could only strengthen his readings. Keeling, on the other hand, while recognizing the beloved as male, recognizes nothing else in "Litany" that could make this observation interesting or worthy of attention.

He bludgeons the homoerotic scenes the poem offers into bland comments on the passage of time. For Keeling, acknowledging Ashbery's sexuality is just a step he makes in order not to be patently wrong.

2. Growing up gay does make it into her list of thematics a decade later when she reviewed *Flow Chart*, "A Steely Glitter Chasing Shadows."

3. Catherine Imbriglio makes the point in " 'Our Days Put on Such Reticence' " that with a living author one can never tell how much critical silence around homosexuality is the explicit or assumed wish of the author and how much is the function of cultural pressures (253). However, peeling the author's agency regarding self-representation from a general cultural silence about homosexuality seems too obviously to exonerate other critics. In the case of Vendler's criticism of *As We Know*, she ignores the gay thematics of the poems in this book. Even if this is at the behest of the author (which seems unlikely), it does not need to be blamed or excused, but simply corrected.

4. Cf. Sedgwick, *Epistemology* 1–63.

5. Cf. Edelman, *Homographesis* 3–23.

6. See Bersani, *Homos* 111–81, in which he examines the relation of the homosexual to society through the lens of an origin story about gay children feeling necessarily, in his telling, apart from any community from the outset.

7. Ashbery has explicitly addressed closure as a site of authorial strategy in the interview I discuss in Chapter 1, when he was asked whether he ever played a joke on his readers and he cited the last word of his collaboratively written novel *A Nest of Ninnies* (with James Schuyler).

8. In citations within the text I will refer to John Ashbery's books of poetry and prose as follows:

ATSWS—*And the Stars Were Shining*
AG—*April Galleons*
AWK—*As We Know*
CYHB—*Can You Hear, Bird?*
DDS—*The Double Dream of Spring*
FC—*Flow Chart*
HD   *Houseboat Days*
HL—*Hotel Lautréamont*
NN—*A Nest of Ninnies* (with James Schuyler)
RM—*Rivers and Mountains*
RS—*Reported Sightings: Art Chronicles 1957–1987*
ShTr—*Shadow Train*
ST—*Some Trees*
SPCM—*Self-Portrait in a Convex Mirror*
TCO—*The Tennis Court Oath*
TP—*Three Poems*
VN—*The Vermont Notebook*
W—*A Wave*

9. In his chapter "Homosexuality and the Matter of Style," Yingling makes a claim similar to Shoptaw's. He explores how gay writers have "often found

literature less a matter of self-expression and more a matter of coding: from Byron to John Ashbery, the consistent locus of parody in gay texts suggests a self-consciousness about what texts may and may not do" (25). I will suggest, taking Yingling and Shoptaw's insights as foundational but not complete, that in Ashbery, coding is not an end point: It serves to particularize gay experience and if not self-express at least self-locate. Coding does not just *not say* to avoid self-nominalization, but in Ashbery particularly, it *avoids saying* in order to declaw the violences of the nominalizing process, thus allowing new forms of identity and identification within gay self-nominalization.

10. For an example of a poem in which lyric movements are wholly based on address and that takes address as a thematic (tracing the theft of a guiding principle of address, an actual "lodestar"), see "The Mandrill on the Turnpike" (*And the Stars Were Shining* 5).

11. This "latticework" appears in many of Ashbery's poems, notably, "Blessing in Disguise," which I will discuss below, and "Litany," in which it stands for a physical but not visual barrier. Ashbery's use of the lattice never explicitly rounds out its imagistic importance: Besides being a barrier, it is also an arrangement of gaps meant to enable vines to climb. The lattice stands for horizontal difficulty but vertical ease and figures a particular effect Ashbery employs: simultaneous glimpses of light through a blockage and sinuous flow from absence to absence.

12. The observation of trees has echoes of the title poem of Ashbery's first book, *Some Trees,* which begins: "These are amazing: each / Joining a neighbor, as though speech / Were a still performance" (51). The way the bushy tops of trees join there figuralizes speech as performance. In "Blessing in Disguise," however, the light from between the speech-performances is at issue. The inexactness of performances in speech that "draw" the reader to the poet gets impacted because the "me" smashes into the plural: "to sing of me / Which are you." And the "remembering" that the speaker commands of himself collides with an uneasily externally directed command to "remember." In this poem, the trees, and their figure for performative speech, are upstaged by the light that comes from the gaps in their overlapping discourse.

Chapter 4   A Mirror at the End of a Long Corridor: Moore, Crane, Closure

1. Margaret Holley, in *The Poetry of Marianne Moore,* traces the influence of Crane's *The Bridge* on Moore's own 1966 poem about the Brooklyn Bridge, "Granite and Steel" (170–5). Interestingly, the loudest echo of Crane in this poem is not from *The Bridge* but instead from his later poem "Key West," published after his death in *Key West: An Island Sheaf,* appearing within his *Collected Works* in 1933. Here, bemoaning literal and figurative mining of the area, Crane ejaculates "O, steel and stone!" which splits into Moore's "O steel! O stone!" Crane's climactic cry of despair becomes Moore's climactic celebration.

2. In fact, the notes to the Liveright edition of Crane's *Complete Poems* do not even remark the oddness of "The Wine Menagerie"'s publication history, noting only the deadpan: "Composed c. October 1925–April 1926; first published in May 1926." Further citations to Crane's *Complete Poems* will refer to Marc Simon's 1986 volume unless otherwise specified.

3. Kalstone finds it "ironic that 'Roosters,' the occasion of a break with Moore, should be the closest Bishop had yet come to the type of poem that made Moore famous" (88). I will suggest that Moore (with her mother's help no doubt) performed her greatest violence to poems she sensed closest to her own project. Moore performed her two most famous rewritings on poems that deeply resemble her own, in technique and in subject. While ironic in terms of Bishop and Moore being driven furthest apart as poets at their moment of poetic collision, it is not ironic that Moore chose "Roosters" to tear apart, reseam, and restuff. Moore's revision of Crane's "The Wine Menagerie" was also famously violent, and, as I will argue, was a poem similarly close to Moore's poetic heart.

4. Hugh Kenner points out how Moore made "The Fish" into a "new poem" without changing a word. This example illustrates just how precise Moore was as a poet, manipulating almost imperceptible aspects of a poem to change it into a wholly different poem. He writes:

> The first three times "The Fish" appeared in print its stanzaic system grouped the syllables not 1, 3, 9, 6, 8, but 1, 3, 8, 1, 6, 8, and in six lines, not five. The poem was twelve years old when the poet made this change and it is not, despite the mechanical ease of retyping with newly set tabulator stops, a trivial change, since it affects the system by which pattern intersects utterance, alters the points at which the intersections occur, provides a new grid of impediments to the over anxious voice, and modifies, moreover, the obtrusiveness of the system itself; the new version actually relents a little of its self-sufficient arbitrariness .... One can nearly say, putting the first and second versions side by side, that we have a *new* poem arrived at in public, without changing a word, by applying a system of transformations to an existing poem. (Bloom, *Moore* 18)

5. Moore herself splits the term "precision" down the middle in her later (1950) poem "Armor's Undermining Modesty" (which I will discuss extensively below), in which she suggests that "illusion" is "more precise than precision" (*Complete Poems* 151). This poem leaps with virtuosity from scene of meditation to scene of meditation: beginning with a huge elaborately and defensively colored moth landing on the speaker's wrist and ending with a "confession" of the desire to talk to a Grail-seeking knight "about excess." It is, in part, an argument about poetics. I dislike simplifying such a complex poem in the same way it has again and again been simplified, because this poem is also "about" loneliness, desire, and pride (to name a few) as they surpass poetry. Poetry is one method, this poem suggests, of self-presentation and access to the other, but not, I think, the only one the poem undertakes

to examine and express. Furthermore, as direct as the statements and meditations in the poem seem, one must not forget that they fly a pennant of multivalency in the form of their title. The apostrophe in the poem's title, "Armor's Undermining Modesty," is both a mark of the possessive and the sign of a contraction. The first suggests that armor possesses the quality of an "undermining" or disarming (both adjectives here) "modesty." The second suggests that armor *is presently* "undermining" modesty, working to undercut it. The poem courts paradox on two levels: explicitly in that armor is an aggressive defense, a kind of obviousness that makes modesty possible, but implicitly as well in the poem's own undermining suggestion that this paradox itself can, in its adoption, become a tool of immodesty. Another way of phrasing this in terms of poetics might be: Poetic correctness is more correct than correctness.

6. Bonnie Costello in *Marianne Moore: Imaginary Possessions,* 169–70, suggests that "Blake" represents what Moore may have taken as a "too slight" example of her "chiasmic wit."

7. Note the similarity of Moore's 1966 ejaculations to Crane's despairing "O, steel and stone!" in his 1927 poem "Key West" (*Complete Poems* 126).

8. Bruhm provides a "queer reading" of the Narcissus myth. He argues that Narcissus is a figure who "rejects not only the dictate to desire another (a socially prescribed and approved other) but also the drive to stabilize a range of binarisms upon which gender in Western Culture is founded" (15). Kopelson offers a different and, to my mind, more richly textured reading of the use of the Narcissus myth that suggests that gay writers have used the myth to describe their desire in ways that resist "the idea that (male) attraction to the same sex is *analogous* to attraction to the same self" (*Litany* 70).

9. The list of ingredients of the "imitation onyx wainscoting," as is delightfully chronicled in Unterecker's biography, used to be different. Bert Ginther remembers: " 'When Hart pressed the front door bell of Florence Manor, I pressed the door release and waited. And I heard Hart coming along the hallway to my apartment—and shouting with mirthful voice his derision of the imitation marble walls of the hallway. The words that Hart shouted are these: "Painted emulsion of snow, eggs, yarn, coal, SHIT." The last word fortissimo ...' " (Unterecker 404). Unterecker sees the change of "shit" in the shouted poem to "manure" in the written one as a function of Crane's poverty and need for the money that came from publication. I disagree that Crane toned down the word out of any single urgency or motive. After all, the two beats of "manure" end the list of single syllables well, and "manure" connects the artificial wainscoting to the flirting that is going on in front of it by the rhyme of "manure" and "her" as well as connecting to rhymes with "cynosures" in the stanza preceding and "assures" in the stanza following it. Also, "manure" has a coarser, more animal, sense to it, a real tactile sense of strands of hay, which is more striking and more exact than "shit."

10. This is incorrectly attributed to Kenneth Burke by Unterecker in *Voyager* (405). It was Matthew Josephson who first commented that Moore wrote all the wine out of the wine menagerie (*Life Among the Surrealists* 296).

11. John Unterecker's comment that Moore "tamed" the menagerie (404) is, in league with his misattribution of Josephson's comment, enough to make one question the care and accuracy of his biographical treatment of "The Wine Menagerie." Clever and incidental as his metaphor is, it suggests that there were animals left to tame and that neatening or correcting wild grammar was all Moore did.

12. I will further examine the figure of Petrushka, a Pierrot figure, featured in a ballet most notably danced by Nijinsky, in Chapter 6. Here, Petrushka provides the fairly simple image of a lifeless, other-controlled marionette. Unlike Holofernes and Orpheus, this figure has not lost his head but has instead lost its figural equivalent, his will.

13. Crane's emphasis on reflection and sameness in his "legend" to his poems suggests that the visual analogy of homosexual sex ("And tremorous / In the white falling flakes / Kisses are,— / The only worth all granting ...") is central to his lyrics and is the basis of many of his meditations on desire. Sameness is the problem of desire for Crane, not simply *what he desires.*

14. One cannot help but recall anecdotes from Crane's biography, in which he closed himself in a room, or in one case, in a barn (at the inception and apparently the completion of "The Wine Menagerie") with a record player blaring while he slugged wine or applejack. In fact, Crane's poem centers around the materiality and specificity of felt reality that encumbers but does not entirely founder ecstasy. The poem itself is the distillate, one cannot help but conjecture, of the very process it illustrates.

15. This phrase has been traced to a letter Warner Moore wrote to his sister while he was in the navy. Bonnie Costello, *Marianne Moore: Imaginary Possessions* (29), attributes this identification to the editors of *The Marianne Moore Newsletter* (Fall 1979).

16. Marie Boroff notes Moore's penchant to "leave[] the last word to someone else" in her poems. Boroff attributes Moore's experiments in "Virginia Britannia," "The Monkeys," "In the Days of Prismatic Color," and "What are Years?" to her experiments with ad and feature article prose. Boroff suggests that the "self-effacement" in Moore's work "is in accord with the conventional self-presentation of the 'expounding I' in promotional prose. The author of the feature article is there to draw our attention to the product" ("Marianne Moore's Promotional Prose," in Bloom, *Moore* 68). Boroff's essay opens up whole new boulevards into Moore's poems based on the conventions she identifies. She concludes that Moore's poetic career was, not in any simple sense, a promotional campaign "waged on behalf ... of that greatest of spiritual forces, a self-effacing love" (72).

Boroff, in conjunction with Bonnie Costello in her "The 'Feminine' Language of Marianne Moore," (also printed in the Bloom volume) offer the most lucid theorizations of Moore's use of "humility." Costello writes, "Moore begins by presenting an object apparently for its own sake, but in the process of describing it she borrows the object as a figure of her own activity. This self-portraiture is not the point of arrival of the poet's search for unity or for the thing itself, but a kind of parting embrace of words and things, a form of possession or appropriation that leaves the thing untouched while its ghost performs the function of analogy" (Costello in Bloom, *Moore* 99).

17. "By Nilus Once I Knew..." is odd in that the character who speaks at the end is a "hieroglyph," a joke that in its significatory compactness and motion proves all machines for understanding inadequate. This hieroglyph is the queerly inflected "Decisive grammar given unto queens." Crane further notes that the hieroglyph, in its difficulty, is no "dumb, deaf mistake." The grammar of queens in this poem is something like the "desire to know the truth about one at the piano" in Ashbery's "The Grapevine." The grammar is designed to create directed indirection: knowing by not knowing. The pleading that ends Crane's poem and is the voice of the hieroglyph itself—"I wish I knew"— is all about sexuality, and how queers as ciphers, and the ciphers created by queers, are powerful precisely because neither satisfy, but endlessly compel, the wish to know.

18. This distinction may seem inexact but is as clear as the difference between the monologue of a ventriloquist's dummy and that of an actor in the character of, say, a tiger. The activity between the two ways of reading the tiger would necessarily inflect the poem after Moore published her famous translations of La Fontaine's fables.

19. This list both rhymes with and shares a kind of emphatic digressive tone with Crane's emulsion of "snow, eggs, yarn, coal, manure." Moore's list is more final due to its final rhyme of "timber" and "fur" that powerfully closes the pattern of rhymes or near rhymes that close each of this poem's stanzas: "it"/"eat," "that"/"cat," "examining"/"thing."

    It is also impossible not to note the similarity between this treatment of the sea in an imperative voice of warning and that employed by Crane in the first section of "Voyages" that is addressed to children playing on the beach and ends with this admonition not to trust the apparently trustworthy and fun- and caress-giving sea:

    > O brilliant kids, frisk with your dog,
    > Fondle your shells and sticks, bleached
    > By time and the elements; but there is a line
    > You must not cross nor ever trust beyond it
    > Spry cordage of your bodies to caresses
    > Too lichen-faithful from too wide a breast.
    > The bottom of the sea is cruel (*Complete Poems* 34).

20. As in "Blake" there is both a vertical and horizontal axis of reflection. The reflection of human interests in the qualities of animals serves as the horizontal axis of this reflective chiasmus, and the reflection of people in the calm ocean serves as the vertical axis. Moore, though, rather than showing reflections dimming or paling in this poem, and instead of urging people to become more exact in their reflections of an original, decries the inappropriate use of the trope of reflection itself. Her thematics suggest that each

relation or comparison, animal to human, and art to nature, are best read with a different legend. She suggests that animals must speak for themselves, which of course is problematic considering the speech she gives the tiger to read.

21. The E. T. A. Hoffmann character to which this passage alludes is from his story "A New Year's Eve Adventure," in which the main character, Erasmus, gives his reflection away as a token of his love.

22. "Self-Portrait" has been read by Anita Sokolsky as Ashbery musing on breaking out of "a framework of narcissistic reflexiveness both for lyric poetry and for the self" (Bloom, *Ashbery* 250). The poem has lead S. P. Mohanty and Jonathan Monroe to suggest that "the most distinctive aspect of Ashbery's work, and its most significant contribution to contemporary poetry in the United States, resides not in its emphasis on the self in isolation but rather in its counter-emphasis on the self as an ineluctably social construction" (45). Both of these readings, though in different critical registers, depict Ashbery's poetry pushing at boundaries of self as psychic and social construct.

Chapter 5   The Magician's Advance: Late Moore

1. Interestingly, five years later, Hart Crane would be lumping Monroe and, Moore together, as the editors of *Poetry* and *The Dial*, in a letter to Allen Tate: "I wonder how much longer our markets will be in the grip of two such hysterical virgins as *The Dial* and *Poetry!*" (Weber 289). This is an oft-quoted remark of Crane's whose ubiquity indicates its usefulness in expressing an easy prejudice against two very different poetic and editorial presences.

2. There are a number of ways to change one's approach in order to read poems that do not concur with the "general laws of shapeliness." For instance, one can declare, as Marjorie Perloff does, that the internal development of a poem is not what is important, but rather the way it fits into a discursive field. Or one can, as Harold Bloom does, note the intertexts of a poem as enormously constitutive of its interior. Neither of these methods, however, have produced truly compelling Moore criticism that deals with her as a lyric poet. These readings of Moore, inevitably it seems, short change the movement of Moore's poems instead by ignoring it rather than bemoaning it.

3. A related problem resides in the operative binary of many critical takes. The critic attacks or defends her shapelessness or shapeliness. The shapely/shapeless binary is a blunt instrument with which to perform critical procedures; embedded within it are notions of the lyric and the relation of theme to form, and embedded within *these* are notions of the reader, the writer, and their relation. In other words, critics do not agree on what shape is, so to judge poems based on its presence or absence seems doomed in advance as a generator of critical discourse. This, I would suggest, also in part accounts for the absence of much real engagement between critics working on Moore.

4. Monroe's allusion to the Pegasus is a rather odd one since it was at the sight of Bellerophon's golden bridle (a gift of Minerva) that Pegasus was willingly tamed, and it was only Bellerophon's pride that lead him to try to fly on the Pegasus into heaven. Pegasus was not unruly, rather he was so tamed and controlled he aided Bellerophon to each of his victories whereupon hubris took Bellerophon and he was thrown from the winged horse who Jupiter had sent a gadfly to sting (*Bullfinch's Mythology* 104–5).

5. Moore was the first recipient (1950) of a 2,500 dollar award from the Bryher Foundation, "established to help artists and writers." As Molesworth tells it in his biography, Moore, in an odd but perfectly Moore-like way, thereupon wrote a letter offering Bryher 500 dollars for a trip to visit her in America. Realizing afterwards that she may have underestimated how much the trip would cost, Moore sent Bryher a check for the more realistic amount (*Moore* 326).

6. For a discussion of "body drag" see Moon and Sedgwick, "Divinity: A Dossier, A Performance Piece, A Little-understood Emotion," in Sedgwick, *Tendencies* 215–51.

7. Moore also was called "Uncle" in her letters from her mother and brother and often referred to herself as Warner's brother.

8. A comic version of this plays out when Moore is asked by an interviewer to react to the comment that William Carlos Williams made in his autobiography about her being a "rafter." Moore tartly responded by taking the refiguration of her body literally: "That's ridiculous! I never held anything up."

9. Frankly, Burke may have been speaking directly to Edmund Wilson's comment (quoted by Allen Tate to Moore when he was hot to curry her favor) that Moore was the "most intellectual woman he had ever met" (Molesworth, *Moore* 316). Burke wrote a fascinating little essay called "She Taught Me to Blush" as his tribute to Moore published in a *Festschrift for Marianne Moore's Seventy Seventh Birthday*. With any document that is meant as an appreciation or celebration of a poet presented to that poet there are of course issues of propriety. Burke explains that he got to know Moore in the editorial office of *The Dial* in the twenties and muses that "she could be extraordinary even in the attempt to be average" (*Festschrift* 61). The final paragraph of this incredibly dense tribute seeks to distill the "Moore effect." Burke writes: "If one may use so unpliant a word, surely the basic 'formula' for her rare personality would stress the spontaneous oneness of her poetizing and her conscientiousness." Burke suggests that Moore is spontaneous in her fastidiousness, a paradox he seeks to illustrate in his essay's central figure: "Marianne Moore even taught me how to blush. (But that was many years ago. I've since had time to again grow sluggish.)" The figure of being taught to blush has two sides, but both depend on the idea of being taught immediacy. The other side is hinted at parenthetically: a quickening of one's sensibility, that things strike harder and surer on the surface of one's senses. This can mean that one is easily offended, but it has the added effect that one's surfaces are supersensitive to contact, instead of making him simply uptight, Moore's teachings also have the effect of making Burke sexy. This take on the

title also includes the implication that not only did Moore provide Burke with a sense of propriety that then lead to blushing, but it also hints at the fact that she provides the material that made him blush. Someone who teaches someone else to blush either provides them with a "sense of decency" or else evidence of the indecent, or perhaps more realistically, both.

10. Molesworth contrasts his own biographical approach to a "psychological, even a psychoanalytic, approach," which he slyly suggests "might be valuable" (Molesworth, *Moore* xxi). He seems to be suggesting that the sexuality of Moore is both separate from her dealings in literature as well as that Moore's sexuality was a matter uniquely suited for analysis—none of it broke the surface in her life. Molesworth's approach disallows or at least brackets sex *in* or *as* "the literary."

11. Charles Altieri, in *Painterly Abstraction in Modernist American Poetry*, offers the most compelling account available of "Omissions are not accidents" in his brilliant reading of Moore's final, shortened version of "Poetry." Altieri reads the final version as inclusive of the earlier version in the "Notes." He hones in on the operations of "it" in the final text that refer to all the attempted metaphorical descriptions of poetry in the version that are present but offstage. Altieri writes, "Omissions are not accidents because they are perhaps the only way of negotiating between the accidental and the essential .... The poet's powers of negation are her richest means of showing what motivates her quest and abides within it ..." (267). Altieri's critical stance emphasizes how Moore's omissions are a negotiation. Omission is an important poetic device in the service of a very complicated and vital poetics, not a tic, that in its compelling simple inclusiveness becomes Moore's self-proclaimed and simply locating trademark.

12. For an example of this see Slatin, 3.

13. See Heuving's chapter in *Omissions Are Not Accidents*, " 'Overstatement': The Later Poems and a Diminished Vision," 140–67.

14. On the other hand, the other side of this structure, imagining Moore's late poems as the *ultimate expression* of her poetics, also seems to depend too heavily on notions of poetic biography's plot line and underregard the way in which Moore's late products are odd in different ways than her earlier ones. As readers of Moore's biography, in order to situate her late work, it seems best to keep in mind the pleasures one finds in reading her poems. If her poems can pleasurably end in the decor, then it seems only appropriate to entertain the notion that that's also perhaps where her oeuvre ends.

15. Moore's poem "Love in America?" was printed in issue 239 (December 31, 1966) of the *Saturday Evening Post* with a question mark in the title. The question mark turned to a dash ("Love in America—"), as the poem made its way into the final version of Moore's *Collected Works*. I will use the original form of the title, with the question mark, because I think it more forcefully directs the poem. The dash has the same effect of making what precedes it into a topic for meditation as well as including the title in the rhetorical workings of the poem. But it does not have the virtue, to my eye,

of as strongly holding a trace of an interlocutor, whose presence helps make this poem vital.

16. In the poem "Voracities and Verities Sometimes are Interacting," the poem's central urgency is to express "love undying" for a book about tigers, *Man-Eaters of Kumaon* (*Complete Poems* 148). Similar to "Tippoo's Tiger," Moore walks a fine line between identifying with the loveliness of the tiger and identifying with and exalting its bloodthirst (241).

17. Kenneth Burke writes that, in Moore's "Four Quartz Crystal Clocks," "... there would be no use in looking for 'symbolist' or 'imagist' motives behind the reference to the fact that precisely *four* clocks are mentioned here. It is an 'objectivist' observation. We read of four, not because the number corresponds, for instance, to the Horsemen of the Apocalypse, but simply because there are actually four of them in the vault" (Burke, *Grammar* 487). The "descriptive" poem seems possessed by its subject in a way that Eliot figures the "lyric" poem as possessed by its own urge to expression.

18. There is a last version of this poem which ends with the line "can't make the owner's loss less hard." This is obviously inferior in sound and not very different in sense. In both versions "one" and "the owner" slip from position to position. The "owner" could be Tipu, the British, the tiger, or the owner of a "tiger-heart."

19. Both Holley and Willis read Moore's central identification as split between the British and Tipu, rather than with none but the tiger.

20. Patricia Willis in *Marianne Moore: Vision into Verse* reproduces Moore's own copies of each of these works. On Moore's "Domain of Lights," clipped from the *New York Times Magazine,* Moore has written "The Magician's Retreat 1969" (Willis, 100). I share Willis's opinion that Moore was as much "renaming" Magritte's painting after her poem as identifying the source of her poem. This title changes the aspect of the painting, making the house's little huddle of light seem more willfully contained, as if house, lamp, and trees (or whatever magician controls them) are in a kind of partnership to keep the sky out. The addition of an agent, a magician, changes the quality of the oil and water layering of light and dark. What before could be taken as an accident becomes purposeful.

Chapter 6   Danced Undone: Performances of Exhaustion and Resignation in Crane's Lyrics

1. John Unterecker tells how, in September 1917, Crane made a trip to Staten Island with Stanislaw, his wife Anna, and Carl Schmitt, after which "Crane's life had seemed to fall together in a coherent pattern. He returned to the boarding house planning not only to stand free of his father but as well to begin the intricate process of untying ... the apron strings of grandmother and mother" (93). The process of untying, as I will show, is central to Crane's poem about his friend.

2. In the spring of 1919, Crane wrote to George Bryan: " 'Stan and Anna no longer interest me very much. They are quite incommunicable and smug, having settled into married life and a flat' " (quoted in Unterecker 137).

3. Unless otherwise noted, quotations from Crane's poetry in this chapter are from Marc Simon, *Complete Poems of Hart Crane,* and will be labeled as "*Complete Poems.*"

4. This poem is also a response to the original "Afternoon of the Faun," a poem by Stéphane Mallarmé (*Selected Poetry and Prose* 33–41). Discussing Mallarmé in a letter to Gorham Munson, Crane writes: "... since Mallarmé and Huysmans were elegant weepers it is up to the following generation to haw-haw gloriously" (Weber 78). Crane's revision of "Afternoon of the Faun" seems just that, a glorious haw-hawing.

5. Françoise Reiss, *Nijinsky: A Biography,* pp. 153–6.

6. I borrow the delightful critical phrase "immiscibility of subjectivity" from Allen Grossman.

7. Edward Brunner revisited this sentiment in his 1984 study entitled *Splendid Failure: Hart Crane and the Making of the Bridge.*

8. Crane's correspondence with Yvor Winters provides an example of the way in which Crane's homosexuality translated quite easily for Winters into failure as a poet. Crane could not be a "complete man." Crane also understood the import of Winters's critiques of his sexuality in the guise of critiques of his poems. Crane wrote: "You need a good drubbing for all your recent easy talk about 'the complete man,' the poet and his ethical place in society, etc. ... One doesn't have to turn to homosexuals to find instances of missing sensibilities" (Parkinson 86–9).

9. The epigram of his first book comes from Rimbaud, "Ce ne peut être que la fin du monde, en avançant." (There can be only the end of the world, in advancing.) It announces its concern with the location, dislocation, and encroachment of endings.

10. It is interesting to read "Reply" as a revisitation and further exploration of the "reply" featured at the closure of Crane's poem "Voyages." In "Voyages," he closes with the "imaged Word ... [which] is the unbetrayable reply / Whose accent no farewell can know" (*Complete Poems* 40). In "Reply," Crane's fame, embodied in the ensured future contact of reader and writer at the site of the text, becomes the "imaged Word," and it is both "unbetrayable" because it incorporates betrayal into its own force and knows "no farewell" because its incorporation of inevitable betrayal ensures it life as long as there is betrayal (that is, for eternity).

11. Simon's volume of Crane's "Complete Poems" spells "syphilitic" with two l's, Waldo Frank's earlier volume spells it with only one, leaving the question open about Crane's original spelling. However, it is an insignificant authorial or editorial error and I have corrected it in the text of the poem rather than remark its error there and break up the already broken-up stream of the poem. Kenneth Lohf in *The Literary Manuscripts of Hart Crane* reports the first line of this poem as "The syphillitic selling violets calmly" (73). Also, Crane misspells "syphilis" as "syphillis" in his letters, cf. *O My Land, My Friends,* Hammer and Weber 464.

12. In the first stanza, each line ends with a peculiar sound repetition. The sound being repeated changes slightly. For instance, the first line ends with

the "alm" and "ly" of "calmly" that jams two different "l" sounds together. A pattern arises when we consider this and the tiny second line's last word "daisies" where "ays" and "ees" are juxtaposed. The third and fourth lines are not so simple in their arrangement although they follow the pattern. In the third line, the "ews" of "news-stand" skews to the "ows" of knows that then smears to the fourth line's "ow" of "how"; "how" serves double when the "hy" of "hyacinths" repeats its "h." As they are patterned, these sounds constantly suggest a doubleness. The rhyme and alliteration is all insistently proximate and insistently partial.

The pattern changes in the second stanza. Here, while the repetition of sound occurs between lines, the rhyming sounds remain hunched at the end of each line as in the first stanza. The first line's "ers" in "offers" links strongly to the "ur" early in "hurriedly" and weakly to the "ed" late in it. The final syllable of "hurriedly" then serves to directly rhyme with "freshly" at the end of the next line. "Bestows," in the fourth line of the second stanza, rhymes with "knows" in the first stanza, a connection that serves to emphasize their common subject while also offering a small pause from the huddled groupings of sounds. In the last two lines of this stanza a trio of repetitions, that echo (though less slanted) the first stanza's concluding trio of rhymes, begins with "purchaser." The first and last syllables of this word exactly rhyme with each other and with the first syllable of "perhaps." The exactness of these rhymes and the slantedness of the rhymes ending the first stanza insist on comparison due to their position in their respective stanzas as well as their threenesses. The proximate rhymes have reached their most orderly, as if the activity of the second stanza, offering and bestowing, overtook the less rigid knowing of the first stanza. This activity manifests itself as sonic order and then is shattered sonically and syntactically in the final stanza where the syphilitic's eyes wander from it.

The glass/pass rhyme dominates the final stanza, overshadowing the slant rhyme of "eyes" and "lilies," but also the midline sound repetitions of crutches/hurtled, mute/sudden, the slant rhyme between the two syllables of "lilies," and roses/no of the ultimate line. These repetitions have notably shifted to the left in each line except for "lilies." The rhymes between lines rather than within lines take the organizational upper hand. These lines buckle in the middle rather than at the end. In line 12 the "uh" sounds in crutches/hurtled/against clutch together in a clump quite separate from the "a" sounds at the end of the line in the rest of "against" and in "glass." In line 13, the blunt bundle of "uh" in "mute and sudden" contrasts with the crisper vowel sounds in "dealing" and "change" at the end of the line. In the final line of the poem, the distilling "oh" sounds of beyond/roses/no starkly contrast with the "eh, ah, a" sounds of the end of the line, "flesh can pass." The effect of the hard emphasis of rhymes from line to line is one of more fluid motion than the motion in the first two stanzas. This stanza has more of a sweep to it while also a very clear sense of its borders. The glass/pass rhyme makes the poem's finish itself impassable; it stops short. The former stanzas slowed but this halts suddenly.

13. Marc Simon reads this poem as a fragment mostly due to its raggedness. It was however published in *Poetry* 41 (January 1933) in the form that I will treat as a finished poem.

14. Barbara Herrnstein Smith offers the connection between closure and aperture as the opening of the book that followed her study of poetic closure. In *On the Margins of Discourse,* she writes, "The turn from closure to openness did not, however, require a turnabout, for ... it is by virtue of its enclosure that the poem achieves its amplitude and infinitude" (ix).

Chapter 7   The End of the Line: Spicer in Love

1. Spicer utilizes the lisp as the closure to a poem in his book *Language*. The final two lines of Section 8 of "Graphemics" read: "... Old / Senses in new thongs." The lisp here indicates that old senses are transported into new songs by the continuity of the lisp as a homosexual mode of expression. That is, lisping queers old senses. This is an example of Spicer's preoccupation with the notion of a queer bridge between the past, present, and future. Furthermore, it is an example of the elasticity of homosexual meanings, as theorized by Lee Edelman in the earlier examined concept of homographesis. In one case, lisping a title is an insult, while in another it is a transformative poetic technique asserting the effect of avowedly homosexual speakers and writers on the meaning of their texts.

2. Lewis Ellingham and Kevin Killian tell the story of Donald Allen and Robin Spicer opening the trunk in which Spicer had stashed his detective novel, now in print and titled, *The Tower of Babel,* and finding "on top of the typescript ... a Zuni fetish, a hex or curse, pointing in the general direction of Duncan's house" (*Tower* 169). This anecdote tells maybe more about how much of a drama queen Blaser is than about Spicer's viciousness. Duncan was, after all, the person who typed the novel for Spicer who couldn't type. And I'm not sure how one reads intention into the location of a chest, which might have been moved, or even jarred after a poet's death. Regardless, the anecdote sneaks under the radar of suspicion because it does sound plausible in relation to other actions Spicer took against those who crossed him.

3. A full account of the Mill Valley reading is given in Ellingham and Killian 123–7.

4. Michael Davidson reads Spicer's reading of "For Joe" as a criticism of Duncan's "female impersonation" group "the Maidens" and a *defense* of Helen Adam (172–3). This reading might be a little too generous to Spicer, but it does indicate that the event doesn't bow to a simple explanation.

5. In his poem, "October 1, 1962," that Lew Ellingham copied from a brown paper bag tacked to the wall of Gino & Carlo's bar, Spicer writes that "This is an ode to John Wieners and Auerhahn Press / Who have driven me away from poetry like a fast car" (*One Night Stand* 87).

6. I want to thank Ms. Andrea Grimes of the Special Collections Department at the San Francisco Public Library for pointing me to this source and particularly to this anecdote.

7. In the final, and eponymous, poem of Spicer's *A Book of Music,* he suggests
   that a sexual encounter, in which two lovers "come at the end" and are
   "exhausted like two swimmers," can be a metaphor for the end of poetry. He
   asks of the sexual situation "Where did it end?" and answers "There is no
   telling." The temporal boundary of the sexual situation leads to questions
   about the boundary between the two lovers and the discreteness of the lovers'
   bodies leads to a notion that poetry ends in discrete strands, which in the body
   of the poem were coiled and presented themselves as one substance: rope.

   > Coming at an end. Rather, I would say, like a length
   > Of coiled rope
   > Which does not disguise in the final twists of its lengths
   > Its endings.
   > But, you will say, we loved
   > And some parts of us loved
   > And the rest of us will remain
   > Two persons. Yes,
   > Poetry ends like a rope. (*Collected Books* 76)

   "Coming" at the end has two senses. An erotic encounter might be declared
   complete upon the successful reaching of orgasm by each of the lovers. This
   completion of a relation at orgasm is something like the sex one might have
   in a Turkish bath or a one night stand. For a while the two lovers are "coiled"
   and "disguised" as a single being, but at the end comes an unraveling. But
   also, at the end, comes a fall from relationality. The metaphor of the rope, in
   another register, maintains a good measure of the danger of verticality. One
   is holding onto a rope, and when one comes to the end, one falls off into the
   void. Poetry ends like something desperately clung to as well as, at its end,
   the disaster it hung over.

   Spicer, it seems, has several different metaphorical renderings of closure.
   Endings, his writing here and elsewhere suggests, are always read backwards.
   In *A Book of Music,* being left alone after sex is presented as inevitable, just
   as being alone as author, separate from the reader. Both reader and author,
   having participated in the construction of the poem, separate, and that is
   how poetry ends. Here, also I must split the word "poetry" itself into two
   strands. A single poem ends like a rope, as I have discussed. But "poetry," the
   category of art, also must be considered to "end like a rope." Poetry ends
   when author and reader are unraveled.

8. Donald Allen dates this poem as "1963?" in *One Night Stand* and *Manroot*
   10 notes that Spicer's "Three Marxist Essays" was published in *The San
   Francisco Capitalist Bloodsucker-N* but does not provide a date or other information.

9. Significantly, the final poem in *After Lorca* (1957), "Radar," carries the ded-
   ication: "A postscript for Marianne Moore." Spicer sent the poem to Moore
   and "was touched and pleased by a postcard she wrote him from Brooklyn
   Heights" (Ellingham and Killian 147).

10. David Gardner's *The California Oath Controversy* details the events before, during, and after the oath was required by the Regents at Berkeley.

11. Paul Naylor in his article "Where Are We Now In Poetry?" makes much of Spicer's mention of pure poetry. He says that "pure poetry," by luring the reader and writer from noticing injustice in the world "finds itself in collusion with injustice" (31). Naylor misses that fact that Spicer was actively political in groups and was political by the fact of his extreme openness about his homosexuality during the very years HUAC was in full swing. In luring *his* reader from Spicer's politics, one could retort, Naylor himself is in "collusion with injustice." Furthermore, as I have already mentioned and Spicer has joined me in asserting, that poets are practitioners of poetry does not give them the final word on its theorization.

12. This is the same "Joe" to whom the poem Spicer read in Mill Valley was dedicated.

13. The thematics of this poem, the powerful "humiliating" babble of the ocean overpowering the mere words of the poet, are similar to those in Whitman's "As I Ebb'd with the Ocean of Life." The poet, faced with the ocean's "blab" is "Oppress'd with myself that I have dared to open my mouth...." (*Leaves of Grass* 394). Whitman compares his lines with drifts of sea garbage as they are rolled up the beach to the feet of the reader.

14. In his 1958 work *Admonitions,* Spicer instructs "Harvey" to whom the poem is directed that "When you break a line nothing / Becomes better. / There is no new... / Measure / ... Break your poem... / ... Like you would a grapefruit..." (*Collected Books* 58). Spicer continues and suggests that each line ought to "Cut itself. Like seaweed thrown / Against the pier." This, rather than displaying nonchalance toward line breaks, indicates that line breaks are integral to the object or activity they are involved in: the grapefruit or the slapping of seaweed on wood. Line breaks do not make things better than they are by being the measure of a breath as Olsen would have it, or any other formula that was popular at the time. They just produce a naturalness or realism about *the things.*

15. Anne Ferry, in *The Title of the Poem,* takes the question of poem-as-unit from the other side. She argues that a title provides a poem a sense of completion, since it is placed after the poem is considered complete enough to carry a name. Either type of unit creation vexes Hejinien's rejection. Closure will always be present when a reader needs to distinguish boundaries for an experience of reading, which is not to say that any particular closure might not open up to the possibility of the noise and chaos of a diverse world. That would be the exercise of a technique at the closure of a poem; to keep a closure "open" is not to reject closure, but rather to produce a particular kind of closure.

16. In the same way that my readings of Spicer's poems argue for the importance of attending to his lyric units as units in groups as opposed to approaching his books of poems as unitless groups, I also want to consider the way in which Spicer's concern with his unitariness or aloneness as a poet relates to a genealogy of poets, specifically a queer one.

17. Whitman's poetics of inclusiveness are not as foreign to Spicer's poetics as they often get pegged. For instance, the first line of the first full-length book on Spicer's poetry reads: "Jack Spicer's poetry is an argument against the American voice that Walt Whitman projects—optimistic, expansive, political" (Foster 5). As we have seen, Foster is just plain wrong about Spicer and his poetry not being political. And poetry is not an "argument" against anything. These quibbles aside, Foster is onto something when he mentions the voice Whitman projects, except here I'm reading "projects" as projecting personalities and persons through space and time.

    Foster is not the only critic to suggest that Spicer has nothing in common with Whitman. Michael Davidson claims that Spicer is against any notion of a Whitmanic ensemble and was instead in favor of a cultish bar community (*Renaissance* 81). James Liddy even describes Whitman as "the country Spicer had to leave," and Burton Hatlen proposes that "in the end, both Lorca and Spicer reject Whitman's totalitarian vision of the 'Self as Kosmos,' a vision that denies the self/other distinction" (Liddy 259; Hatlen 128).

18. Damon's mention of "bridging" immediately conjures Crane. Hart Crane shows up as a ghost, "The Crane of Hearts," in an early poem entitled "The Bridge Game," but then also later in the "Love Poems" section of *Language,* which I will discuss later, in which Spicer writes, "My heart's in the highlands / A-chasing the deer" (*Collected Books* 228); the heart chasing a hart (deer).

Bibliography

Allen, Donald, ed. *The New American Poetry, 1945–1960.* Berkeley: University of California Press, 1999.

Altieri, Charles. "Motives in Metaphor: John Ashbery and the Modernist Long Poem." *Genre* XI, 4 (1978): 653–87.

———. *Enlarging the Temple: New Directions in American Poetry during the 1960s.* London: Associated University Presses, 1979.

———. *Self and Sensibility in Contemporary American Poetry.* Cambridge: Cambridge University Press, 1984.

———. *Canons and Consequences: Reflections on the Ethical Force of Imaginative Ideals.* Evanston: Northwestern University Press, 1990.

———. "Contemporary Poetry as Philosophy: Subjective Agency in John Ashbery and C. K. Williams." *Contemporary Literature* 33 (1992): 214–42.

——— "Ashbery as Love Poet." *The Tribe of John: Ashbery and Contemporary Poetry.* Ed. Susan Schultz. Tuscaloosa: The University of Alabama Press, 1995. 26–32.

———. *Painterly Abstraction in Modernist American Poetry.* University Park: The Pennsylvania State University Press, 1995.

Ashbery, John. *Some Trees.* New York: The Ecco Press, 1956.

———. "The Impossible." *Poetry* 90:4 (July 1957): 250–4.

———. *The Tennis Court Oath.* Middletown: Wesleyan University Press, 1962.

———. *Rivers and Mountains.* New York: The Ecco Press, 1966.

———. "Straight Lines Over Rough Terrain." *The New York Times Book Review* (November 26, 1967): 1, 42.

——— and James Schuyler. *A Nest of Ninnies.* New York: E. P. Dutton & Co., Inc., 1969.

———. *The Double Dream of Spring.* New York: The Ecco Press, 1970.

———. *Three Poems.* New York: Penguin Books, 1972.

———. *Self-Portrait in a Convex Mirror.* New York: Penguin Books, 1975.

———. *The Vermont Notebook.* Illus. by Joe Brainard. Los Angeles: Black Sparrow Press, 1975.

———. *As We Know.* New York: Penguin Books, 1979.

———. *Shadow Train.* New York: Penguin, 1981.

———. *A Wave.* New York: The Viking Press, 1984.

———. *April Galleons.* New York: Penguin Books, 1988.

Ashbery, John. *Three Plays.* Manchester: Carcanet Press Limited, 1988.
———. *Flow Chart.* New York: Alfred A. Knopf, 1991.
———. *Reported Sightings: Art Chronicles 1957–1987.* Ed. David Bergman. Cambridge: Harvard University Press, 1991.
———. *Hotel Lautréamont.* New York: Alfred A. Knopf, 1992.
———. *Three Books: Houseboat Days, Shadow Train, and A Wave.* New York: Penguin Books, 1993.
———. *And the Stars Were Shining.* New York: Farrar, Straus and Giroux, 1994.
———. *Can You Hear, Bird?* New York: Farrar, Straus and Giroux, 1995.
Auden, W. H. *The Dyer's Hand and Other Essays.* New York: Random House, 1962.
Bahti, Timothy. *Ends of the Lyric: Direction and Consequence in Western Poetry.* Baltimore: The Johns Hopkins University, 1996.
Bayley, John. "The Poetry of John Ashbery." *John Ashbery: Modern Critical Views.* Ed. Harold Bloom. New York: Chelsea House, 1985. 195–206.
Bedient, Calvin. "Walt Whitman: Overruled." *Salmagundi* 58–9 (Fall 1982–Winter 1983): 326–46.
Berger, Charles. "The Sum." *Raritan* XI.4 (1992): 123–36.
Bergman, David. "Marianne Moore and the Problem of 'Marriage.'" *American Literature* 60: 2 (May 1988): 241–54.
———. "Choosing Our Fathers: Gender and Identity in Whitman, Ashbery and Richard Howard." *American Literary History* (Summer 1989): 383–403.
———. *Gaiety Transfigured: Gay Self-Representation in American Literature.* Madison: The University of Wisconsin Press, 1991.
Bersani, Leo. *Homos.* Cambridge: Harvard University Press, 1995.
Berthoff, Warner. *Hart Crane: A Re-Introduction.* Minneapolis: University of Minnesota Press, 1989.
Bewley, Marcus. "Hart Crane's Last Poem." *Modern Critical Views: Hart Crane.* Ed. Harold Bloom. New York: Chelsea House Publishers, 1986. 31–42.
Bishop, Elizabeth. *One Art.* Ed. Robert Giroux. New York: Farrar, Straus and Giroux, 1994.
———. *The Collected Prose.* Ed. Robert Giroux. New York: Farrar, Straus and Giroux, 1984.
Blackmur, R. P. "The Method of Marianne Moore." *Marianne Moore: A Collection of Critical Essays.* Ed. Charles Tomlinson. Englewood Cliffs, N.J.: Prentice-Hall, Inc., 1969. 66–86.
———. "New Thesholds, New Anatomies: Notes on a Text of Hart Crane." *Hart Crane: Modern Critical Views.* Ed. Harold Bloom. New York: Chelsea House Publishers, 1986. 17–31.
Blaser, Robin. "The Practice of Outside." *The Collected Books of Jack Spicer.* Ed. Robin Blaser. Santa Rosa: Black Sparrow Press, 1975. 271–326.
Bloom, Harold. *The Anxiety of Influence: A Theory of Poetry.* London: Oxford University Press, 1973.
———. *Poetry and Repression: Revisionism from Blake to Stevens.* New Haven: Yale University Press, 1976.

————. "The Breaking of Form." *Deconstruction and Criticism.* Ed. Harold Bloom. New York: Continuum Publishing Company, 1979.

————. *Agon: Towards a Theory of Revisionism.* Oxford: Oxford University Press, 1982.

————, ed. *John Ashbery: Modern Critical Views.* New York: Chelsea House, 1985.

————, ed. *Hart Crane: Modern Critical Views.* New York: Chelsea House Publishers, 1986.

————, ed. *Marianne Moore: Modern Critical Views.* New York: Chelsea House Publishers, 1987.

Bogan, Louise. *Achievement in American Poetry.* Chicago: Gateway Editions, Inc., 1951.

Boone, Bruce. "Spicer's Writing in Context." *Ironwood* 14: 2 (1986): 202–5.

Boroff, Marie. "Marianne Moore's Promotional Prose." *Marianne Moore: Modern Critical Views.* Ed. Harold Bloom. New York: Chelsea House Publishers, 1987. 43–72.

Breslin, Paul. *The Psycho-Political Muse: American Poetry Since the Fifties.* Chicago: University of Chicago Press, 1987.

Bromwich, David. "Marianne Moore's Poems." *Poetry* 139: 6 (March 1982): 340–52.

————. "John Ashbery: The Self Against Its Images." *Raritan* V.4 (Spring 1986): 36–58.

————. "That Weapon, Self-Protectiveness." *Marianne Moore: The Art of a Modernist.* Ed. Joseph Parisi. Ann Arbor: University of Michigan Research Press, 1990. 67–82.

Brown, Susan Jenkins. *Robber Rocks: Letters and Memories of Hart Crane, 1923–1932.* Middletown, Conn.: Wesleyan University Press, 1969.

Bruhm, Steven. *Reflecting Narcissus: A Queer Aesthetic.* Minneapolis: University of Minnesota Press, 2001.

Brunner, Edward. *Splendid Failure: Hart Crane and the Making of The Bridge.* Urbana: University of Illinois Press, 1985.

Bryher, Winifred. *West.* London: Jonathan Cape Ltd., 1925.

Bulfinch, Thomas. *Bulfinch's Mythology.* New York: HarperCollins, 1991.

Burke, Kenneth. *The Philosophy of Literary Form: Studies in Symbolic Action.* New York: Vintage Books, 1957.

————. "Motives and Motifs in the Poetry of Marianne Moore." *A Grammar of Motives.* Berkeley: University of California Press, 1969.

————. "She taught me to blush." *Festschrift for Marianne Moore's Seventy Seventh Birthday.* Ed. Tambimuttu. New York: Tambimuttu and Mass., 1964.

Butler, Judith. *Gender Trouble: Feminism and the Subversion of Identity.* New York: Routledge, 1990.

Butterfield, R. W. *The Broken Arc: A Study of Hart Crane.* Edinburgh: Oliver & Boyd, 1969.

Cady, Edwin H. and Budd, Louis J., eds. *On Whitman: The Best from American Literature.* Durham: Duke University Press, 1987.

Cameron, Sharon. *Lyric Time: Dickinson and the Limits of Genre*. Baltimore: The Johns Hopkins University Press, 1979.

———. *Choosing Not Choosing: Dickinson's Fascicles*. Chicago: The University of Chicago Press, 1992.

Coote, Stephen, ed. *The Penguin Book of Homosexual Verse*. New York: Penguin, 1986.

Corn, Alfred. "A Magma of Interiors." *Parnassus* 4: 2 (Fall/Winter 1975): 223–33.

Costello, Bonnie. *Marianne Moore: Imaginary Possessions*. Cambridge: Harvard University Press, 1981.

———. "John Ashbery and the Idea of the Reader." *Contemporary Literature* 23 (Fall 1982): 493–514.

———. "Marianne Moore and Elizabeth Bishop: Friendship and Influence." *Twentieth Century Literature* 30:2/3 (Summer/Fall 1984): 130–49.

———. "Marianne Moore and the Sublime." *Sagetrieb* 6: 3 (Winter 1987): 5–13.

———. "The 'Feminine' Language of Marianne Moore." *Marianne Moore: Modern Critical Views*. Ed. Harold Bloom. New York: Chelsea House Publishers, 1987. 89–106.

Cowley, Malcolm. "Walt Whitman: The Secret." *The New Republic* 114 (1946): 481–84.

———. *Exile's Return: A Literary Odyssey of the 1920s*. Ed. Donald W. Faulkner. New York: Penguin Books, 1994.

Crane, Hart. *The Letters of Hart Crane 1916–1932*. Ed. Brom Weber. New York: Hermitage House, 1952.

———. *The Complete Poems of Hart Crane*. Ed. Waldo Frank. Garden City, N.Y.: Doubleday & Company, Inc., 1958.

———. "General Aims and Theories." *The Complete Poems and Selected Letters and Prose of Hart Crane*. Ed. Brom Weber. New York: Liveright Publishing Corporation, 1966.

———. *Complete Poems of Hart Crane*. Ed. Marc Simon. New York: Liveright, 1986.

———. *O My Land, My Friends: The Selected Letters of Hart Crane*. Eds. Langdon Hammer and Brom Weber. New York: Four Walls Eight Windows, 1997.

Crase, Douglas. "The Prophetic Ashbery." *John Ashbery: Modern Critical Views*. Ed. Harold Bloom. New York: Chelsea House, 1985. 127–44.

Culler, Jonathan. *Structuralist Poetics, Structuralism, Linguistics, and the Study of Literature*. Ithaca: Cornell University Press, 1975.

———. *On Deconstruction: Theory and Criticism after Structuralism*. Ithaca: Cornell University Press, 1982.

Damon, Maria. *The Dark End of the Street: Margins in American Vanguard Poetry*. Minneapolis: University of Minnesota Press, 1993.

Davidson, Michael. *The San Francisco Renaissance: Poetics and Community at Mid-Century*. Cambridge: Cambridge University Press, 1989.

Davis, Robert Leigh. *Whitman and the Romance of Medicine.* Berkeley: University of California Press, 1997.

DeChirico, Georgio. *Hebdomeros.* Trans. John Ashbery, Louise Bourgeois, Robert Goldwater, Damon Krukowski, and Mark Polizzotti. Cambridge: Exact Change, 1992.

deMan, Paul. *Allegories of Reading: Figural Language in Rousseau, Nietzsche, Rilke, and Proust.* New Haven: Yale University Press, 1979.

———. *Blindness and Insight: Essays in the Rhetoric of Contemporary Criticism.* Intro. by Wlad Godzich. Minneapolis: University of Minnesota Press, 1983.

Dickinson, Emily. *The Complete Poems of Emily Dickinson.* Ed. Thomas H. Johnson. Boston: Little, Brown and Company, 1960.

Diehl, Joanne Feit. *Elizabeth Bishop and Marianne Moore: The Psychodynamics of Creativity.* Princeton: Princeton University Press, 1993.

Duncan, Robert. *Caesar's Gate, Poems 1949–50.* With paste-ups by Jess. Berkeley: Sand Dollar, 1972.

Edelman, Lee. "The Pose of Imposture: Ashbery's 'Self-Portrait in a Convex Mirror.'" *Twentieth Century Literature* 32:1 (Spring 1986): 95–113.

———. *Transmemberment of Song: Hart Crane's Anatomies of Rhetoric and Desire.* Stanford: Stanford University Press, 1987.

———. *Homographesis: Essays in Gay Literary and Cultural History.* New York: Routledge, 1994.

Ellingham, Lewis, and Kevin Killian. *Poet Be Like God.* Hanover, N.H.: University Press of New England, 1998.

Eliot, T. S. *On Poetry and Poets.* New York: Farrar, Straus and Cudahy, 1957.

———. "Introduction to *Selected Poems.*" *Marianne Moore: A Collection of Critical Essays.* Ed. Charles Tomlinson. Englewood Cliffs, N.J.: Prentice-Hall, Inc., 1969. 60–5.

———. "Marianne Moore (1923)." *Marianne Moore: A Collection of Critical Essays.* Ed. Charles Tomlinson. Englewood Cliffs, N.J.: Prentice-Hall, Inc., 1969. 48–51.

Erickson, Darlene Williams. *Illusion is More Precise Than Precision: The Poetry of Marianne Moore.* Tuscaloosa: The University of Alabama Press, 1992.

Erkkila, Betsy and Jay Grossman, eds. *Breaking Bounds: Whitman and American Cultural Studies.* New York: Oxford University Press, 1996.

Erwin, John W. "The Reader is the Medium: Ashbery and Ammons Ensphered." *Contemporary Literature* 21 (Autumn 1980): 588–610.

Eshelman, Clayton, ed. *Caterpillar* 12 (July 1970).

Fast, Robin Riley. "Moore, Bishop, and Oliver: Thinking Back, Re-Seeing the Sea." *Twentieth Century Literature* 39: 3 (Fall 1993): 364–79.

Feld, Ross. "Lowghost to Lowghost." *Parnassus: Poetry in Review* 4: 2 (1976): 5–30.

Fenton, James. "Becoming Marianne Moore." *New York Review of Books* XLIV:7 (April 24, 1997), 40–5.

Ferry, Anne. *The Title of the Poem.* Stanford: Stanford University Press, 1996.

Folsom, Ed, ed. *Walt Whitman: The Centennial Essays.* Iowa City: University of Iowa Press, 1994.

Fone, Byrne R. S. *Masculine Landscapes: Walt Whitman and the Homoerotic Text.* Carbondale: Southern Illinois University Press, 1992.

Foster, Edward. *Jack Spicer.* Boise: Boise State University Western Writers Series, 1991.

Frank, Waldo, ed. *The Complete Poems of Hart Crane.* Garden City, N.Y.: Doubleday & Company, Inc., 1958.

Frye, Northrop. *Anatomy of Criticism: Four Essays.* Princeton: Princeton University Press, 1957.

———. "Approaching the Lyric." *Lyric Poetry: Beyond New Criticism.* Eds. Chaviva Hosek and Patricia Parker. Ithaca: Cornell University Press, 1985.

Gardner, David. *The California Oath Controversy.* Berkeley: University of California Press, 1967.

Gilbert, Sandra M. "Marianne Moore as a Female Female Impersonator." *Marianne Moore: The Art of a Modernist.* Ed. Joseph Parisi. Ann Arbor: University of Michigan Research Press, 1990. 27–48.

Giles, Paul. *The Contexts of The Bridge.* Cambridge: Cambridge University Press, 1986.

Gizzi, Peter, ed. *The House That Jack Built: The Collected Lectures of Jack Spicer.* Hanover, N.H.: University Press of New England, 1998.

Goodridge, Celeste. "Towards a Poetics of Disclosure: Marianne Moore and Henry James." *Sagetrieb* 6: 3 (Winter 1987): 31–43.

Graham, Vicki. "Whetted to Brilliance." *Sagetrieb* 6: 3 (Winter 1987): 127–46.

———. "'The Power of the Visible': Marianne Moore and the 'Mimetic Faculty.'" *Sagetrieb* 12: 2 (Fall 1993): 33–50.

Griffith, Clark. "Sex and Death: The Significance of Whitman's *Calamus* Themes." *Philological Quarterly* 39 (1960): 18–38.

Grossman, Allen. "Hart Crane and Poetry: A Consideration of Crane's Intense Poetics." *Hart Crane: Modern Critical Views.* Ed. Harold Bloom. New York: Chelsea House Publishers, 1986. 221–54.

———. "Whitman's 'Whoever You Are Holding Me Now in Hand': Remarks on the Endlessly Repeated Rediscovery of the Incommensurability of the Person." *Breaking Bounds.* Eds. Betsy Erkkila and Jay Grossman. Oxford: Oxford University Press, 1996. 112–22.

Guest, Barbara. *Herself Defined: The Poet H. D. and Her World.* New York: Quill, 1984.

Hadas, Pamela White. *Marianne Moore: Poet of Affection.* Syracuse: Syracuse University Press, 1977.

Hall, Donald. *Marianne Moore: The Cage and the Animal.* New York: Pegasus, 1970.

Hammer, Langdon. *Hart Crane & Allen Tate: Janus-Faced Modernism.* Princeton: Princeton University Press, 1993.

Hanley, Alfred. *Hart Crane's Holy Vision: "White Buildings."* Pittsburgh: Duquesne University Press, 1981.

Hatlen, Burton. "Crawling into Bed with Sorrow: Jack Spicer's *After Lorca.*" *Ironwood* 28 (1987): 118–35.

Hazelwood, Dave. *A Bibliography of the Auerhahn Press.* Berkeley: Poltroon Press, 1976.

Hejinian, Lyn. *The Language of Inquiry.* Berkeley: University of California Press, 2000.

Helms, Alan. "Whitman Revised." *Études Anglaises* 37 (1984): 257–71.

———. "Whitman's 'Live Oak with Moss.'" *The Continuing Presence of Walt Whitman: The Life after the Life.* Ed. Robert K. Martin. Iowa City: University of Iowa Press, 1992. 185–205.

——— and Hershel Parker. "Commentary." *Nineteenth-Century Literature* 52:3 (December 1997): 413–6.

Herscovitz, Marcia. "Visionary Architects of the 18th Century." *Art Magazine* (December/January 1967–68): 22–6.

Heuving, Jeanne. "Gender in Marianne Moore's Art: Can'ts and Refusals." *Sagetrieb* 6:3 (Winter 1987): 117–26.

———. *Omissions Are Not Accidents: Gender in the Art of Marianne Moore.* Detroit: Wayne State University Press, 1992.

Holden, Jonathan. *The Rhetoric of the Contemporary Lyric.* Bloomington: Indiana University Press, 1980.

Holley, Margaret. *The Poetry of Marianne Moore: A Study in Voice and Value.* Cambridge: Cambridge University Press, 1987.

Holls, C. Carroll. *Language and Style in Leaves of Grass.* Baton Rouge: Louisiana State University Press, 1983.

Horton, Philip. *Hart Crane: The Life of an American Poet.* New York: W.W. Norton & Company, Inc., 1937.

Hosek, Chaviva and Patricia Parker, eds. *Lyric Poetry: Beyond New Criticism.* Ithaca: Cornell University Press, 1985.

Howard, Richard. *Alone with America: Essays on the Art of Poetry since 1950.* New York: Atheneum, 1969.

———. "Marianne Moore and the Monkey Business of Modernism." *Marianne Moore: The Art of a Modernist.* Ed. Joseph Parisi. Ann Arbor: University of Michigan Research Press, 1990. 1–12.

Imbroglio, Catherine. "'Our Days Put On Such Reticence': the Rhetoric of the Closet in John Ashbery's *Some Trees.*" *Contemporary Literature* 36:2 (1995): 249–89.

Jarman, Mark. "The Curse of Discursiveness." *The Hudson Review* 45 (1992): 158–66.

Jarraway, David R. "'Vanilla Hemorrhages': The Queer Perversities of Frank O'Hara." *GLQ* 4: 1 (1998): 67–108.

Jarrell, Randall. *Poetry and the Age.* New York: Vintage Books, 1955.

Josephson, Matthew. *Life Among the Surrealists.* New York: Holt, Rinehart and Winston, 1962.

Kalstone, David. *Five Temperaments.* New York: Oxford University Press, 1977.

———. *Becoming a Poet: Elizabeth Bishop with Marianne Moore and Robert Lowell.* Ed. Robert Hemenway. New York: Farrar, Straus and Giroux, 1989.

Kappel, Andrew J. "The Achievement of Marianne Moore." *Twentieth Century Literature* 30: 2/3 (Summer/Fall 1984): v–xxx.

Kearns, Cleo McNelly. "Consanguinities: T. S. Eliot and Marianne Moore." *Sagetrieb* 6: 3 (Winter 1987): 45–56.

Keats, John. *The Complete Poems of John Keats*. New York: The Modern Library, 1994.

Keeling, John. "The Moment Unravels: Reading John Ashbery's 'Litany.'" *Twentieth Century Literature* 38: 2 (Summer 1992): 125–51.

Keenaghan, Eric. "Jack Spicer's Pricks and Cocksuckers: Translating Homosexuality into Visibility." *The Translator* 4: 2 (1998): 273–94.

Keller, Karl. "Walt Whitman Camping." *Camp Grounds: Style and Homosexuality*. Ed. David Bergman. Amherst: University of Massachusetts Press, 1993.

Keller, Lynn. "'Thinkers Without Final Thoughts': John Ashbery's Evolving Debt to Wallace Stevens." *ELH* 49 (1982): 125–51.

——— and Christine Miller. "'The Tooth of Disputation': Marianne Moore's 'Marriage.'" *Sagetrieb* 6: 3 (Winter 1987): 99–115.

Kenner, Hugh. "Meditation and Enactment." *Marianne Moore: A Collection of Critical Essays*. Ed. Charles Tomlinson. Englewood Cliffs, N.J.: Prentice-Hall, Inc., 1969. 159–64.

———. "Supreme in Her Abnormality." *Marianne Moore: A Collection of Critical Essays*. Ed. Charles Tomlinson. Englewood Cliffs, N.J.: Prentice-Hall, Inc., 1969. 139–43.

———. "The Experience of the Eye." *Marianne Moore: Modern Critical Views*. Ed. Harold Bloom. New York: Chelsea House Publishers, 1987. 11–24.

Kent, Kathryn. *Making Girls into Women: American Women's Writing and the Rise of Lesbian Identity*. Durham: Duke University Press, 2003.

Kevorkian, Martin. "John Ashbery's *Flow Chart*: John Ashbery and The Theorists on John Ashbery against The Critics against John Ashbery." *New Literary History* 25 (1994): 459–76.

Killingsworth, M. Jimmie. "Sentimentality and Homosexuality in Whitman's 'Calamus.'" *ESQ, A Journal of the American Renaissance* 29 (1983): 144–53.

———. *Whitman's Poetry of the Body: Sexuality, Politics, and the Text*. Chapel Hill: The University of North Carolina Press, 1989.

Kopelson, Kevin. "Wilde, Barthes, and the Orgasmics of Truth." *Genders* 7 (March 1990): 22–31.

———. *Love's Litany: The Writing of Modern Homoerotics*. Stanford: Stanford University Press, 1994.

———. *The Queer Afterlife of Vaslav Nijinsky*. Stanford: Stanford University Press, 1997.

Leavell, Linda. *Marianne Moore and the Visual Arts: Prismatic Color*. Baton Rouge: Louisiana State University Press, 1995.

Leckie, Ross. "Art, Mimesis, and John Ashbery's 'Self-Portrait in a Convex Mirror.'" *Essays in Literature* 19: 1 (Spring 1992): 114–31.

Lehman, David, ed. *Beyond Amazement: New Essays on John Ashbery*. Ithaca: Cornell University Press, 1980.

Lemagny, J.-C. *Visionary Architects: Boulee, Ledoux, Lequeu*. Houston: University of St. Thomas, 1968.

Lewis, R. W. B. *The Poetry of Hart Crane: A Critical Study.* Princeton: Princeton University Press, 1967.

Liddy, James. "A Problem with Sparrows: Jack Spicer's Last Stance." *Boundary* 6 (1977): 259–66.

Lieberman, Lawrence. *Unassigned Frequencies: American Poetry in Review.* Urbana: University of Illinois Press, 1977.

Lodge, David. *The Modes of Modern Writing: Metaphor, Metonymy, and the Typology of Modern Literature.* Chicago: University of Chicago Press, 1988.

Lohf, Kenneth A. *The Literary Manuscripts of Hart Crane.* Columbus: Ohio State University Press, 1967.

Lourdeaux, Stanley. "Marianne Moore and a Psychoanalytic Paradigm for the Dissociated Image." *Twentieth Century Literature* 30: 2/3 (Summer/Fall 1984): 366–71.

Lynch, Michael. " 'Here is Adhesiveness': From Friendship to Homosexuality." *Victorian Studies* 29 (1985): 67–96.

Mallarmé, Stéphane. *Selected Poetry and Prose.* Ed. Mary Ann Caws. New York: New Directions, 1982.

Marek, Jayne. "Marianne Moore's Editorship of *The Dial.*" *Sagetrieb* 11: 1–2 (Spring–Fall 1992): 181–205.

Mariah, Paul, ed. *The Jack Spicer Issue. Manroot* 10 (Fall 1974/Winter 1975).

Martin, Robert K. "Whitman's 'Song of Myself': Homosexual Dream and Vision." *Partisan Review* 42 (1975): 80–96.

———. *The Homosexual Tradition in American Poetry.* Austin: University of Texas Press, 1979.

———, ed. *The Continuing Presence of Walt Whitman.* Iowa City: University of Iowa Press, 1992.

Martin, Taffy. "Portrait of a Writing Master: Beyond the Myth of Marianne Moore." *Twentieth Century Literature* 30: 2/3 (Summer/Fall 1984): 192–209.

———. *Marianne Moore: Subversive Modernist.* Austin: University of Texas Press, 1986.

Miller, Christanne. *Marianne Moore: Questions of Authority.* Cambridge: Harvard University Press, 1995.

Mohanty, S. P. and Jonathan Monroe. "John Ashbery and the Articulation of the Social." *Diacritics* 17: 2 (1987): 37–63.

Molesworth, Charles. " 'This Leaving-Out Business': The Poetry of John Ashbery." *Salmagundi* 38/39 (1970): 20–41.

———. "In Earnest of Merit: Moore's Early Fiction." *Sagetrieb* 6: 3 (Winter 1987): 57–66.

———. *Marianne Moore: A Literary Life.* New York: Atheneum, 1990.

Monroe, Harriet. "A Symposium on Marianne Moore." *Poetry* 19 (January 1922): 208–16.

Moon, Michael. "Flaming Closets." *October* 51 (Winter 1989): 19–54.

———. *Disseminating Whitman: Revision and Corporeality in Leaves of Grass.* Cambridge: Harvard University Press, 1991.

Moore, Marianne. "Blake." *Others* 1: 6 (December 1915): 105.

Moore, Marianne. *Poems*. London: The Egoist Press, 1921.

———. *Selected Poems*. London: Faber, 1935.

———. *Collected Poems*. New York: The Macmillan Company, 1953.

———. *The Complete Poems of Marianne Moore*. New York: The Viking Press, 1967.

———. *The Complete Prose of Marianne Moore*. Ed. Patricia C. Willis. New York: Viking Penguin Inc., 1986.

———. *The Selected Letters of Marianne Moore*. General ed. Bonnie Costello. Associate eds. Celeste Goodridge and Christanne Miller. New York: Alfred A. Knopf, 1997.

Moramarco, Fred. "John Ashbery and Frank O'Hara: The Painterly Poets." *Journal of Modern Literature* 5 (September 1976): 436–62.

Musil, Robert. *The Man Without Qualities*. Trans. Sophie Wilkins. New York: Alfred A. Knopf, 1995.

Nathanson, Tenney. *Whitman's Presence: Body, Voice, and Writing in Leaves of Grass*. New York: New York University Press, 1992.

Naylor, Paul Kenneth. "Where Are We Now In Poetry?" *Sagetrieb* 10: 1–2 (Spring–Fall 1991): 29–44.

O'Hara, Frank. "Rare Modern." *Poetry* (February 1957): 306–16.

Packard, William, ed. *The Craft of Poetry: Interviews from the New York Quarterly.* Garden City: Doubleday, Inc., 1974.

Parisi, Joseph, ed. *Marianne Moore: The Art of a Modernist*. Ann Arbor: University of Michigan Research Press, 1990.

Parker, Hershel. "The Real 'Live Oak with Moss': Straight Talk about Whitman's 'Gay Manifesto.'" *Nineteenth-Century Literature* 51: 2 (September 1996): 145–60.

Parkinson, Thomas. *Hart Crane and Yvor Winters: Their Literary Correspondence.* Berkeley: University of California Press, 1982.

Paul, Sherman. *Hart's Bridge*. Urbana: University of Illinois Press, 1972.

Pease, Donald. "Blake, Crane, Whitman, and Modernism: A Poetics of Pure Possibility." *Hart Crane: Modern Critical Views*. Ed. Harold Bloom. New York: Chelsea House Publishers, 1986. 189–220.

Perloff, Marjorie. *The Poetics of Indeterminacy: Rimbaud to Cage*. Princeton: Princeton University Press, 1981.

———. *Poetic License: Essays on Modernist and Postmodernist Lyric*. Evanston, Ill.: Northwestern University Press, 1990.

Preminger, Alex and T. V. F. Brogan, eds. *The New Princeton Encyclopedia of Poetry and Poetics*. Princeton, N.J.: Princeton University Press, 1993.

Press, John. *The Chequer'd Shade: Reflections on Obscurity in Poetry.* New York: Oxford University Press, 1958.

Pritchard, William H. *Lives of the Modern Poets*. New York: Oxford University Press, 1980.

Ranta, Jerrald. "Marianne Moore's Sea and the Sentence." *Essays in Literature* 15: 2 (Fall 1988): 245–57.

Reiss, Françoise. *Nijinsky: A Biography*. Trans. Helen and Stephen Haskell. London: Adam & Charles Black, 1960.

Riddel, Joseph. "Hart Crane's Poetics of Failure." *Hart Crane: Modern Critical Views*. Ed. Harold Bloom. New York: Chelsea House Publishers, 1986. 91–110.

Schulman, Grace. *Marianne Moore: The Poetry of Engagement*. Urbana: University of Illinois Press, 1986.

———. "Marianne Moore and E. McKnight Kauffer: Their Friendship, Their Concerns." *Conversant Essays: Contemporary Poets on Poetry*. Ed. James McCorkle. Detroit: Wayne State University Press, 1990.

Schultz, Susan M. " 'The Lyric Crash': The Theater of Subjectivity in John Ashbery's *Three Poems*." *Sagetrieb* 12: 2 (1993): 137–48.

———. " 'Returning to Bloom': John Ashbery's Critique of Harold Bloom." *Contemporary Literature* 36 (1995): 24–48.

———, ed. *The Tribe of John: Ashbery and Contemporary Poetry*. Tuscaloosa: The University of Alabama Press, 1995.

Schwartz, Joseph. *Hart Crane: A Reference Guide*. Boston: G. K. Hall & Co., 1983.

Schwartz, Joseph and Robert C. Stew. *Hart Crane: A Descriptive Biography*. Pittsburgh: University of Pittsburgh Press, 1972.

Sedgwick, Eve Kosofsky. *Between Men: English Literature and Male Homosocial Desire*. New York: Columbia University Press, 1985.

———. *Epistemology of the Closet*. Berkeley: University of California Press, 1990.

———. *Tendencies*. Durham: Duke University Press, 1993.

Shapiro, David. *John Ashbery: An Introduction to the Poetry*. Columbia Introductions to Twentieth-Century American Poetry. New York: Columbia University Press, 1979.

Sheehy, Eugene and Kenneth Lohf. *The Achievement of Marianne Moore: A Bibliography 1907–1957*. New York: The New York Public Library, 1958.

Shetley, Vernon. *After the Death of Poetry: Poet and Audience in Contemporary America*. Durham: Duke University Press, 1993.

Shively, Charley. *Drum Beats: Walt Whitman's Civil War Boy Lovers*. San Francisco: Gay Sunshine Press, 1987.

Shoptaw, John. *On the Outside Looking Out: John Ashbery's Poetry*. Cambridge: Harvard University Press, 1994.

Simon, Marc. *Samuel Greenberg, Hart Crane and the Lost Manuscripts*. Atlantic Highlands, N.J.: Humanities Press, 1978.

Slatin, John M. *The Savage's Romance: The Poetry of Marianne Moore*. University Park: The Pennsylvania State University Press, 1986.

Smith, Barbara Herrnstein. *Poetic Closure: A Study of How Poems End*. Chicago: The University of Chicago Press, 1968.

———. *On the Margins of Discourse: The Relation of Literature to Language*. Chicago: University of Chicago Press, 1978.

Smith, Ernest. *"The Imaged Word": The Infrastructure of Hart Crane's White Buildings*. New York: Peter Lang, 1989.

Sokolsky, Anita. " 'A Commission that Never Materialized': Narcissism and Lucidity in Ashbery's 'Self-Portrait in a Convex Mirror.' " *John Ashbery: Modern Critical Views*. Ed. Harold Bloom. New York: Chelsea House, 1985. 233–50.

Sommer, Piotr. "An Interview in Warsaw." *Code of Signals: Recent Writings in Poetics.* Ed. Michael Palmer. Berkeley: North Atlantic Books, 1983. 294–313.

Spanos, William and Robert Kroetsch, eds. "Jack Spicer." *Boundary* 2 VI, no. 1 (Fall 1977).

Spicer, Jack. *Book of Magazine Verse.* Berkeley: White Rabbit Press, 1966.

———. *Some Things from Jack.* Ed. Richard Rummonds. Verona, Italy: Plain Wrapper Press, 1972.

——— and Robert Duncan. *An Ode and Arcadia.* Berkeley: Ark Press, 1974.

———. *One Night Stand & Other Poems.* Ed. Donald Allen. San Francisco: Grey Fox Press, 1980.

———. *Collected Poems 1945–1946.* Berkeley: Oyez, 1981.

———. *A Book of Correspondences for Jack Spicer.* Eds. David Strauss and Benjamin Hollander. *Acts* 6 (1987): 18.

———. *The Collected Books of Jack Spicer.* Ed. Robin Blaser. Santa Rosa: Black Sparrow Press, 1989.

———. *The Tower of Babel: Jack Spicer's Detective Novel.* With an afterword by Lew Ellingham and Kevin Killian. Hoboken, N.J.: Talisman House Publishers, 1994.

———. *The House that Jack Built: The Collected Lectures of Jack Spicer.* Ed. Peter Gizzi. Hanover, N.H.: University Press of New England, 1998.

———. *Golem.* Collages by Fran Herndon. New York: Granary Books, 1999.

Stamelman, Richard. "Critical Reflections: Poetry and Art Criticism in Ashbery's 'Self-Portrait in a Convex Mirror.'" *New Literary History* 15 (Spring 1984): 607–30.

Stapleton, Laurence. *Marianne Moore: The Poet's Advance.* Princeton: Princeton University Press, 1978.

Steiner, George. *On Difficulty and Other Essays.* New York: Oxford University Press, 1978.

Steinman, Lisa M. "Modern America, Modernism, and Marianne Moore." *Twentieth Century Literature* 30: 2/3 (Summer/Fall 1984): 210–230.

Stevens, Wallace. *The Necessary Angel: Essays on Reality and the Imagination.* New York: Vintage Books, 1951.

———. *Opus Posthumous.* Ed. Milton J. Bates. New York: Alfred A. Knopf, 1989.

Stitt, Peter. "The Art of Poetry XXXIII: An Interview with John Ashbery." *The Paris Review* 90 (Winter 1983): 30–59.

Strauss, David Levi and Benjamin Hollander, eds. *A Book of Correspondences for Jack Spicer. Acts* 6 (1987).

Tambimuttu, ed. *Festschrift for Marianne Moore's Seventy Seventh Birthday.* New York: Tambimuttu & Mass, 1964.

Tomlinson, Charles. *Marianne Moore: A Collection of Critical Essays.* Englewood Cliffs, N.J.: Prentice-Hall, Inc., 1969.

Trachtenberg, Alan, ed. *Hart Crane: A Collection of Critical Essays.* Englewood Cliffs, N.J.: Prentice-Hall, Inc., 1982.

Unterecker, John. *Voyager: A Life of Hart Crane.* New York: Farrar, Straus and Giroux, 1969.

Uroff, M. D. *Hart Crane: The Patterns of His Poetry.* Urbana: University of Illinois Press, 1974.

Valéry, Paul. *The Art of Poetry.* Ed. Jackson Matthews. Trans. Denise Folliot. Bollingen Series XLV, 7. Princeton: Princeton University Press, 1989.

Vendler, Helen. *Part of Nature, Part of Us.* Cambridge: Harvard University Press, 1980.

———. "Understanding Ashbery." *The New Yorker* (March 16, 1981): 108–36.

———. *The Music of What Happens.* Cambridge: Harvard University Press, 1988.

———. "A Steely Glitter Chasing Shadows: John Ashbery's *Flow Chart.*" *Soul Says: On Recent Poetry.* Cambridge: Harvard University Press, 1995.

Vincent, John. "Reports of Looting and Insane Buggery Behind Altars: John Ashbery's Queer Poetics." *Twentieth Century Literature* 44: 2 (Summer 1998): 155–75.

———. "Pulling Close and Pushing Away: Rhetorical Suspense, Sexuality and Death in Whitman's 'Calamus' Poems." *Arizona Quarterly* 56: 1 (Spring 2000): 29–48.

Vogler, Thomas A. "A New View of Hart Crane's Bridge." *Hart Crane: Modern Critical Views.* Ed. Harold Bloom. New York: Chelsea House Publishers, 1986. 69–90.

Warner, Michael. *The Trouble with Normal: Sex, Politics, and the Ethics of Queer Life.* Cambridge: Harvard University Press, 1999.

———. "Whitman Drunk." *Breaking Bounds.* Eds. Betsy Erkkila and Jay Grossman. New York: Oxford University Press, 1996. 30–43.

Wasserman, Rosanne. "Marianne Moore and The New York School: O'Hara, Ashbery, Koch." *Sagetrieb* 6: 3 (Winter 1987): 67–77.

Weber, Brom. *Hart Crane: A Biographical and Critical Study.* New York: The Bodley Press, 1948.

Whitman, Walt. *Leaves of Grass.* Intro. by John Hollander. New York: Vintage Books/The Library of America, 1992.

Williams, William Carlos. "Marianne Moore (1925)." *Marianne Moore: A Collection of Critical Essays.* Ed. Charles Tomlinson. Englewood Cliffs, N.J.: Prentice-Hall, Inc., 1969. 52–9.

———. "Marianne Moore (1948)." *Marianne Moore: A Collection of Critical Essays.* Ed. Charles Tomlinson. Englewood Cliffs, N.J.: Prentice-Hall, Inc., 1969. 112–13.

Williamson, Alan. *Introspection and Contemporary Poetry.* Cambridge: Harvard University Press, 1989.

Willis, Patricia C. *Marianne Moore: Vision into Verse.* Philadelphia: The Rosenbach Museum & Library, 1987.

Winters, Yvor. *On Modern Poets.* New York: Meridian Books, Inc., 1959.

———. "Hart Crane's Poems." *The Uncollected Essays and Reviews of Yvor Winters.* Ed. Francis Murphy. Chicago: The Swallow Press, Inc., 1973. 47–50.

Woods, Gregory. *Articulate Flesh: Male Homo-eroticism and Modern Poetry.* New Haven: Yale University Press, 1987.

Yingling, Thomas. *Hart Crane and the Homosexual Text.* Chicago: The University of Chicago Press, 1990.
———. "Homosexuality and Utopian Discourse in American Poetry." Introduction by Robyn Wiegman. *Breaking Bounds.* Eds. Betsy Erkkila and Jay Grossman. New York: Oxford University Press, 1996. 135–46.

Index